P. Anstadt

Luther's smaller Catechism explained

P. Anstadt

Luther's smaller Catechism explained

ISBN/EAN: 9783337127114

Printed in Europe, USA, Canada, Australia, Japan

Cover: Foto ©Lupo / pixelio.de

More available books at **www.hansebooks.com**

DR. MARTIN LUTHER.

LUTHER'S
Smaller Catechism,

EXPLAINED, ANALYZED & ILLUSTRATED

WITH APPROPRIATE

ANECDOTES, PROVERBS AND EXAMPLES,

Drawn from Scripture History, Biography, Nature, and Remarks of Distinguished Persons,

BY

P. ANSTADT, D. D.,

EDITOR TEACHERS' JOURNAL, CHRISTIAN'S GUIDE, AUTHOR OF BIBLE WINE, COMMUNION ADDRESSES, CHRISTIAN CATECHISM, ETC., ETC.

YORK, PA.
P. ANSTADT & SONS,
1894.

Entered according to Act of Congress, in the year 1894, by
P. ANSTADT & SONS,
In the office of the Librarian of Congress, at Washington.

PREFACE.

The instruction of the young in the truths of our holy religion has in all ages been regarded as an important duty. In the Old Testament the Lord said of Abraham, "I know him, that he will command his children, and his household after him, and they shall keep the way of the Lord, to do justice and judgment." Gen. xviii. 19. Solomon says, "Train up a child in the way he should go, and when he is old he will not depart from it." Prov. xxii. 6. Paul commends the mother and grandmother of Timothy, who had instructed him in the holy Scriptures from his youth up.

In the early Christian church the converts from heathenism were generally very ignorant, and required careful instruction in the truths of the Christian religion, before they were baptized and admitted into full membership. Even the more educated and learned among them required more or less instruction in the fundamentals of religion. In large cities special schools were founded for this purpose. The catechetical school of Alexandria in Egypt became the first theological seminary, in which Clement and Origen were the teachers.

The prevailing ignorance of the people at the time of the Reformation made instruction necessary and gave rise to the preparation of Catechisms. Nearly all the reformers, Luther, Brenz, Justus Jonas, Aecolampadius, Calvin, Ursinus, and Olevianus prepared such works.

Of the value and importance of Catechetical instruction, Dr. Abdel Green speaks thus in his admirable lectures: "It is exactly this kind of instruction which is at the present time most urgently needed in many, perhaps in most of our congregations. It is needed to imbue effectually the minds of the people with 'the first principles of the oracles of God;' to indoctrinate them soundly and systematically in revealed truth, and thus to guard them against being 'carried about by every wind of doctrine,' as well as to qualify them to join in the weekly services of the sanctuary with full understanding, and with minds in all respects prepared for the right and deep impression of what they hear."

In Scotland John Craig compiled a catechism in 1581.

The Anglican Catechism was prepared in 1549 and enlarged in 1604 for the use of the Episcopal church.

PREFACE.

The Westminster Catechisms, Longer and Shorter, were prepared by the Westminster assembly for the use of the Presbyterians of England and Scottland.

The Heidelberg Catechism was prepared by Ursinus, a pupil of Melanchton, and Olevianus, a pupil of Calvin, in 1563, for the Reformed churches of the Palatinate.

"When we compare these catechisms of the leading churches of Christendom," says Dr. Schaff, "it is remarkable, how much more they agree, than they differ in the essential articles of the Christian faith and duty."

We give specimens from the larger Catechism of Craig, first printed in Edinburgh by Henrie Charteris in 1581, and in London in 1589. It has recently been reprinted by the Rev Dr. H. Bonar in his work on the Catechisms of the Scottish Reformation, with historical preface.

FIRST QUESTIONS.

Ques. Who made man and woman?
Ans. The Eternal God, of his goodness.
Ques. Whereof made he them?
Ans. Of an earthly body and an heavenly spirit.
Ques. To whose image made he them?
Ans. To his own image.
Ques. What is the image of God?
Ans. Perfect uprightness in body and soul.
Ques. To what end were they made?
Ans. To acknowledge and serve their maker.
Ques. How should they have served him?
Ans. According to his holy will.
Ques. How did they know his will?
Ans. By his works, word, and sacraments.
Ques. What liberty had they to obey his will?
Ans. They had free will to obey and disobey.

OF THE SACRAMENTS.

Ques. What is a sacrament?
Ans. A sensible sign and seal of God's favor offered and given to us.
Ques. To what end are the sacraments given?
Ans. To nourish our faith in the promise of God.
Ques. How can sensible signs do this?
Ans. They have this office of God, not of themselves.
Ques. How do the sacraments differ from the word?
Ans. They speak to the eye, and the word to the ear.

Ques. Speak they other things than the word?
Ans. No; but the same diversely.
Ques. But the word doth teach us sufficiently?
Ans. Yet the sacraments with the word do it more effectually.
Ques. What, then, are the sacraments to the word?
Ans. They are sure and authentic seals given by God.
Ques. May the sacraments be without the word?
Ans. No; for the word is their life
Ques. May the word be fruitful without the sacraments?
Ans. Yes, no doubt; but it worketh more plenteously with them.
Ques. What is the cause of that?
Ans. Because more senses are moved, to the comfort of our faith.
—*Steel.*

Luther's Catechisms, a large one for teachers, and a small one for children, were prepared in 1529, to meet the lamentable ignorance which then prevailed in Saxony and throughout Germany. The Small Catechism appeals directly to the heart, and is a model of child-like simplicity.

"Luther's Catechism became the household book of German families. It marked an epoch in religious teaching. His Smaller Catechism, which chiefly deserves the name, 'is truly a great little book,' with as many thoughts as words, and every word telling and sticking to the heart as well as the memory."—*Schaff's Church History*, Vol. VI. pp. 550-557.

"It was an immense boon to the people and would alone have immortalized its author."—*Rev. Robert Steel.*

This work claims to be an explanation of Luther's Smaller Catechism, with Scripture Examples, and Anecdotes and Illustrations, drawn from Biography, History, Nature, Science, etc., etc., etc.

There are a number of German books of this kind, but so far as we know, there has never been a book printed in the English language, giving illustrations and anecdotes of Luther's Smaller Catechism. The publisher of this book of illustrations has used many of them during his early ministry, and found them very helpful in fastening abstract truths on the minds of his Catechumens. No doubt, many pastors have had the same experience. A number of our ministerial brethren have encouraged us to publish these illustrations in book form, and have engaged copies in advance.

Dr. P. Born, Prof. of Theology, Selinsgrove, Pa., kindly read some of the proof sheets and writes as follows:

"I am pleased with your method, especially in regard to the analysis of the several articles. It simplifies and aids in impressing and remembering the several points given under the respective heads. Your illustrations and anecdotes are pertinent and certainly add interest and value to the work. They give to abstract truths, vividness and living forms. I hope the work will have an extensive circulation, for I think it is well calculated to do good."

The importance of combining history with Christian instruction has long since been recognized.

"In histories we find all doctrines and laws living."—*Sebastian Frank.*

"*Verba docent, exempla trahunt.*"—*Jacob Balde.*

One important use of anecdotes and illustrations in religious instruction is to attract attention. In this respect they are of great value. How far superior is this means to the impatient, oft repeated, and useless admonition, "Please pay attention!" "Look this way;" "Stop talking." Dry bread is not relished by the children, and abstract truth cannot hold their attention long. But the mere promise of "a story" arouses the attention like an electric shock and directs all eyes and ears toward the speaker.

But the attraction of attention is not the only, nor the most important use of this mode of imparting instruction. Its great value consists in the means which it affords of enlightening the understanding. What faithful teacher has not often sought for a suitable comparison, an example, a definition, or demonstration in order to set an important truth in its proper light? Very learned men, even, who are accustomed to abstract thought, often find it necessary to make themselves understood by means of this popular method. The teacher should not usually begin his instructions by anecdotes and illustrations, which would simply amuse or interest his hearers, but he should teach first the doctrine or precept, and then impress the truth upon the minds and hearts of his hearers by appropriate anecdotes and illustrations. There is something overwhelming in the expression when it is said, not thus it is written and demonstrated, but "Thus it was lived, thus it was done!"

Even in the divine Revelation instruction, doctrine and history go hand in hand; they permeate each other and are seldom separated. No one would now teach Bible History without connecting it with doctrine. Why then, should Bible doctrines and systematic instruction be imparted only in an abstract manner? Why should doctrine not be made perspicuous, plain and vivid by examples?

"One of the most important duties of the Christian pastor is undoubtedly that of preparing all the baptized members of his church, and all other persons properly within the reach of his influence, for

the solemn duty of making a public profession of religion, and a worthy approach to the table of the Lord. In the instruction of children in the family, and in the Sabbath-school, the elements of Christian truth and duty are taught by means of a smaller catechism, such as that of Luther. But in the different Lutheran countries of Europe, as well as in many churches in America, larger catechisms, adapted to more developed minds, are employed to prepare catechumens for *confirmation*. It was in order to furnish a suitable work of this kind, more copious in matter and systematic in arrangement, that the author was induced to undertake the present work. In executing it, his aim has been to take the pupil by the hand, and, in familiar language, to conduct him through the popular course of religious truth; teaching him his lost condition by nature and practice, and persuading him to an entire surrender of his heart to the Savior, as his only hope. In short, the object of the writer in composing this catechism was the same as that at which every faithful minister aims in his course of catechetical instruction—the conversion, edification, and salvation of his pupils."
—*Preface to Schmucker's Class-book of Religious Instruction.*

"A catechism on the Christian religion should present the articles of faith fresh from the fountain of the word of God to the mind and heart of the pupil for his instruction and comfort in life and in death. It should move in the central current of Christian truth. The more important denominational differences may be stated for historical information, but in a kind and charitable spirit, and with a view to promote, rather than to diminish, unity and harmony among the various branches of the kingdom of Christ."—*Dr Schaff.*

The reader will notice that we have made use of popular proverbs in connection with some of the doctrines discussed. These often make a very striking and lasting impression, when given in illustration of a particular truth. Says A. Fricke: "Even the Talmud says, 'Do not look with contempt upon the proverb. By the use of these it becomes easy to instruct men in morals and religion. When the king has lost a gold piece or a pearl, may he not be able to find them by the help of a little candle, that is hardly worth a penny?' And on this point the Talmud is doubtless correct: as the little candle is sufficient to find a pearl, so the little proverb is often sufficient to bring back him, who has gone astray, and is in danger of making shipwreck of faith and virtue. Therefore we should make diligent use of the proverb in religious instruction."

This manual has been prepared for the special use of ministers, students, S. S. teachers, heads of families and intelligent laymen, who we hope will be interested and benefitted by its careful perusal.

We have been aided in our work by two English books on the Presbyterian Shorter Catechism, one by John Whitcross, 1848, and the other by Rev. Robert Steel, D. D., both of Edinburg, Scotland. But the bulk of the work is compiled from such German books as Woelbling's Christliche Geschichten; Muehe, Konfirmanden Unterricht; Nissen, Unterredungen ueber den Katechismus; Caspari, Geistliches und Weltliches. J. H. Abbert Fricke, Handbuch des Katechismus Unterrichts, 1892, kindly lent us by Prof. J. W. Richard, came too late for practical use on this work.

This book was prepared at longer or shorter intervals, with many interruptions, during the busy hours of our editorial labors, and we, therefore, beg the indulgence of the reader for any imperfections or errors that may be discovered therein. We send it forth with the prayer, that our readers may receive as much instruction and enjoyment in its perusal, as we have received in its preparation.

P. ANSTADT.

York, Pa., 1894.

INTRODUCTION.

1. What is religion?

True religion is a knowledge of God, and a proper manner of worshiping him. As there is but one true God, there can be but one true religion.

2. How many principal religions are there in the world?

There may be named four principal religions in the world; namely, the Heathen, the Jewish, the Mahomedan and the Christian, which is the true religion.

3. What is the character of the Heathen religion?

The heathen people are those who do not know the true God, but serve false gods and idols. Their understandings are darkened, and they are alienated from the life of God, through the ignorance that is in them, because of the blindness of their hearts. Eph. iv. 18.

4. Why did the heathen fall into this deplorable condition?

The heathen fell into their deplorable condition because, when they knew God they did not glorify him as God, neither were they thankful; but they became vain in their imaginations and their foolish hearts were darkened. Romans i. 21.

5. What duty does this deplorable condition of the heathen impose upon us?

It is the duty of the Christian church to send missionaries into heathen lands, as Christ commanded, Go ye, therefore, and teach all nations, baptizing them in the name of the Father and the Son and the Holy Ghost. Matt. xxviii. 19. We should remember, also, that our forefathers were heathen, and we are indebted for our Christianity and civilization to christian missions.

6. *What is the history of the Jewish people?*

God chose Abraham and his family, and the children of Israel, to whom he revealed himself in the bestowment of great blessings. From this people the knowledge of the true God was to go out unto all nations. Therefore glorious institutions were established, and wonderful works of God were performed. Wonderful and significant is the history of this people; their disgraceful apostacies; their rejection of Christ; their present dispersion over the earth, and their stiffnecked unbelief.

They know the Father in a manner, but cannot come to him, because they have rejected the Son. Jesus saith ... I am the way, the truth and the life; no man cometh unto the Father, but by me. John xiv. 6. Yet, it is believed, a glorious future awaits the Jewish people. In the last times, which may be very near, great multitudes will be converted to the faith of Christ and be restored to their ancient inheritance, the land of Palestine. Read in this connection Gen. xvii. 8; Isa. xi. 15, 16; Isa. xxxv. 10; Jer. xxx. 3, 10, 16; Rom. xi; Rev. vii. 4-8.

7. *What was the nature of the Jewish religion?*

The Jews believed in one true God, and their doctrines and forms of worship are laid down in the Old Testament Scriptures. Their worship consisted largely of ceremonies and sacrifices, which were types of the promised Messiah, or Christ, whom they rejected and crucified.

8. *Why is the Jewish not now the true religion?*

Because all the types of the Old Testament were fulfilled in Christ, and therefore, those types have passed away, and the ceremonies connected with them should no longer be observed.

9. *What is the character of the Mahomedan religion?*

The Mahomedan religion was founded by Mahomed, who was the son of a merchant in Mekka, Arabia. He claimed to be a prophet in the year 611 of the christian era. His religion is a mixture of Christianity, Judaism, heathenism and his pretended revelations. His religious system is called Islam and his followers are called Moslems. His father-in-law, Abu-Bekr, collected his teachings into a book, called the *Koran*, which is divided into 114 chapters. Mahomed's flight from Mekka to Medina occurred on July 15, 622, and is called the Hegira.

The Mahomedans date their time from the Hegira. They extended their religion by force of arms. In the year 630, they conquered and occupied Mekka and dedicated the old heathen Haaba, as their triumph. At the time of Mahomed's death, the whole of Arabia was subdued by them. In 637 they took Jerusalem, in 707 they occupied all of North Africa, in 711 they occupied Spain, in 1453 they occupied Constantinople and advanced as far as Vienna.

The Mahomedan religion teaches false doctrines and impure morality, such as hatred of enemies and polygamy. They have no correct knowledge of the Father, much less of the Son.

10. *How are the inhabitants of the earth divided among these four principal religions?*

The number of adherents of the different great religions of the world, respectively, are given as follows:

Jews, 7,000,000; Mahomedans, 185,000,000; Christians, 445,000,000; Heathen, 830,000,000; converts at heathen mission stations, 2,887,500.

LUTHER'S SMALL CATECHISM IS DIVIDED INTO FIVE PARTS.

The first part teaches us, in the Ten Commandments, our *duties* to God and to our neighbor.

The second part embraces in the three articles of the Creed the *motives* that should impel us to the performance of those duties.

The third part teaches us in the Lord's Prayer, whence and how we derive strength for the performance of our duties.

The fourth and fifth parts contain, in the Holy Sacraments, the strengthening means for the performance of our duties.

PART I.

THE TEN COMMANDMENTS.

11. What does the first part of the Catechism embrace?

The first part of the Catechism embraces the Ten Commandments, as they are recorded in Exodus xx. and Deut. vi. 9, 20, 25.

12. How were the Ten Commandments given?

The Ten Commandments were spoken by God himself from Mount Sinai in the hearing of the children of Israel, amid thunderings and lightnings. They were then written by the finger of God on two tables of stone and delivered unto Moses.

Exodus xxxi. 18. And he (God) gave unto Moses two tables of testimony, tables of stone, written with the finger of God.

13. How many commandments were written on the first table?

According to the Augustinian division the first, second and third commandments are contained on the first table.

14. What is inculcated by the commandments on the first table?

The commandments on the first table inculcate love for and worship of God.

15. Which commandments are contained on the second table?

The second table, according to the Augustinian division, contains the fourth, fifth, sixth, seventh, eighth, ninth and tenth commandments.

16. What do the commandments of the second table inculcate?

The commandments of the second table inculcate love and good will to our neighbor.

17. How were the commandments originally divided in the Bible?

The Scriptures were originally written without any division of chapters or verses; hence we cannot determine with certainty, how many commandments were contained on each table.

THE FIRST COMMANDMENT.

18. Repeat the first commandment.

"I am the Lord thy God. Thou shalt have no other gods before me. Thou shalt not make unto thee any graven image, or any likeness of anything that is in heaven above, or that is in the earth beneath, or that is in the water under the earth: thou shalt not bow down thyself to them, nor serve them: for I the Lord thy God am a jealous God, visiting the iniquity of the fathers upon the children unto the third and fourth generation of them that hate me; and showing mercy unto thousands of them that love me, and keep my commandments."

19. What is meant by this commandment in general?

In general this commandment means, that we should *fear, love* and *trust* God above all things.

20. Why should you fear, love and trust God above all things?

1. He is my *Lord;* therefore I should fear him;
2. He is *God*, the supreme good; therefore I should *love* him;
3. He is *my* God; therefore I should *trust* him;
4. And this above *all* things, because there is none other so *great*, so *loving* and so *true* as the Lord, my God.

21. *What is forbidden in the first commandment?*
The first commandment forbids idolatry.

22. *How many kinds of idolatry are there?*
There are two kinds of idolatry; namely:
1. Gross or open idolatry, and
2. Refined or secret idolatry.

23. *What is gross, or open idolatry?*
Gross idolatry consists in exalting any thing that is not God, upon God's throne, and honoring, and worshiping it as God, such as wood, stone, gold, silver, pictures, angels, saints, the sun, moon, stars, animals, reptiles, etc.

Rev. xxii. 8, 9. And I, John, fell down to worship before the feet of the angel, which showed me these things. Then said he, See thou do it not, for I am thy fellow servant . . . worship God.

24. *When is refined or secret idolatry committed?*
Refined or secret idolatry is committed when we fear, love, and trust anything else more than God.

25. *What is required in the first commandment?*
In the first commandment we are required not only to gain a knowledge of God from nature, and the Holy Scriptures; but also to honor him; that is, to live according to our knowledge of God.

26. *Wherein does the fear of God consist?*
The fear of God consists in a reverential awe of his omnipresence, power and justice. It is, indeed, not a slavish fear of punishment, but it is a filial fear, which restrains from sin through the love of God.

27. *Wherein does the love of God consist?*
The love of God consists
1. In joy in God, who is our greatest benefactor.
2. In a heartfelt longing after God.
3. Which leads to the obedience of God.
4. And keeps God constantly in our thoughts.
5. Which obedience is the true evidence of our love to God.

6. The observance of all the commandments is derived from this filial fear and love of God.

28. How do we put our trust in God?

We put our trust in God,

1. When we expect everything good from him.
2. And therefore never despair in time of trouble.

29. What other motives have we for the observance of this commandment?

We should obey this commandment, because,

1. God is *our* God.
2. We are indebted to him for our whole being and existence.
3. We have received from him every blessing we have ever enjoyed, and we look to him for every blessing we hope to enjoy in this world, and the world to come.

ANECDOTES AND ILLUSTRATIONS.

Scriptural Examples. God revealed himself and conversed with Adam and Eve, Gen. ii. 16, 17; Cain, iv. 6-15; Noah, vi. 13; vii. 1; viii. 15 17; Abraham, xii. 1-3; xvii. 1; Samuel, 1 Sam. iii., etc; to all the Patriarchs and Prophets. He revealed himself by visions to Abraham, Gen. xv. 1; Jacob, xlvi. 2; Isa. i. 1; Ananias, Acts ix. 10; Peter, xi. 5, etc. He revealed himself in dreams to Jacob, Gen. xxviii. 12, etc.; Joseph, xxxvii. 5, etc.; the wise men from the East, Matt. ii. 12. He revealed himself through the Angel of the Lord to Hagar, Gen. xvi. 7, etc.; Abraham and Lot, xviii. and xix; Moses, Ex. iii. 2, 6. He revealed himself through the *Word*, the Son, to the whole world, John i., etc., xiv. 9; Heb. i. 1 3.

The following is the occasion which induced Luther to write the Small Catechism:

The Elector of Saxony had ordered a visitation of the churches and schools. Luther writes: "The deplorable condition in which I found religious affairs during a recent visitation, impelled me to publish this catechism. Alas! what misery I found! The people, especially those who live in the villages, seem to have no knowledge of christian doctrine, and many of the pastors are ignorant and incompetent teachers. And yet, they all maintain that they are christians, have been baptized and received the Lord's Supper. Yet they cannot recite the Lord's Prayer, the Creed or the Ten Commandments."

Luther one day asked his little son what he had learned. The son replied, "I have learned the whole catechism." "My dear son," said Luther, "if you have learned, or understand the whole catechism, then you have learned more than I have. For, although I am an old Doctor, yet I must still continue to study and learn every day."

Luther calls the catechism the true layman's Bible, which contains everything that is necessary to our salvation. He says:

1. The Ten Commandments are the *doctrina doctrinarum*, that is, the doctrines above all others.

2. The Creed is the *historia historiarum*, that is, the history above all histories.

3. The Lord's Prayer is *oratio orationum*, that is, the prayer above all prayers, and

4. The Holy Sacraments are *ceremoniae ceremoniarum*, that is, ceremonies above all ceremonies.

The Ten Commandments teach us, what, according to God's will, man should be, but is not.

The Creed teaches us what God is towards man, the sinner.

The Lord's Prayer teaches us, how the sinner seeks God and draws near to him.

The Sacraments show us how God seeks the sinner and draws near to him.

Dr. Jonas called the catechism "The children's Bible."

Joachim, Duke of Anhalt, was a learned man. He wrote with his own hand in his catechism: "Next to the Bible, this is my best book."

John George, Duke of Mecklenburg, said on his death bed (1675), "When I was a boy I learned the catechism, and I have not yet forgotten it."

An atheist wanted to dispute with a christian on the existence of God. The christian replied, that he would dispute with him on one condition; namely, that the atheist would go out into the grave yard at midnight, alone, into a secluded spot, and there lift up his hands toward the starry heavens and exclaim, "There is no God." The atheist did not comply with the conditions, and there was no dispute.

"I am." Luther says: "I have several times tried to comprehend the ten commandments, but when I only began with the first word, I almost stuck fast with the little word 'I,' and I could not comprehend the word 'I.'"

The Existence of God. The fool hath said in his heart, there is no God. Ps. xiv. 1.

The following anecdote will illustrate that the man who says there is no God is a fool: The famous astronomer Athenasius Kircher, having an acquaintance who denied the existence of God, took the following method to convince him of his error, upon his own principles. Expecting him on a visit, he procured a very handsome globe of the starry heavens, which being placed in a corner of the room in which it could not escape his friend's observation, the latter seized the first occasion to ask, whence it came and to whom it belonged. "Not to me," said Kircher, "nor was it ever made by any person, but it came here by '*mere chance.*'" "That," replied his skeptical friend, "is absolutely impossible; you surely jest." Kircher, however, seriously persisted in his assertion, took occasion to reason with his friend upon his own atheistical principles "You will not believe," said he, "that this small body came here by *mere chance;* and yet you will contend that those heavenly bodies, of which it is only a faint and diminutive resemblance, came into existence without order or design." Pursuing this chain of reasoning, his friend was at first confounded, in the next place convinced, ultimately joined in a cordial acknowledgement of the absurdity of denying the existence of a God. The Poet Young says: "An undevout astronomer is mad."

A poor Arabian of the desert being asked how he came to be assured that there was a God, replied: "In the same way that I am able to tell the foot-prints impressed on the sand, whether it was a man, or a beast that passed that way."

Lord Rochester was one day at an atheistical meeting in the house of a person of quality. He undertook to manage the cause and was the principal disputant against God and religion, and for his performance received the applause of the whole company; "upon which," he says, "my mind was terribly struck, and I immediately replied thus to myself; Good God! that a man that walks upright, that sees the wonderful works of God, and has the use of his senses and reason, should use them to the defying of his Creator!"

Mr. Collins, the deist, met one day with a plain countryman going to church. He inquired where he was going. "To church, sir." "What to do there?" "To worship God." "Pray whether, is your God a great or a little God?" "He is so great, sir, that the heaven of heavens cannot contain him: and so little, that he can dwell in my heart." Collins declared, that this simple answer by the countryman, had more effect upon his mind than all the learned volumes which the learned doctors had written against him.

An Atheistical Anatomist. When Galen, a celebrated physician, but atheistically inclined, had anatomised the human body, and carefully surveyed the frame of it, viewed the fitness and usefulness of every part of it and the many several intentions of every little vein, bone and muscle, and the beauty of the whole, he fell into a fit of devotion and wrote a hymn to his Creator.

The pious Bishop Barowsky, of Kœnigsburg, was once asked by a boasting Atheist: "How will you convince me of the contrary, when I tell you into your face: 'There is no God!'" "That does not cause me much trouble," replied the bishop, "as I can safely intrust the answer to the sacred Scriptures, which make mention of you." "Of me!" "Yes, yes, of you: in Psalms xiv. 1." The Bible was brought and the passage audibly read: "*The fool hath said in his heart, there is no God.*"

When Robespiere, the French atheist and bloodthirsty persecutor, was after his fall, lying speechless on a table, with a bloody and half-bandaged face, a poor laboring man stepped up to him, and after looking at him for some time in mute astonishment, exclaimed: "*Yes, Robespiere, there is a God!*"

I am the Lord thy God. "The Lord," says Luther; "this sounds like a peal of thunder, when we remember how many thunderbolts and strokes of lightning this Lord God has in his hands, with which he can crush and destroy; but then the words, '*thy God*,' sound so mild and lovely, when we think how many blessings and how much goodness this Lord God holds in his hands to pour out over those who fear him; yea, this he does daily over all kinds of people. 'Thy God,' that is, he will treat you as a mother does her child, he will act towards *thee* as though there were no other human being in the world but thou."

"Thou shalt have no other gods before me." A gentleman in England, who had a chapel attached to his house, was visited by a person from London, to whom he showed the chapel. "What a glorious kitchen this would make!" said the visitor. "When I make a God of my belly," replied the gentleman, "I will make a kitchen of my chapel."

A lady once told the Rev. Romaine that she thought she could comply with his doctrine, and give up everything but one. "And what is that, madam?" "Cards, sir." "You think you could not be happy without them?" "No, sir; I know I could not." "Then, madam, they are your god, and they must save you." This pointed and just reply is said to have resulted in her conversion.

An Indian chief having sent for Hiacomus, a converted native, with a view of receiving religious instruction of him, asked him how many gods the English worshiped. Hiacomus answered, "One and no more." On this the chief reckoned up about thirty-seven principal gods which he had; "and shall I," said he, "throw away all these thirty-seven for the sake of one only?" "What do you yourself think?" said Hiacomus; "for my part, I have thrown away all these and many more, some years ago, and yet I am preserved, as you see, to this day." "You speak true," said the chief, "and therefore, I will throw away all my gods, too, and serve that one God with you."

"How does it come," says some one "that the heathen worship the creature instead of the Creator?" And he was answered: "They are like the little boy, who for the first time came to the court of a king, and took every one, whom he saw clothed in attractive garments, to be the king himself. Thus weak, unenlightened man now regards the sun, moon and stars, and then some other glorious creature as God himself."

It is a bad thing, when one man is the other's devil, but equally bad, when one man becomes another's god.

A miser, who was shipwrecked, sat down upon his money chest and exclaimed: "Where this goes, there I will go, too!"

A golden key can unlock all doors, except the door of heaven.—*Proverb*.

Many men are like a certain king, (Redwald), who caused two altars to be erected in his temple; on one of these he sacrificed to Christ and upon the other to the Devil, in order that he may not offend either, but retain the favor of both.

A poor heathen had placed all his trust in his two cows. Therefore he once remarked to Moffat, the missionary: "Your religion may be good enough for you, but I have never seen that it fills the stomach."

When the emperor Frederick III. was asked which of his ministers he liked best, he answered: "Those who fear God more than me."

Cardinal Woolsey, having fallen under the displeasure of his monarch, made the following sad reflection a little before his death: "Had I served my God as diligently as I served my king, he would not have forsaken me now in my gray hairs. But this is the just reward that I must receive for my indulgent pains and study, not regarding my service to God, but only to my prince."

Whenever the conscience of Henry VIII. ouched, he was in the habit of drowning its monitions by gormandizing and drunkenness.

On his death-bed he ordered a glass full of wine to be brought to him. He drank it out and said to the bystanders: "*Amici, nunc pudidimus, omnia—regnum, vitam, animam!*" (Now sirs, all is gone, my crown, my body and my soul?")

Thou shalt not make unto thee any graven image, or any likeness of anything that is in heaven above, or that is in the earth beneath, or that is in the water under the earth. A native of India, who came to London, very much censured the want of images in the churches; he said the worshipers had nothing upon which to fix their attention, and hence they were often gazing at each other, and often at mere inanity. "We," he said, "have in our temples an image of the Deity to look at, with large eyes, huge ears, great hands and long feet. Not that we believe this very image to be the Deity, but we use it only to fix our attention, and to remind us that that Being, which it represents, can see everything, hear everything, etc."

A Protestant, who had rented a small farm under Alexander II., Duke of Gorden, having fallen behind in his payments, a vigilant steward, in his grace's absence, seized the farmers stock and advertized it to be sold at auction, and fixed a day. The duke happily returned home in the interval, and the tenant went to him to supplicate for indulgence. "What is the matter, Donald?" said the duke as he saw him enter with downcast looks. Donald told his story in a concise, natural manner; it touched the duke's heart and produced a formal acquittance of the debt. Donald, as he cheerfully withdrew, was staring at the pictures and images which he saw in the ducal hall, and expressed to the duke in a homely way, a wish to know what they were. "These," said the duke, who was a Roman Catholic, "are the saints who intercede with God for me." "My lord Duke," said Donald, "would it not be better to apply yourself directly to God? I went to muckle Sawney Gordon, and little Sawney Gordon; but if I had not come to your Grace's self, I could not have got my discharge, and both I and my bairns had been turned out of house and home."

Thou shalt have no other gods before me. A little boy being asked, "how many gods are there?" replied "One." "How do you know that?" "Because," said the boy, "there is room for only one, and he fills heaven and earth."

THE SECOND COMMANDMENT.

30. Repeat the second commandment?

"Thou shalt not take the name of the Lord thy God in vain; for the Lord will not hold him guiltless that taketh his name in vain."

31. What is required of us in this commandment?

That we should so fear and love God, as not to curse, swear, conjure, lie or deceive in his name; but call upon him in every time of need, and worship him with prayer, praise and thanksgiving.

32. What is forbidden in this commandment?

The second commandment forbids the taking of God's name in vain.

33. What do you understand by God's name?

The name of God is that by which he himself is represented, and by which he is distinguished from all creatures.

34. How is God's name represented?

God is represented

1. By his appropriate names, God, Jehovah, Lord, or,
2. By his attributes.

Exodus xxxiv. 6. And the Lord passed by before him, and proclaimed, The Lord, The Lord God, merciful and gracious, long suffering, and abundant in goodness and truth.

Isaiah xlii. 8. I *am* the Lord: that *is* my name: and my glory will I not give to another, neither my praise to graven images.

3. By his word.

Acts ix. 15. But the Lord said unto him, Go thy way: for he is a chosen vessel unto me, to bear my name before the Gentiles, and kings, and the children of Israel.

4. By his sacraments.

Ex. xx. 24. An altar of earth thou shalt make unto me, and shalt sacrifice thereon thy burnt-offerings, and thy peace offerings, thy sheep, and thine oxen: in all places where I record my name I will come unto thee, and I will bless thee.

35. In how many ways may the name of God be taken in vain?

The name of God may be taken in vain, openly and secretly.

36. By whom is God's name openly taken in vain?

God's name is openly taken in vain

    I. By those who deny the being, or existence of God. Ps. xiv. 1.

Psalms xiv. 1. The fool hath said in his heart, *There* is no God. They are corrupt, they have done abominable works, *there* is none that doeth good.

    II. By those who live as though there was no God.

Psalms x. 4. The wicked, through the pride of his countenance, will not seek *after God:* God *is* not in all his thoughts.

Isaiah iii. 9. The shew of their countenance doth witness against them; and they declare their sin as Sodom, they hide it not. Woe unto their soul! for they have rewarded evil unto themselves.

    III. By those who disregard his word or the Holy Scriptures, and the Holy Sacraments, upon which God has placed his name.

Ex. v. 1. And afterward Moses and Aaron went in, and told Pharaoh, Thus saith the Lord God of Israel, Let my people go, that they may hold a feast unto me in the wilderness.

Ex. v. 2. And Pharaoh said, Who *is* the Lord, that I should obey his voice to let Israel go? I know not the Lord, neither will I let Israel go.

Jer. vi. 10. To whom shall I speak, and give warning, that they may hear? Behold, their ear *is* uncircumcised, and they cannot hearken: behold, the word of the Lord is unto them a reproach; they have no delight in it.

    IV. By those who carelessly speak of God and his attributes and ordinances from mere habit or for adornment of their speech or mere merriment.

    V. By those who use that holy name to their own harm and the injury of others,

        a. By cursing, wherein they wish evil either to

themselves or others, thus showing that they cannot control their tongues.

James iii. 5. Even so the tongue is a little member, and boasteth great things. Behold, how great a matter a little fire kindleth.

James iii. 6. And the tongue *is* a fire, a world of iniquity : so is the tongue among our members, that it defileth the whole body, and setteth on fire the course of nature ; and it is set on fire of hell.

  b. By swearing, wherein they falsely, or without necessity, call God to witness for the truth of their assertions.

  c. By conjuring, that is, using the name of God in seeking to accomplish extraordinary things.

  d. By lying, when God's word is perverted to their own or other's injury.

2 Peter iii. 3. Knowing this first, that there shall come in the last days scoffers, walking after their own lusts,

2 Peter iii. 4. And saying, Where is the promise of his coming ? for since the fathers fell asleep, all things continue as *they were* from the beginning of the creation.

37. How is God's name secretly taken in vain ?

God's name is secretly taken in vain when his name, his attributes, his word and sacraments are improperly used or misappropriated.

38. What is required in this commandment ?

In this commandment the proper use of God's name is required,

  1. Internally, that we should keep God always in our mind. Ps. cix. 72 ; Ps. l. 15.

Ps. cxix. 72. The law of thy mouth *is* better unto me than thousands of gold and silver.

Ps. l. 15. And call upon me in the day of trouble : I will deliver thee, and thou shalt glorify me.

  2. Externally, that we should confess him with our lips, diligently read his word, and make a faithful use of the sacraments.

Psalm x. 4. The wicked, through the pride of his countenance, will not seek *after God :* God *is* not in all his thoughts.

Ps. xci. 15. He shall call upon me, and I will answer him: I *will be* with him in trouble; I will deliver him, and honor him.

Ps. xci. 16. With long life will I satisfy him, and shew him my salvation,

3. And apply all this to the glory of God and the good of our own souls.

Prov. xviii. 10. The name of the Lord *is* a strong tower: the righteous runneth into it, and is safe.

39. What are the motives for the observance of this commandment?

The motives for the observance of this commandment are

1. The punishment threatened against its transgressors.

Lev. xxiv. 14. Bring forth him that hath cursed without the camp, and let all that heard *him* lay their hands upon his head, and let all the congregation stone him.

2. The reward promised to those who faithfully obey it.

Acts ii. 21. And it shall come to pass, *that* whosoever shall call on the name of the Lord, shall be saved.

ANECDOTES AND ILLUSTRATIONS.

Scriptural Examples. The Divine Curse: Gen. iii. 17; Gen. iv. 11; Deut. xxvii. 16-26; Noah, Gen. ix. 25; Isaac, Gen. xxvii. 29; Joshua vi. 26; Elisha, 2 Kings ii. 24; David, Ps. cix; Christ, Mark xi. 13, 14, 20, 21; Matt. xxv. 41; Paul, Gal. i. 8.

Sinful cursing. Goliath against David, 1 Sam. xvii. 43; Job iii; Shimei against David, 2 Sam. xvi. 5, 7, 13, 19, 21; Peter, Matt. xxvi. 74.

Divine swearing. To Abraham, Gen. xxii. 16; Isaac, Gen. xxvi. 3; David, Psa. lxxxix., iv., xxxvi., cxxxii., xi; Israelites, Num. xiv. 23, 28, 35; Heb. iii. 14; Abraham, Gen. xxi. 23, 24; Elieser, Gen. xxiv. 1-9; Joseph, Gen. xlvii. 31; Paul, Rom. iv. 4.

The judicial oath. Christ, Matt. xxvi. 63, 64.

Sinful oaths. Peter, Matt. xxvi. 74; Herod, Mark vi. 23.

Perjury. (Compare Jos. ix. 15-19;) 2 Chron. xxxvi. 11-13; Zech. viii. 17; Ezekiel xvii. 19; Absalom, 2 Sam. xv 8; 2 Chron. xxxvi. 11-13.

"That horse, sir," said a coachman to a pious man traveling with him, "that horse knows when I swear at him." "Yes," said the traveller, "and so does One above." The rebuke silenced the profane man.

A wealthy man had been stung in the face by a bee. This caused him intense pain and he called for a doctor to relieve him. The doctor told him to be patient and the pain would subside. But the man cursed and blasphemed in a shocking manner. The doctor then told him the bee had not stung him in the right place. "Where," said the man, "should the bee have stung me?" "At the end of your tongue," replied the doctor.

A king of Egypt sent an animal for sacrifice to Pittakus, one of the seven wise men of Greece, with the request that he should send back to him the *best* and the *worst* piece of it. The wise man sent back to the king the *tongue* of the animal, thereby indicating that the tongue is the *best* part of man when properly used, but the *worst* part of man when improperly used.

James iii. 8 10. The tongue can no man tame; it is an unruly evil, full of deadly poison. Therewith bless we God, even the Father; and therewith curse we men, which are made after the similitude of God. Out of the same mouth proceedeth blessing and cursing. My brethren, these things ought not so to be.

A man in Shelton could not speak without cursing. This distressed his little daughter, who was only four years old. One day she heard him repeat the Lord's Prayer. Yet on the same day she heard him cursing most dreadfully, and said to him. "Did you say the Lord's Prayer to-day?" The man did not answer a word, but from that day he was not heard to curse again.

Prince Henry, the son of James I. of England, had a particular aversion to the vice of swearing and profanation of the name of God. When at play he never swore, and on being asked why he did not swear at play as did others, he answered that he knew of no game worthy of an oath. Again, when a butcher's dog had killed a stag that he was hunting, he remarked, "How could the butcher help it?" One of his huntsmen said that if his father had been served thus, he would have sworn so as no man could have endured it. "Away!" said the prince, "all the pleasure of the world is not worth an oath."

The learned and pious Dr. Desaguliers was once in the company of gentlemen of rank, one of whom swore habitually, yet at every oath asked the doctor's pardon. "Sir," at length said the doctor, "you have taken some pains to render me ridiculous by your pointed apologies; now, sir, I must tell you, that if God Almighty does not hear you, I assure you I will never tell him."

It is related of the venerable Dr. Matthews, President of Hanover College, America, that on one occasion he was walking near the college, with his slow and noiseless step. A youth who had not observed him approach, while engaged in cutting wood, began to swear profanely in his vexation. The doctor stepped up and said, "Give me the axe," and then quietly chopped the wood himself. Returning the axe to the young man, he said, in his peculiar manner, "You see now the wood may be cut without swearing." The reproof was effectual, and led the young man to abandon his impious habit.

"Sir," said a lady travelling in Scotland with a gentleman who swore often, "can you talk Gaelic?" "Yes," said he, "and I will be happy to converse with you." The lady politely asked him to use that language for his oaths, as swearing was offensive to herself and others who knew the English language.

When the Elector of Cologne, who was also an archbishop, was one day swearing profanely, a peasant standing beside him looked amazed. The archbishop asked what he was surprised at. "To hear an archbishop swear," he replied. "I swear not as an archbishop, but as a prince," said the dignitary. "But, my lord," said the peasant, "when the prince goes to the devil, what will become of the archbishop?"

Two soldiers at Chatham once laid a wager on the greatest oaths they could respectively utter. After one of them had uttered many shocking and blasphemous expressions, he hesitated, and said that one more would be his last, when he was instantly struck speechless, and died in three hours. The officers made his body a public spectacle, as a warning to others.

John Howard used to button his pockets when he heard men swearing, saying that if men could take God's name in vain, they might also steal.

An American planter was in the habit of using the name of God frequently in his talk, whereupon one of his slaves made a solemn bow as often as he heard him. On being asked why he did so, he said that the name of God filled his soul with awe. The master took the hint, and was reclaimed from his profane habit.

Two men of learning were conversing together, about the method they should take in reference to a certain regulation imposed upon them by the higher powers, and to which they had conscientious scruples. One of them thoughtlessly and impiously swore, "By my faith," said he, "I must live." The other calmly and pleasantly replied, "I hope to live by my faith too, though I dare not swear by it." The result was that the man who resolved by grace, to venture his temporal interest for conscience-sake, lived in prosperity to see the other begging, and to contribute to his relief.

In the year 1796, when the ship Duff was preparing to take out the missionaries from the London Missionary Society, Mr. Cox, one of the Directors, was one day walking in the street; he was there met by a very fine looking boy, about fourteen years of age, who, stopping him, said, "Pray sir, have you not some management in the ship that is going out with the missionaries?" "Yes, I have, my young man," said Mr. Cox. "I should like very much, sir, to go out with her as a cabin boy." "Would you?" said Mr. Cox, "have you any parents?" "I have a mother," said the boy, "but no father." "And is your mother willing you should go?" "O yes, sir, very willing." Mr. Cox then desired the boy to call at his house and to bring his mother along with him, that she might speak for herself. At the time appointed, the boy and his mother came, who, having declared her willingness that her son should go, the matter was accordingly settled. In the course of the conversation, a gentleman who was present, in order to try the boy, said to him, "So you wish to go to sea?" "Yes, sir, in the missionary ship." "And you can swear a good round hand, I suppose?" Shocked at the very idea of such a thing, the ingenuous little fellow bursts into tears, and exclaimed, "*If I thought there would be swearing on board at all, I would not go.*"

Mr. John Howe, being at dinner with some persons of fashion, a gentleman expatiated largely in praise of Charles I., and made some disagreeable reflections upon others. Mr. Howe, observing that he mixed many horrid oaths with his discourse, took the liberty to say that in his humble opinion, he had omitted one great excellence in the character of that prince, which, when the gentleman had pressed him to mention, and waited with impatience to hear it, he told him it was this: "that he was never heard to swear an oath in common conversation." The gentleman took the reproof, and promised to break off the practice.

The late Rev. John Brown of Haddington, once passing the Firth of Forth, between Leith and Kinghorn, had for a fellow-passenger, one who appeared to be a Highland nobleman. Mr. B. observed with grief, that he frequently took the name of God in vain: but suspecting, that to reprove him in the presence of the other passengers, might tend only to irritate him, he forebore saying anything till he reached the opposite shore. After landing, Mr. B., observing the nobleman walking alone, stepped up to him and said, "Sir, I was sorry to hear you swearing while on our passage. You know it is written, 'Thou shalt not take the name of the Lord thy God in vain.'" On this the nobleman, lifting his hat, and bowing to Mr. B., made the following reply: "Sir, I return you thanks for the reproof you have now given me, and shall endeavor to attend to it in the future, but," added he, "had you said this to me while in the boat, I believe I should have run you through with my sword."

The Rev. John Maclaurin, of Glasgow, well known to the christian world by his valuable writings, in passing one day along the street, was disturbed by the noise of some disorderly soldiers. One of them particularly, just as Mr. Maclaurin approached them, uttered this awful imprecation, "God damn my soul, for Christ's sake!" The good man, shocked with hearing such blasphemous language, went up to him, and laying his hand on the shoulder of the man, said to him with peculiar mildness and solemnity, "Friend, God has already done much for Christ's sake; suppose he should do that too, what would become of you?" It was a word in season, and it came with power. The conscience of the soldier sunk under the reproof. He was lead not only to reform the evil habit of swearing, to which he had long been addicted, but to reflect on his ways, and to turn to the Lord. He became a real Christian; and proved the soundness of his conversion by maintaining to the end of his life, a conversation becoming the gospel.

A minister of the gospel, one day finding a servant beating his master's horses, and taking the name of God in vain, he stood still and reproved him sharply. The servant made no reply, but prompted by curiosity, came next Lord's day to hear his reprover preach. "Swear not at all," said the preacher, when concluding his discourse, "is a divine command that binds both master and servant. I knew a man, not long ago, who surprised one of the swearing tribe of servants, in the very act of damning his master's horses. The son of Belial, though challenged, durst not open his mouth for his father's interest; but hung down his head like a coward in the devil's service. He passed by, and had not the manners to thank his reprover, or grace to promise amendment. Is he here? Do I see him? Shall I name him?" After some pause, he added, "We shall rather pray for him." The servant was sitting trembling before him; and may it be proper to add, that he came forward to the minister, confessed his fault, gave signs of true repentance, was added to the church, and never after heard to blaspheme that worthy name.

THE THIRD COMMANDMENT.

40. Repeat the third commandment?

"Remember the Sabbath day to keep it holy. Six days shalt thou labor, and do all thy work: But the seventh day *is* the Sabbath of the Lord thy God.

In it thou shalt not do any work, thou, nor thy son, nor thy daughter, thy man-servant, nor thy maid-servant, nor thy cattle, nor thy stranger that *is* within thy gates.

For *in* six days the Lord made heaven and earth, the sea, and all that in them *is*, and rested the seventh day:

Wherefore the Lord blessed the Sabbath-day, and hallowed it.

41. What is enjoined in this commandment?

That we should so fear and love God, as not to despise his word and day, and the preaching of his gospel; but deem it holy, and willingly hear, learn and obey it.

42. What is the meaning of the word Sabbath?

Sabbath is the Hebrew word for rest.

43. When and by whom was the Sabbath appointed?

God appointed and hallowed the Sabbath day after his six day's work of creation, because he rested on the seventh day.

44. What is meant by God's resting on the seventh day?

By this expression is meant, that God ceased from his work of creation on the seventh day.

45. What day of the week is required to be kept holy as the Sabbath day?

In the Old Testament dispensation the seventh day was required to be kept holy in honor of a finished creation. But in the New Testament dispensation, the first day of the week is required to be kept holy in honor of a finished redemption.

46. Why was the Sabbath changed from the seventh to the first day of the week?

In the christian church the first day of the week is appointed to be kept as a holy Sabbath day, because

1. Christ rose from the dead on the first day of the week. Matt. xxviii. 1-7.

2. During the forty days between his resurrection and ascension he frequently met with his disciples on the first day of the week, and thus sanctioned their assembling on that day by his presence.

John xx. 1. The first *day* of the week cometh Mary Magdalene early, when it was yet dark, unto the sepulchre, and seeth the stone taken away from the sepulchre.

John xx. 19. Then the same day at evening, being the first *day* of the week, when the doors were shut where the disciples were assembled for fear of the Jews, then came Jesus and stood in the midst, and saith unto them, Peace be unto you.

John xx. 26. And after eight days again his disciples were within, and Thomas with them : *then* came Jesus, the doors being shut, and stood in the midst, and said, Peace *be* unto you.

3. The Holy Ghost was poured out upon the disciples on the day of Pentecost, which was also on the first day of the week.

4. In Scripture it is called The Lord's Day.

Rev. i. 9. I John, who also am your brother, and companion in tribulation, and in the kingdom and patience of Jesus Christ, was in the isle that is called Patmos, for the word of God, and for the testimony of Jesus Christ.

Rev. i. 10. I was in the Spirit on the Lord's day, and heard behind me a great voice, as of a trumpet,

Rev. i. 11. Saying, I am Alpha and Omega, the first and the last: and, what thou seest, write in a book, and send *it* unto the seven churches which are in Asia; Unto Ephesus, and unto Smyrna, and unto Pergamos, and unto Thyatira, and unto Sardis, and unto Philadelphia, and unto Laodicea.

5. The inspired apostles and early Christians met on the first day of the week for public worship. Acts ii. 1-41; Rev. i. 1-11.

1 Cor. xvi. 1. Now concerning the collection for the saints, as I have given order to the churches of Galatia, even so do ye.

1 Cor. xvi. 2. Upon the first *day* of the week let every one of you lay by him in store, as God hath prospered him, that there be no gathering when I come.

6. Ignatius, the disciple of St. John, says: "Let us not Jewishly sabbatize, but let us rest spiritually; and instead of the old Sabbath, let every lover of Christ celebrate the Lord's day, the best and most eminent of days, on which our Lord arose."

47. Has the Sabbath or any part of it ever been abolished?

The ceremonial aspect of the Third Commandment, which pertained especially to the Jewish people, has been abolished, because it was fulfilled in Christ; but the moral aspect of the Sabbath has not been abolished, because the Sabbath is necessary for our bodily health as well as our spiritual welfare.

48. How does the third commandment differ from the other commandments?

The third commandment differs from the preceding, and most of the following commandments, which are put *negatively*,—" Thou shalt *not*," while this one is *positive*, and says, " Remember the Sabbath day to keep it holy." It is a positive enactment and a special revelation from God.

49. What is meant by keeping the Sabbath day holy?

We keep the Sabbath day holy, when we devote the whole day to bodily rest and religious duties.

50. What religious exercises should we engage in on the Sabbath?

1. In the morning we should have family worship, engage in religious meditation, reading of the Scripture or good books, then

2. Attend public worship, hear the word with a prayful heart, and regard it as a great privilege to enjoy the means of grace.

Luke x. 16. He that heareth you, heareth me; and he that despiseth you, despiseth me; and he that despiseth me, despiseth him that sent me.

2 Cor. v. 20. Now then we are ambassadors for Christ, as though God did beseech *you* by us: we pray *you* in Christ's stead, be ye reconciled to God.

3. After the public worship we should search the scriptures, apply the truths, which we have heard, to our hearts and carry them out in practice.

51. What other religious duties should we engage in on the Sabbath?

As we may have opportunity we should unite with our fellow christians in social prayer, take an active part in Sunday-school, visit the sick, etc.

52. How is the Sabbath day profaned?

We profane the Sabbath,

1. When by excessive bodily labors we so exhaust our strength as to unfit ourselves to receive the word.

Luke viii. 6. And some fell upon a rock; and as soon as it was sprung up, it withered away, because it lacked moisture.

Luke viii. 7. And some fell among thorns; and the thorns sprang up with it, and choked it.

Luke viii. 8. And other fell on good ground, and sprang up, and bare fruit a hundred-fold. And when he had said these things, he cried, He that hath ears to hear, let him hear.

2. When during the public worship we whisper, pay no attention, sleep, or occupy our thoughts with worldly business.

3. When we neglect public worship without a reasonable excuse.

4. When we spend the day in worldly amusements, such as dancing, Sunday excursions, games, formal visits in which the conversation is mainly on our worldly business, or politics.

Isaiah lviii. 13. If thou turn away thy foot from the Sabbath, *from* doing thy pleasure on my holy day; and call the sabbath a delight, the holy of the Lord, honorable; and shalt honor him, not doing thine own ways, nor finding thine own pleasure, nor speaking *thine own* words.

53. What works are allowed to be done on the Sabbath?

Works of necessity, charity or mercy are allowed and commanded to be done on the Sabbath; such as

1. Attending to the wants of our domestic animals.

2. Keeping ourselves comfortable in our clothing and houses, and preparing our food.

3. Ministering to the sick and needy.

4. Rescuing men or beasts from peril, through accident, fire or flood.

<small>Matt. xii. 11. And he said unto them, What man shall there be among you, that shall have one sheep, and if it fall into a pit on the sabbath-day, will he not lay hold on it, and lift *it* out?</small>

54. What are the motives for keeping this commandment?

We should keep this commandment, because

1. God says, "Remember the Sabbath day to keep it holy."

2. God gave this command already in Paradise. It is therefore obligatory on the whole human race.

3. God has given us six days to do all our own work, but the seventh day is the Sabbath of the Lord, our God, on which he has commanded us to do no work.

ANECDOTES AND ILLUSTRATIONS.

Scripture Examples. John. Rev. i. 10; The Israelites do not gather manna on the Sabbath. Exodus xvi. 22-24. The man who gathered fire-wood on the Sabbath. Numbers xv. 32-36. Christ heals the sick on the Sabbath. Mark iii. 3-5; Luke xiii. 10-17; Luke xiv. 1-6; John v. 1; etc. Nehemiah xiii. 15-23. Christ, Matt. iv. 1-11. The disciples. John ii. 22. Philip and the Eunuck. Acts viii. 26, etc. The Bereans. Acts xviii. 11. Apollo. Acts. xviii. 24. Love to the house of God. David. 1 Chron. xvii. 7-36; Psalms xxvi. 6-8; xxvii. 4; lxxxiv. 2-5. David and the people. 1 Chron. xxx. Solomon. 1 Kings v. 8; The first christians. Acts ii. 46. Desecration of the house of God by the heathen. 2 Malkabus vi. 4. The Jews, xix. 45, 46.

A German once visited a rich manufacturer in England and remarked that it must be a great loss which he must sustain to have the work in his factory stopped on Sunday. But the manufacturer replied, "It has been my experience, that what is gained on Sunday is lost on Monday."

A planter in Surinam asked his negroes why they must always come together to pray. He thought each one might as well pray by himself. He was just standing before a coal-fire, and one of the negroes said, "Massa, if you would lay these coals each by itself, they would all go out, but what a grand fire they make when they all burn together.

King Charles, of England, was once interrupted in the midst of the sermon in church by a nobleman who wanted to engage in conversation with him. "Dear sir," said the king, "do not hinder me from hearing God when he speaks to me, in order that on the other hand, he may hear me when I speak to him."

Luther attended public worship in a village one Sunday and listened attentively to the sermon. Some one criticised the sermon in Luther's presence. But Luther said, "O, if a preacher simply preaches Christ according to the Gospel as explained in the catechism, then he is a blessed preacher. In the time of Moses they had not only gold and silver vessels in the tabernacle, but also copper and iron ones, yet they all served the eternal Son of God."

That great man, Sir Matthew Hale, thus speaks of the Sabbath: "I have," says he, "by long and sound experience, found that the due observance of this day, and of the duties of it, have been of singular comfort and advantage to me. The observance of this day hath ever had joined to it, a blessing upon the rest of my time; and the week that hath been so begun, hath been blessed and prosperous to me; and, on the other side, when I have been negligent of the duties of this day, the rest of the week has been unsuccessful and unhappy to my own secular employments; so that I could easily make an estimate of my successes the week following, by the manner of my passing of this day: and this I do not write lightly or inconsiderately, but upon a long and sound observation and experience."

It is said of the pious and learned Mr. Gouge, that as he forbore providing suppers on the eve before the Sabbath, that servants might not be kept up too late, so he would never suffer any servant to tarry at home to dress any meat on the Lord's day for any friends, whether they were mean or great, few or many.

Mr. Philip Henry used to call the Lord's day, the queen of days, the pearl of the week, and observed it accordingly. His common salutation of his family or friends, on the Lord's day in the morning, was that of the primitive Christians; "the Lord is risen! he is risen indeed!" making it his chief business on that day to celebrate the memory of Christ's resurrection; and he would say sometimes, "Every Lord's day is a true Christian's Easterday."

Mr. John Knox, a little before his death, rose out of his bed, and being asked, "Why he rose, being so sick?" he answered, "That he had had in the night sweet meditations on the resurrection of Jesus Christ; and now he would go into the pulpit, and impart to others the comforts he felt in his soul."

A woman who always used to attend public worship with great punctuality, and took care to be always in time, was asked, how it was she could always come so early, she answered very wisely, "that it was part of her religion not to disturb the religion of others."

One Lord's day, as a man was passing through Haworth on horseback, his horse lost a shoe; he applied to a blacksmith, who told him, "that he could not shoe a horse on the Lord's day, without the ministers permission." They went together to Mr. Grimshaw, the minister of the place, and the man, satisfying him that he really was in haste, going for a midwife, Mr. Grimshaw permitted the blacksmith to shoe the horse, which otherwise he would not have done for double pay.

It was the frequent and almost constant custom of Mr. Grimshaw to leave his church while the psalm was singing, to see if any were absent from worship and idling their time in the church-yard, the street or the ale-house: and many of those whom he so found he would drive into the church before him. "A friend of mine," says Mr. Newton, "passing a public-house in Haworth, on a Lord's day morning, saw several persons making their escape out of it, some jumping out of the lower windows, and some over a low wall; he was at first alarmed, fearing the house was on fire; but, on inquiring what was the cause of the commotion, he was told that they saw the parson coming. They were more afraid of their parson than they were of a justice of peace. His reproofs were so authoritative, and yet so mild and friendly that the stoutest sinners could not stand before him."

A minister, observing that some of his people made a practice of coming in very late, and after a considerable part of the sermon was over, determined that they should feel the force of public reproof. One day, therefore, as they entered the place of worship at their usual late hour, the minister, addressing his congregation, said, "But, my hearers, it is time for us now to conclude, for here are our friends just come to fetch us home." We may easily conjecture what the parties felt at this curious but pointed address.

In the year, 1809, a youth about seventeen years of age, the son of a respectable tradesman in London, went out for the purpose of shooting birds *on a Lord's day in the afternoon*. He had done so more than once before, which coming to the knowledge of his father, he expressly enjoined him never to do the like again. But the lad, disregarding this command, and taking advantage of his father's absence, borrowed a gun from a person in the neighborhood, and went out as usual. While he was watching the birds, the gun by some accident, went off, and killed him on the spot. Not returning at the accustomed time, his friends were alarmed; a search was made, and at length his body was discovered in a barn, in a state too shocking to be described.

On a Lord's day, at the time of the great frost in the year 1634, fourteen young men were playing at football, on the river Trent, near Gainsborough; while thus engaged, in the open violation of God's command, they met together in a scuffle; the ice suddenly broke, and they were all drowned.

When a minister of the gospel was spending a few weeks in Edinburg, there came on business to the house where he was, a man of the world—one of those modern scoffers who are so constantly fulfilling Peter's prediction, 2 Peter iii. 3. He was introduced to the preacher in the following manner: "This is Mr. ———, an acquaintance of mine, and I am sorry to add, though young and healthy, never attends public worship." "I am almost tempted to hope," replied the minister, "that you are bearing false witness against your neighbor." "By no means," said the infidel, "for I always spend my Sunday in settling accounts." The minister immediately replied, "You will find, sir, that the day of judgment will be spent in exactly the same manner."

The eccentric preacher, Rowland Hill (died 1833), once took a large stone with him to church and laid it on the pulpit beside the Bible. When he noticed that the people were uncommonly attentive and astonished, he remarked, "As you are so very attentive to this common, cold, dead stone, how much more should you be attentive to the word of God."

Leigh Leigton, bishop of Glasgow, went to church one Sunday during unpleasant weather, notwithstanding his ill health. He said, "If the weather had been fair, I would have remained at home, but as it is unpleasant, I dare not stay away, for it might appear, as if by my example I sanctioned the bad practice of neglecting public worship for slight hindrances."

The Pilgrim Fathers, who landed on Plymouth Rock in the bleak month of December, were conscientious keepers of the Sabbath. The first Sabbath was spent on the island, within half an hour's sail of the harbor. They moored, and dedicated the day of sacred rest to God on the frost-bound shore, and beneath a snowy sky. "There they stood; there they praised God; there arose to heaven from New England's soil the first Sabbath hymn of praise and the first united prayer of faith, from child-like, patient, submissive hearts—from men in resolution and endurance, children in faith and obedience."—*Dr. Cheever.*

A gentleman in England, who was in the habit for more than twenty years of daily visiting convicts, states that almost universally, when brought to a sense of their condition, they lamented their neglect of the Sabbath, and pointed to the violation of it as the principal cause of their ruin.

Of 1232 convicts in the Auburn State Prison, previously to 1837, as many as 447 had been watermen, boatmen or sailors, who had been kept at work on the Sabbath. Of these, only 26 had conscientiously kept the Sabbath.

When Captain Palmer of Her Majesty's ship *Rosario*, was at Tanna, in the New Hebrides, he was anxious to see what effect the few years' residence of the missionary, the Rev. Thomas Neilson, had had upon the savage people. He told all his men that there was to be no trading on Sabbath. To his surprise not a canoe came to the ship. Some of the boys went in a boat to the shore, and wished the natives to give them some cocoanuts. They replied, "To-morrow!" Yet these same men were not then baptized Christians.

David Brainerd, a devoted and successful missionary to the North American Indians, speaking of the Sabbath, says: "I was born on a Sabbath day; I was new-born on a Sabbath-day; and I hope I shall die on a Sabbath-day. I long for the time. Oh, why is his chariot so long in coming?"

When the miners first crowded into California, to dig for gold, they worked seven days in the week, until they found they were digging more than gold—they were digging graves. They therefore, resolved to rest one day in seven, and found that it was to their temporal advantage to have a Sabbath.

In the city of Bath a barber pursued his craft, as so many in his trade do, on the Sabbath-day. One day he happened to look into a church just as the minister was giving out his text, "Remember the Sabbath-day, to keep it holy." He listened long enough to be convinced that he was habitually violating one of God's commands. After a struggle he gave up his Sabbath work. God blessed him afterwards.

LUTHER ON THE SABBATH.

The following are extracts from Luther's writings as quoted by the *Lutheran Observer,*

Its Institutions and Sacredness. "It is the demand of nature," says Luther, "that man should refrain from labor, and rest one day in the week, ... which natural cause Moses also sets forth in the Sabbath, in order that he may set the Sabbath among men, as Christ also does (Matthew xii. 8; Mark ii. 27). The Sabbath existed before the law of Moses came, and had, indeed, been ordained from the beginning of the world for the service of God. If Adam had remained steadfast in his innocence, he yet would have kept holy the seventh day. Where the law of Moses and the law of nature are one thing, there the law remains. God sanctified the seventh day unto himself. The force and might of the third [fourth] commandment lie, not in the *resting*, but in the *sanctifying* of the day; for the proper idea of the Sabbath is, that we should teach and hear the word on God's day, in order that we may sanctify both the day and ourselves. The Sabbath is in itself a command for all the world. God will have this commandment strictly kept, and will punish those who break it."

The Change of the Sabbath. "Christians have always kept Sunday, not Saturday, and I believe that the Apostles transferred the Sabbath to Sunday (from the seventh to the first day of the week), otherwise no man would have been so audacious as to dare to do it. And I believe that they were moved thereto by the resurrection of Christ our Lord, and the sending of the Holy Ghost on Pentecost. The Sabbath (seventh day) is now changed for us into Sunday (the first day), and the other days are work days. Sunday (the Christian Sabbath) is the day of rest, or holy day, or sacred day. Would to God that there were no other holy day except Sunday in Christendom, and that all the festivals were put on Sunday! and the half day of the afternoon should be holy to God, as well as the half day of the forenoon."

Works of Mercy and Charity. "Works of necessity are, however, allowable on the Sabbath day; but such necessity must not be devised by men, but thrust upon them. Physicians, messengers and others are all excusable in case of necessity. But here it may be asked whether our Wittenbergers are excusable for shooting at the popinjay with the cross-bow on the sacred day, for that could be done on another day, and there is no necessity, nor love, nor requirement to excuse such a thing. The practice of inspecting arms and accoutrements on Sunday is to be regarded in the same way, as if that too could not be done on a week day ; and to this matter the attention of the magistrates should be directed."

These quotations taken from the writings of Luther, speak for themselves. They are clear, discriminating, consistent with each other, and cover the whole ground. They prove that Luther regarded the Sabbath—*i. e.*, setting apart one day for rest in seven—as founded in nature and demanded by the physical and spiritual wants of man. He distinguished between its moral aspects which were perpetual and unchahangeable, and its ceremonial aspects which were temporal and changeable. As founded upon the eternal fitness of things, he maintained that its observance was obligatory upon all men before the law was promulgated from Sinai, even from the creation, and will continue to be obligatory upon them to the end of time. While he insisted that the Jewish Sabbath, as an arbitrary institution, was abrogated, he insisted just as stoutly that the Christian Sabbath, as a moral institution, was substituted for the Jewish, and that all that pertained to the Sabbath originally as founded upon nature, and all that was contained in the Sabbatic commandment as a moral statute, had been transferred by the Apostles, under divine inspiration, to Sunday, the Christian Sabbath. The late Dr. C. P. Krauth, of Philadelphia, after a careful examination of Luther's writings on the Sabbath, forcibly remarks : "If Germany has not enjoyed a Christian Sabbath, it is because she has refused what the principles of Luther would have given her. The Sunday of Luther was an entire day, not a morning for the church and an afternoon for the beer saloon or the dance or idle saunter ; but a day for holy works and holy thoughts, a holy day, not a holiday. When, in his own matchless manner, he has overthrown the idea of intrinsic or ceremonial or meritorious sacredness in days or places or outward things under the New Dispensation, he regards no language too strong to mark how blessed and how necessary is the day of the Lord, nor how great is the guilt and peril of those who profane and neglect it."

Violations of the Sabbath. "Those violate the Sabbath who do manual labor and business ; those who engage in feasting, surfeiting, drunkenness, dancing and wantonness; those who indulge in sloth, sleep, idle talk and loitering about; those who do not pray, meditate nor mourn over their sins, and who neglect the ordinances of God and lose the blessings of the sacred day."

We may also add the testimony of Christ, who, as "Lord of the Sabbath," recognized its divine institution by declaring that "the Sabbath was made for man." And by rising from the dead, pouring out the Holy Spirit on the first day of the week, and by meeting with his Apostles assembled on that day for religious services, he sanctioned the change of the Sabbath from the seventh to the first day of the week, and by his example enforced its observance as the Christian Sabbath upon all his disciples until the end of the world.

THE FOURTH COMMANDMENT.

55. Repeat the fourth commandment?

"Honor thy father and thy mother, that thy days may be long upon the land which the Lord thy God giveth thee.

Ephesians vi. 1. Children, obey your parents in the Lord: for this is right.

Ephesians vi. 2. Honor thy father and mother, (which is the first commandment with promise.)

Ephesians vi. 3. That it may be well with thee, and thou mayest live long on the earth.

56. What is the signification of this commandment?

That we should so fear and love God, as not to despise or displease our parents or superiors; but honor, serve, obey, love and esteem them.

57. What is required in the fourth commandment?

In the fourth commandment we are required to honor our father and our mother, and those who are placed over us, as our superiors, or associated with us as our equals, or placed under us as our inferiors.

58. Of whom do our superiors consist?

Our superiors consist of our parents, masters, teachers or pastors, magistrates or rulers.

59. Of whom do our equals consist?

Our equals consist of our brothers and sisters, classmates, and persons of the same rank with us.

60. Of whom do our inferiors consist?

Our inferiors consist of our children, servants, scholars and subjects.

61. By whom were these relations appointed?

These relations were appointed by God, and are therefore wise, and good, and right.

62. *What does this commandment require more particularly of children towards their parents?*

This commandment requires more particularly that children should honor their parents, because they are dependent on them and receive much love and care from them.

Children should also love, obey and respect their parents, and do this more so, as they grow in age and intelligence.

63. *How should this honor to parents be manifested?*

The honor toward our parents should be manifested,
1. Internally.
2. Externally.

64. *In what way do we honor our parents internally?*

We honor our parents internally by esteeming them highly on account of their piety, intelligence and experience, and because God has confided us to their care to nourish, protect and clothe us.

65. *In what way do we honor our parents externally?*

Externally we honor our parents,
1. By our behavior, words and actions.
2. By our obedience and cheerful services in all things pleasing to God.
3. But especially by comforting and supporting them when they need our help in poverty, sickness or old age.

66. *Should we obey our superiors when they command us to sin?*

When our parents or superiors command us to sin, we should not obey them, for we must obey God, rather than man.

67. *How should we act towards our equals?*

We should love, comfort, assist and respect our equals.

68. *How should we act toward our inferiors?*

Towards our inferiors we should be condescending, kind, just and exemplary.

69. *What is forbidden in this commandment?*

The fourth commandment forbids the neglect of the honor and duty which we owe to others who stand in relation to us.

70. *How do parents and superiors transgress this commandment?*

Parents transgress this commandment when they neglect the welfare of their children, and superiors when they neglect the welfare of their inferiors.

71. *How do equals transgress this commandment?*

Equals, such as brothers and sisters, transgress this commandment when they omit brotherly kindness and mutual respect.

72. *How do inferiors transgress this commandment?*

Children transgress this commandment when they do not honor their parents, servants their masters, learners their teachers or pastors, subjects their rulers.

73. *What farther does this commandment more especially forbid?*

The fourth commandment forbids tyranny over inferiors; disobedience by inferiors, and envy and malice by equals. This also applies to disobedience of parents by children, of employers by servants, and to strife between brethren.

74. *What are the motives for the observance of this commandment?*

The motives for the observance of this commandment are the following:

1. The promise of long life and the divine blessing on those who honor their father and their mother.

Ephesians vi. 1. Children, obey your parents in the Lord: for this is right.

2. The punishment threatened against violaters of this commandment.

Prov. xix. 26. He that wasteth *his* father, *and* chaseth away *his* mother, *is* a son that causeth shame, and bringeth reproach.

3. And gratitude for the benefits received from our parents.

ANECDOTES AND ILLUSTRATIONS.

Scriptural Examples. Honor due to parents; Shem and Japheth, Gen. ix. 23; Joseph, Gen. xlv. 9. Solomon, 1 Kings ii. 19, 20. Love: Joseph, Gen. xlvi. 29. Elisha, 1 Kings xix. 20. Obedience: Isaac, Gen. xxii. 6; Jacob, xxviii. 1; Joseph, xxxvii. 13. The Rechabites, Jer. xxxv. 18, 19. Jesus, Luke ii. 51. Gratitude: Joseph, Gen. xlv. 11. David, 1 Sam. xxii. 3. Jesus: John, xix. 25-27. Jonathan, 1 Sam. xix. Bad children: Cain, Gen. iv; Ham, ix. 2; Jocob's sons, xxxvii. Eli's sons, 1 Sam ii. 12, 15, 22-25 Samuels sons, Joel and Obia, viii. 1-5. Absalom, 2 Sam. xiii. 1. Manasseh, 2 Chron. xxxiii. 1.

Children should provide for the wants of their aged parents, A farmer was one day ploughing near the summer residence of a king. The king happening to ride past the place where he was laboring, called to him in a kind tone, "You appear to be very industrious, my friend. Does this field belong to you, in which you are ploughing so busily?" "No sir," said the farmer, who did not know the king, "I am ploughing for wages." "And how much do you get for your labors." "Eight groats." "And what do you do with these eight groats?" "Two groats are for me and my wife; with two I pay my debts, two I invest in hope, and two I give away."

The king did not quite understand the farmer's answer, and desired an explanation, which he gave as follows: "I have my parents at home with me, who are now old and feeble; but as they nourished me in my childhood and brought me up to manhood, I am now also bound to sustain them in their old age; this debt I daily pay off with two groats. The third pair of groats, which I invest in hope, I devote to the education of my children, for I hope, that when I cannot labor any longer, they will also support me. With the last two groats, which I give away, I support my two sickly sisters." The king was so much pleased with the way in which this poor laborer laid out his wages, that he gave him rich presents, and this enabled him to treat his aged parents and sick sisters with still greater kindness, and to give his children a more liberal education.

Frederick, the late king of Prussia, having rung his bell one day, and nobody answering, opened the door, and found the page in waiting, asleep on a sofa. He was just going to awake him when he perceived the end of a paper out of his pocket, on which something was written; this excited his curiosity; he pulled it out and found it to be a letter from the mother of the page, thanking him for having sent her a part of his wages, which had proved a very timely assistance to her, and, in conclusion, beseeching God to bless him for his filial duty. The king stepped softly to his room, took a roll of ducats, and slipped them with the letter into the page's pocket. Returning to his apartment, he rung so violently that the page awoke, opened the door and entered. "You have been asleep," said the king. The page attempted to excuse himself; and in his embarrassment, happened to put his hand into his pocket, felt with astonishment the roll. He drew it out, turned pale, and looking at the king, burst into tears, without being able to speak a word. "What is the matter?" said the king, "what ails you?" "Oh! sire," said the young man, throwing himself at his majesty's feet, "somebody wishes to ruin me. I know not how I came by this money in my pocket." "What God bestows," resumed the king, "he bestows in sleep; * send the money to your mother; salute her in my name, and assure her, that I shall take care of both her and you."

The danger occasioned by an awful eruption of Mount Etna, many years since, obliged the inhabitants of the adjacent country to flee in every direction for safety. Amidst the hurry and confusion of this scene, everyone carrying away what he deemed most precious, two sons, the one named Anaphias, the other Amphonimus, in the height of their solicitude for the preservation of their wealth and goods, recollected their father and mother, who, being both very old, were unable to save themselves by flight. Filial tenderness overcame every other consideration. "Where!" exclaimed the generous youths, "shall we find a more precious treasure than our parents?" This said, the one took up his father on his shoulders, the other his mother, and so made their way through the surrounding smoke and flames.

The judicious Hooker used to say, "If I had no other reason and motive for being religious, I would earnestly strive to be so for the sake of my aged mother, that I might requite her care of me, and cause the widow's heart to sing for joy."

---

* A German proverb.

Among the multitude of persons who were proscribed under the second triumvirate of Rome, were the celebrated orator Cicero, and his brother Quintus. The latter found means to conceal himself so effectually at home that the soldiers could not find him. Enraged at their disappointment, they put his son to the torture in order to make him discover the place of his father's concealment; but filial affection was proof against the most exquisite torments. An involuntary sigh, and sometimes a deep groan were all that could be extorted from the youth. His agonies were increased, but with amazing fortitude he still persisted in his resolution of not betraying his father. Quintus was not far off, and it may be imagined better than can be expressed how his heart must have been affected with the sighs and groans of a son expiring in torture to save his life. He could bear it no longer, but, quitting the place of his concealment, he presented himself to the assassins, begging them to put him to death and dismiss the innocent youth. But the inhuman monsters, without being the least affected with the tears either of the father or of the son, answered that they must both die; the father because he was proscribed, and the son, because he had concealed the father. Then a new contest of tenderness arose, who should die first; but this the assassins soon decided, by beheading them both at the same time.

Ancient history records that a certain city was besieged, and at length obliged to surrender. In the city there were two brothers who had in some way obliged the conquering general, and in consequence of this, received permission to leave the city before it was set on fire, taking with them as much of their property as each could carry about his person. Accordingly the generous youths appeared at the gates of the city, one of them carrying their father, and the other their mother.

Pomponius Atticus, who pronounced a funeral oration on the death of his mother, protested that though he had resided with her sixty-seven years, he was never once reconciled to her; "because," said he, "there never happened the least discord between us, and consequently there was no need of reconciliation."

Olympias, the mother of Alexander, was of so very unhappy and morose a disposition that he could not employ her in any of the affairs of government. She, however, narrowly inspected the conduct of others, and made many complaints to her son, which he always bore with patience. Antipater, Alexander's deputy to Europe, once wrote a long letter to him complaining of her conduct, to whom Alexander returned this answer: "Knowest thou not, that one tear of my mother's will blot out a thousand such letters."

When Epaminondas had won three battles over the Lacedemonians, the subject which gave him the most pleasure was that his father was living to enjoy the news.

A deaf and dumb boy, thirteen years of age, educated in the school for such persons at Edinburg, after an absence of four years, went home to see his mother. When he entered her house in company with his benefactor, she was sitting in a state of intoxication, which greatly affected him. He took his pencil and attempted to show her the evil and danger of such conduct, and gave her much good advice. After retiring with his friend, at whose house he went to lodge, his countenance became very sorrowful and the tears trickled down his cheeks. His friend asked him the occasion of all this, when he wrote that he was thinking if he got to heaven, how sorry he should be, not to find his mother there.

A negro of one of the kingdoms on the African coast, who had become insolvent, surrendered himself to his creditors, who, according to the established custom of the country, sold him to the Danes. This affected his son so much that he came and reproached his father for not selling his children to pay his debts; and after much entreaty, he prevailed on the captain to accept him, and liberate his father. The son was put in chains, and on the point of sailing to the West Indies; when the circumstance coming to the knowledge of the Governor, through the means of Mr. Isert, he sent for the owner of the slaves, paid the money that he had given for the old man, and restored the son to his father.

General George Washington, when quite young, was about to go to sea as a midshipman; everything was arranged, the vessel lay opposite his father's house, the little boat had come on shore to take him off, and his whole heart was bent on going. After his trunk had been carried down to the boat, he went to bid his mother farewell, and saw the tears bursting from her eyes. However, he said nothing to her, but he saw that his mother would be distressed if he went, and perhaps never be happy again. He just turned round to the servant and said, "Go and tell them to fetch my trunk back. I will not go away to break my mother's heart." His mother was struck with his decision, and she said to him, "George, God has promised to bless the children that honor their parents, and I believe he will bless you."

Valerius Maximus relates that a woman of distinction, having been condemned to be strangled, was delivered to the triumvir, who caused her to be carried to prison in order to be put to death. The jailer who was ordered to execute her, was struck with compunction, and could not resolve to kill her. He chose, however, to let her die with hunger; but meanwhile suffering her daughter to visit her in prison, taking care that she brought her nothing to eat. Many days passed over in this manner, when the jailer at length, surprised that the prisoner lived so long without food, took means of secretly observing their interviews. He then discovered that the affectionate daughter had all the while been nourishing her mother with her own milk. Amazed at so tender and at the same time so ingenious an artifice, he related it to the triumvir, and the triumvir to the proctor, who thought the fact merited stating in the assembly of the people. This produced the happiest effects; the criminal was pardoned, and a decree passed that the mother and daughter should be maintained for the remainder of their lives, at the expense of the public; and that a temple, sacred to filial piety, should be erected near the prison.

A certain farmer in Connecticut, possessing a small estate, was persuaded by his only son (who was married and lived with his father), to give him a deed of the property. It was accordingly executed. Soon the father began to find himself neglected; next removed from the common table to a block in the chimney corner, to take the morsel of food reluctantly given him. At last the unnatural son resolved one day, to try to break the afflicted heart of his sire. He procured a block and began to hollow it. While at work, he was questioned by one of his children what he was doing. "I am making a trough for your grandfather to eat out of," was the reply. "Ah," says the child, "and when you are as old as grandfather, shall I have to make a trough for you to eat out of?" The instrument he was using fell from his hand, the block was cast on the fire; the old man's forgiveness asked, and he was restored to the situation to which his age and worth entitled him.

There was once a man who had an only son, to whom he was very kind, and gave everything that he had. When his son grew up and got a house, he was very unkind to his poor old father, whom he refused to support and turned out of the house. The old man said to his grandson, "Go and fetch the covering from my bed, that I may go and sit by the wayside and beg." The child burst into tears, and ran for the covering. He met his father, to whom he said, "I am going to fetch the rug from my grandfather's bed, that he may wrap it around him and go a begging!" Tommy went for the rug and brought it to his father, and said to him, "Pray, father, cut it in two, the half of it will be large enough for grandfather, and perhaps you may want the other half, when I grow a man and turn you out of doors." The words of the child struck him so forcibly that he immediately ran to his father, and asked forgiveness, and was very kind to him till he died.

A certain farmer in England had an only son, to whom he was greatly attached, and never could think of chastising him for his faults. When he arrived at the age of twelve years, he bade adieu to his father's house, and went with a band of gypsies. For nearly twenty years he was never heard of. It happened, however, that the old man was under the necessity of taking a journey a considerable way, with a large sum of money. He had to pass a wood, and as he went on, a man rushed from it, seized his horse, and demanded his money. The old man remonstrated with him. He would not hear, but again demanded his money. Most reluctantly he gave it up. The robber gazing at him, said, "Do you know me?" "No," said the old man. "Do you not know me?" he repeated. "No, I do not know you." "Well," said the robber, "I am your son!" and returning his money, added, "Had you corrected me when young, I might have been a comfort to you; but now I am a disgrace to you, and a pest to society!"

The Rev. Mr. Berridge being once visited by a loquacious young lady, who, forgetting the modesty of her sex, and the superior gravity of an aged divine, engrossed all the conversation of the interview with small talk concerning herself. When she rose to retire, he said, "Madam, before you withdraw, I have one piece of advice to give you; and that is, when you go into company again, after you have talked *half an hour* without intermission, I recommend it to you to stop awhile, and see if any other of the company has anything to say."

A clergyman was asked, when examined for orders by the bishop's chaplain, whether he had made divinity his study? he replied, that he had not particularly studied it; "but," said he, "my mother tought me the scriptures." "Ah!" said the chaplain, "mothers can do great things!" The young man was examined with respect to the extent of his knowledge, was approved, ordained and desired to preach before the bishop. The excellent mother alluded to, in writing to another of her sons, on the birth of his eldest child, says, "Give him an education that his life may be useful—teach him religion that his death may be happy?"

Children are required to obey their parents in the Lord, for this is right. Eph. vi. 1. It is important, however, that parents agree in their authority. The following anecdote will illustrate this necessity: A little girl, six years old, was repeating the fourth commandment in Sunday-school. Her teacher endeavored to show her in what way she was to honor her parents, and said, "You must honor your parents by obeying them." "O ma'am," she said, "I cannot keep this commandment." "Why cannot you keep it, my dear?" "Because, when my mother tells me to do one thing, my father tells me to do another. Now, just before I came here, my mother told me to stay upstairs and learn my lessons, and my father told me to come down and play. Now, how can I obey both? I cannot keep this commandment."

When the Rev. Richard Cecil was but a little boy, his father had occasion to go to the India House in London, and he took his son with him. While he was transacting business the little fellow was dismissed, and told to wait at one of the doors. His father, on finishing his business, went out at another door, and entirely forgot his son. In the evening, his mother, missing the child, inquired where he was; on which his father, suddenly recollecting that he directed him to wait at a certain door, said, "You may depend upon it he is still waiting where I appointed him." He immediately returned to the India House, and found his dear boy on the very spot where he had ordered him to remain. He knew that his father expected him to wait, and therefore he would not disappoint him.

The disobedience rendered to parents is a fruitful source of crime and ruin to character. A young man was sentenced to a penitentiary for four years When he was about to be sentenced, he stated publicly that his downward course began in disobedience to his parents —that he thought he knew as much of tne world as his father did, and needed not his aid or advice; but as soon as he turned his back upon his home, then temptations came round him like a drove of hyenas, and hurried him on to ruin.

An undutiful son, who had given his father much trouble and uneasiness, and had almost brought down his gray hairs with sorrow to the grave, once called on his father on his birthday, to do him honor. "Ah, my son," said his father, "the best way to honor me is to turn from the error of your ways. If you really respect me, learn to respect yourself: till then I can have no faith in your professions; for how can I expect him to honor his father on earth, who dishonors his Father who is in heaven?"

"The promise announces the general purpose of God and a general principle of his providential government. 'The hand of the diligent maketh rich;' that is the general rule, which is not invalidated if here and there a diligent man remains poor. It is well with obedient children; they prosper in the world. Such is fact, and such is the divine promise. The family being the corner-stone of social order and prosperity, it follows that those families are blessed in which God's plan and purpose are most fully carried out and realized.''—*Dr. Hodge.*

The pious Æneas, in the epic poem of Virgil, obtained his honorable title from the care which he bestowed on his father at the siege of Troy, carrying him on his back till they were clear of danger.

Christopherus Jonas, son of Justus Jonas the great theologian, and friend of Luther, was a talented young man. He enjoyed his learned and pious father's instructions, and also studied much in the schools and universities. But all this time he had despised his father's admonitions and filled his heart with sorrow. In the year 1567, he was publicly beheaded in Copenhagen, on account of a great crime which he had committed. As they tied up his eyes, he exclaimed, "What benefit was it, that I studied much and did not do right?"

When your pastor reproves you for your sins, he wishes to rescue you from temporal and eternal ruin. Do not act like the dog in the fable who fell into a well and showed his teeth and wanted to bite the hand of the farmer who tried to rescue him. But thank him, as you would a man who sees you lost in a dark forest and calls and guides you safely out, or as you would thank a man who had rescued you from a watery or fiery death.

"Well, the master is gone," said a heathen slave to his christian fellow-slave, "now let us stop working and enjoy ourselves." "My Master is here yet," replied the christian slave, "from yonder heaven he looks down to see whether he shall reward or punish; so I think I shall continue to work."

Ambrosius says, pastors and teachers should receive such salaries, that on the one hand they may not be proud and on the other hand, that they may not be discouraged. Labor for souls cannot be done like that of a common day-laborer, but it requires enthusiasm, love, and a free and cheerful mind.

A wicked son had once taken his father by the hair of his head and dragged him through the room. When he had dragged him as far as the door-step, the father cried out, "Drag me no farther, my son, for just this far I also once dragged my father."

A widow in Marienburg, Prusia, bequeathed $1000 to the Mission Treasury, shortly before her death. Although she had made this bequest only verbally, yet her son in-law hastened to pay the money into the treasury soon after her death.

The cavalry captain Kurtzhagen, was invited to dine with King Frederick II. "From what noble house are you descended?" asked the king. "From none whatever," replied Kurtzhagen. "My parents are only poor country people, but I would not exchange them for any other parents in the world." "Well said," replied the king, "Woe to him who is so mean as to be ashamed of his parents."

A heathen boy who attended the mission-school of the sainted Rhenius, took sick. His father brought an idol image to him and urged him to sacrifice to the idol in order that he might get well. But the son took an axe and broke the idol to pieces to demonstrate to his father that the idol could not help him.

As kind and loving as Luther was toward his children, so strict was he in the discipline of his family. He remarked, "I would rather have a dead, than a worthless and disobedient son."

The theological students in one of our American Seminaries, were requested to report how many of them had pious mothers. They were surprised to learn that out of 120 students, 100 had pious mothers who had taught them to pray and exhorted them to lead christian lives.

Nona, the pious mother of Gregory Nazianzen, took her first born to the church and consecrated him to God, praying that his life might be devoted to religion, and as it was often done in those days, she placed a New Testament in the child's hands. The recollection of this consecration made a deep impression on Gregory's mind.

Monica, the mother of St. Augustine, prayed with tears for the conversion of her son, and also urged pious christians to interest themselves in his behalf. A bishop to whom she appealed, said to her, "Be of good comport, the son for whom you shed so many tears, and offer so many prayers to God, cannot be lost." And afterwards, when he really did become a devoted christian, he said to his mother, "I believe that I am indebted to your prayers for my faith in Christ."

A father reproved his son for cursing and swearing, telling him to remember that God hears everything. "Does he, indeed," said the boy, "and can he also see everything?" "Certainly," said the father. "Then," said the boy, "I am sorry for you, father, for he also saw you drunk yesterday evening."

The son of a heathen father attended the mission-school of Rev. Rhenius in the East Indies. One day the father came to the teacher and said, "If my son remains much longer in your school, he will not get along in the world, because he will not tell any more lies, but always speaks the truth."

One day Pastor Oberlin asked his servant girl the cause of the sadness which he saw in her face. "O sir," said she, "I have just been thinking that there will be no servants in heaven, and then I was so sorry to think that I should not be able to serve you when we get to heaven."

An English minister was urged at a banquet to drink the health of the king. He replied, "I beg your pardon, my lords, I will pray for the health of the king."

THE FIFTH COMMANDMENT.

75. Repeat the Fifth Commandment.
"Thou shalt not kill."

Genesis ix. 6. Whoso sheddeth man's blood, by man shall his blood be shed : for in the image of God made he man.

Matt. v 21. Ye have heard that it was said by them of old time, Thou shalt not kill ; and whosoever shall kill, shall be in danger of the judgment.

Numbers xxxv. 16. And if he smite him with an instrument of iron, so that he die, he *is* a murderer : the murderer shall surely be put to death.

76. What is the meaning of this commandment?

That we should so fear and love God, as not to do our neighbor any bodily injury; but rather assist and comfort him in danger or want.

77. What is the design of this commandment?

The design of the fifth commandment is the protection of human life.

78. What is forbidden in this commandment?

The fifth commandment forbids

1. Murder, whereby the lives of human beings are unlawfully taken.

2. Suicide, whereby persons become their own murderers, and for which their is no more opportunity for repentance.

3. Whatever is injurious to our health, such as intemperance in eating or drinking, unhealthy fashions, bad ventilation and uncleanliness.

4. Whatever is injurious to our own or others health, such as selling or giving intoxicating liquors to drink, or adulterated food to eat, or overworking those who are in our employ.

79. *In what ways may this commandment be violated?*
The fifth commandment may be violated,
1. Internally, in our hearts, or
2. Externally, by our actions.

80. *How is this commandment violated internally or in our hearts?*
The fifth commandment may be violated internally or in our hearts,
1. By angry feelings against our neighbors.
2. By hatred of our neighbor.
3. By envy of our neighbor.

81. *How is this commandment violated externally?*
The fifth commandment may be violated externally
1. Designedly, or
2. Undesignedly.

82. *How may this commandment be violated designedly?*
The fifth commandment may be violated externally and designedly by
1. Angry, hypocritical or mocking gesticulations.

Genesis iv. 5. But unto Cain, and to his offering, he had not respect. And Cain was very wroth, and his countenance fell.

Genesis iv. 6. And the Lord said unto Cain, Why art thou wroth? and why is thy countenance fallen?

Jeremiah ix. 8. Their tongue *is as* an arrow shot out; it speaketh deceit: *one* speaketh peaceably to his neighbor with his mouth, but in heart he layeth his wait.

Matt. xxvii. 29. And when they had platted a crown of thorns, they put *it* upon his head, and a reed in his right hand and they bowed the knee before him, and mocked him, saying, Hail, King of the Jews!

2. Hard, insulting or bitter words; also by treachery, revilings and slanderings, whereby others may be mortally grieved.

Jeremiah xviii. 18. Then said they, Come, and let us devise devices against Jeremiah; for the law shall not perish from the priest, nor counsel from the wise, nor the word from the prophet. Come, and let us smite him with the tongue, and let us not give heed to any of his words

Rom. iii. 13. Their throat *is* an open sepulchre; with their tongues they have used deceit; the poison of asps *is* under their lips.

3. Actions, when we purposely injure ourselves or others in body or soul.

2 Sam. xi. 15 And he wrote in the letter, saying, Set ye Uriah in the forefront of the hottest battle, and retire ye from him, that he may be smitten, and die.

83. How may this commandment be undesignedly violated?

The fifth commandment may be undesignedly violated by

1. Intemperance in eating or drinking.
2. Lust. Sir. xix. 2. *
3. Immoderate grief.

2 Cor. vii. 10. For godly sorrow worketh repentance to salvation not to be repented of: but the sorrow of the world worketh death.

4. Rashness, or unnecessary exposure to danger. Sir. iii. 27.

84. What is required of us in this commandment?

In the fifth commandment we are required to seek the preservation of our own and others' bodily and spiritual life, as in cases of sickness or temptations.

Romans xiii 14. But put ye on the Lord Jesus Christ, and make not provision for the flesh, to *fulfill* the lusts *thereof*.

James v. 9. Grudge not one against another, brethren, lest ye be condemned: behold, the Judge standeth before the door.

James v. 12. But above all things, my brethren, swear not, neither by heaven, neither by the earth, neither by any other oath: but let your yea, be yea; and *your* nay, nay; lest ye fall into condemnation.

---

* These quotations are from the Apocrypha, and are not given as scripture proof-texts.

85. *Who may lawfully take away human life?*

1. Magistrates, as "God's ministers in executing vengeance," are commanded to put murderers to death. "Whoso sheddeth man's blood, by man shall his blood be shed."

2. Witnesses and executioners may also concur in such capital punishment.

3. It is also lawful to take another's life in self-defence, when he attempts to murder us, for by this he forfeits his own life, and there is no opportunity of referring the cause to a civil magistrate.

4. Some wars, especially defensive wars, when our country is invaded, are necessary and unavoidable, and the blood shed in them is not computed as murder. But all wars waged merely for conquest or revenge are wholesale murders.

86. *What particular classes may farther be designated as murderers?*

1. Duelists are murderers, for each duelist is intent upon murdering his antagonist.

2. Prize fighters are murderers, and the blood shed by them is murder.

3. Liquor sellers are murderers, for they know that their business ruins thousands of people in soul and body.

87. *What are the motives for the observance of this commandment?*

1. The blood shed by the murderer crieth up to God for vengeance.

Genesis iv. 10. And he said, What hast thou done? the voice of thy brother's blood crieth unto me from the ground.

2. God has threatened to punish the murderer. Whoso sheddeth mans blood, etc.

Ezekiel iii. 17. Son of man, I have made thee a watchman unto the house of Israel: therefore hear the word at my mouth, and give them warning from me.

Ezekiel iii. 18. When I say unto the wicked, Thou shalt surely die; and thou givest him not warning, nor speakest to warn the wicked from his wicked way, to save his life; the same wicked *man* shall die in his iniquity; but his blood will I require at thy hand.

Ezekiel iii. 21. Nevertheless, if thou warn the righteous *man*, that the righteous sin not, and he doth not sin, he shall surely live, because he is warned; also thou hast delivered thy soul.

3. The ruin of the soul brings with it unspeakable woe, occasioned by provocation or evil example.

Matthew xviii. 6. But, whoso shall offend one of these little ones which believe in me, it were better for him that a millstone were hanged about his neck, and *that* he were drowned in the depth of the sea.

Matthew xviii. 7. Woe unto the world because of offences! for it must needs be that offences come; but woe to that man by whom the offence cometh!

Romans xiv. 15. But if thy brother be grieved with *thy* meat, now walkest thou not charitably. Destroy not him with thy meat, for whom Christ died.

ANECDOTES AND ILLUSTRATIONS.

Scriptural Examples. *1. Love to our neighbor.* The Good Samaritan, Luke x 33 36. Abraham and Lot, Gen. xiv. 14-16. Joseph and his fellow prisoners, Gen. xl. 7. Moses and his brethren, Ex. ii. 11-15. David mourns over Saul, 2 Sam. i. 12. Absalom, 2 Sam. xviii. 33. Christ laments over Israel, Matt. xxiii. 27. Cain is jealous of Abel, Gen. iv. 4, 5. Joseph's brethren jealous, Gen. xxxvii. 11. Ahab jealous of Naboth, 1 Kings xxi. 4. The high priests envious of Christ, Matt. xxvii. 18.

2. Injure no one in body or soul. Joseph's brethren transgress this commandment, Gen. xxxvii. 18. The high priests, John xi. 53. Saul, Acts viii. 1. The Jews, Acts ix. 23. Actual murder, Cain, Gen. iv. Abimelech, Judges ix. 1-5. As accomplices to murder, David, 2 Sam. xi. Jezebel, 1 Kings xxi. Judas and Pilate, Matt. xxvi.

3. Punished with death by the command of God. Profane swearers, Levit. xxiv. 10 14. The Sabbath desecrator, Num. xv. 32-36. The destruction of Jericho, Joshua vi. Achan, Joshua vii. 25. Elijah slaughters the priests of Baal, 1 Kings xviii.

Life is considered precious in the sight of God.

I. We are to use all lawful endeavors to preserve our own life.

1. The life of the body, by proper food, raiment and residence; by self-defence against injury; by self-defence against irregular appetites and passions.

2. The life of the soul, by seeking salvation from sin, and by doing the will of God.

II. We are to use all lawful endeavors to preserve the life of others.
    1. Their bodily life, by kindness, protection, and provision in time of need.
    2. Their spiritual life, by prayer, instruction in the gospel, and christian sympathy.

III. Endeavors to preserve life must be lawful. We are not to break one law to keep another, or to do evil that good may come. Sinful compliance to save life endangers the soul and dishonors God. Martyrs died rather than deny Christ.
    1. God is to be glorified with our bodies and spirits, which are his.
    2. Each man is his brother's keeper.
    3. The science and practice of medicine are followed for the purpose of preserving life.
    4. Philanthropic institutions have arisen for the same end.

In the fifth commandment is forbidden
  I. The taking away of our own life.
    1. By violence—as Ahithophel and all suicides.
    2. By sinful indulgences—such as intemperance, carnal pleasures.
    3. By neglecting proper means for health.
    4. By neglecting the salvation of the soul.
  II. The taking away of our neighbor's life unjustly.
    1. This is done by murder, as Cain did.
    2. By persecution and oppression.
    3. By tempting to sin, as to drink or any crime.
  III. Life may sometimes be taken justly, as in defence of one's own life or the life of others, or in defensive war, or for murder.
    1. "No murderer hath eternal life abiding in him." 1 John iii. 15.
    2. The neglect of sanitary laws may cause the loss of life.
    3. It is an awful thing to be guilty of the ruin of others, in soul or body, or both.

Sir Theodore Mayem on his death-bed, gave this advice to a noble friend who asked counsel regarding the preservation of his health: "Be moderate in your diet, use much exercise and little physic."

The old adage will not be out of place here,—
    "Early to bed, and early to rise,
      Will make a man healthy, wealthy and wise."

The preaching of the Gospel has been the means of saving many souls, and of making life more precious, both in this world and in the world to come.

"It is conceivable that men who do not believe in God or in a future state of existence, should think it allowable to take refuge in annihilation from the miseries of this life; but it is unaccountable, except on the assumption of temporary or permanent insanity, that any man should rush uncalled into the retribution of eternity. Suicide, therefore, is self murder. It is the desertion of the post which God has assigned us; it is a deliberate refusal to submit to his will; it is a crime which admits of no repentance, and consequently involves the loss of the soul." —*Dr. Hodge*.

Alexander the Great once invited several of his friends and officers to a feast, and offered a reward to him who would drink most. Promachus won the prize, having swallowed fourteen measures of wine—that is, eighteen pints. He received a crown worth a talent, but survived his victory only three days. Of the rest, forty died from excessive drinking. Alexander also soon drank himself to death.

Anger among boys has often led to crime, and sometimes to murder.

The worship of Juggernaut has often led to suicide in India.

The great Spanish captain Gonsalvo was asked on his death-bed what had given him the greatest satisfaction in the course of his long and glorious life. He replied, that it was the consideration that he never drew his sword but in the service of God and of his sovereign.

The Apostle John attained to a very high age. In the latter years of his life he could no longer walk to the church. Young men, therefore, carried him there; at last he could no longer preach a sermon to the congregation; then he constantly repeated these words, "Little children, love one another." When asked why he so constantly repeated these words, he replied, "Because it is the command of the Lord, and if this command is kept, all the others will be obeyed also."

When St. Patrick, the apostle to the Irish, began his mission from Brittain to Ireland, in the 5th century, many exclaimed, "Why does he expose himself to danger among the heathen who know not the Lord."

Bishop Spangenberg, of the Moravian Church, preached on one occasion in Lancaster, Pa., on the text, "Father, forgive them; they know not what they do," whilst stones were thrown at his head. A justice of the peace was present, and expected every moment that the preacher would denounce those wicked people. But when he heard him pray for them, the prayer was the occasion of his own conversion, and the enemies ceased their opposition.

When Charles the V. (the same before whom Luther stood at the diet of Worms), occupied Halle, a Spanish captain was quartered in the house of Justus Jonas, with the secret order to murder him, as he was one of the strongest pillars of the Protestant religion. But after Jonas had received the captain so very kindly, he said to him, "Doctor Jonas, I cannot conceal from you that I was ordered to put you to death, but I see that you are such an honest and pious man, that I cannot possibly do you any harm."

In 1750 intemperance had increased to such a degree, that the liquor dealers gave the following notice on their signs, "For ten pennies, whiskey enough to intoxicate; twenty pennies, enough to make dead drunk, and straw to lie upon till you get sober again."

A liquor dealer who had become a member of a temperance society, felt himself driven by conscience to throw his large stock of liquors into the sea, because he saw no other way to dispose of them without causing injury to his fellow-men, even if he had sold the liquors and devoted the amount to benevolent purposes.

Alfred, king of England, kept a wax candle in his room which burned twenty-four hours; every hour was marked upon the candle, and a servant was appointed to announce to the king when an hour's length was burned down.

A Hottentot who was a great drinker and slave of every vice, was converted to Christianity. He took his last bottle of whiskey and broke it to pieces. Some of his tribe told him it would be injurious to his health to stop drinking so suddenly. But he replied, "Rather that the body should die, than that soul and body should perish."

One of the old church fathers was asked how old he was, and he replied, "Forty-five years" The questioner said, "I took you to be seventy years old." "That may be," replied the church father, "Yet you must know that I do not count the foolish, sinful years of my youth, as a part of my age, because they cannot properly be called life."

A foolish woman in France bequeathed a certain amount for the support and keeping of her favorite cat, but also ordered in her will that all heirs must pay a weekly visit to this cat on pain of loosing their inheritance. In consequence, a great law suit ensued, but the cat lost the case.

The capuchin monk, Felix, once saw a Roman lady hug and kiss her lap dog, and said to her, "How much better it would be for you if you would love your God as much as you love this beast."

It is the divine order that the blood of the murderer shall be shed on the place of execution. By the hand of the hangman he receives his doom. Therefore, God often arranges in his providence, that the murderers frequently reveal or betray themselves, or that their crimes are discovered in a wonderful way.

When Meinhard, the duke of Sulgard, in Suabia, had retired from the world, built a cell for himself in a dark forest and became a hermit, two robbers came and murdered him in the hope of finding gold or treasure in his cell. As he was dying by their hands, he saw two ravens flying and said, "The ravens will testify against you." Sometime afterwards, while they were sitting in a restaurant, they saw some ravens flying around the house, and one of them said, "See, there are some of Meinhard's witnesses flying about." This remark was reported to the officers; they were arrested, and when they confessed the crime, they were put to death and their bodies consumed with fire.

When the Swiss confederates were defeated by the French, near Basle, in a battle which lasted a whole day, a French officer rode over the battle-field among the slain with uncovered head, that he might keep cool and enjoyed seeing the blood streaming over the ground, he exclaimed, "See here! we are wading through beds of roses!" These shameful words were heard by a deeply wounded confederate, who raised himself up on his knees, grasped a big stone and hurled it it with such force against the officer's head that he fell from his horse and died.

Lewis XIII had many enemies before he became king of France, who had always opposed him. After he became king he had a list of them made out and made a black cross before each name When his enemies heard this they were very much alarmed and fled in haste. But the king had them called back with the assurance of his forgiveness, and said to them, "Be of good cheer, my friends. I put a cross before each of your names, in order that I might be constantly reminded of the cross of Christ, and think of the words he spoke on the cross, "Father, forgive them, for they know not what they do.

The Romans had a law, that no person should approach the emperor's tent in the night, upon pain of death; but it once happened, that a soldier was found in that situation, with a petition in his hand, waiting for an opportunity of presenting it. He was apprehended, and going to be immediately executed; but the emperor having overheard the matter in his pavilion, cried aloud, saying, "If the petition be for himself, let him die; if for another, spare his life." Upon inquiry, it was found that the generous soldier prayed for the lives of his two comrades who had been taken asleep on the watch. The emperor nobly forgave them all.

It is recorded of John Dod, that one night, very late, he felt strongly moved to visit a gentleman of his acquaintance, who lived at some distance. Not knowing what might be the design of Providence in this, he went. Having come to the house and knocked at the door, the gentleman himself opened it; to whom Mr. Dod said, "I am come to you, I know not why myself, but I was restless in my spirit till I had done it." The gentleman replied, "You know not why you came; but God knew why he sent you." On which he pulled out the halter with which he intended to take away his own life, which by this means was happily prevented.

THE SIXTH COMMANDMENT.

88. Repeat the sixth commandment.

"Thou shalt not commit adultery."

Heb. xiii. 4. Marriage *is* honorable in all, and the bed undefiled: but whoremongers and adulterers God will judge.

Matt. v. 27. Ye have heard that it was said by them of old time, Thou shalt not commit adultery:

Matt. v. 32. But I say unto you, That whosoever shall put away his wife, saving for the cause of fornication, causeth her to commit adultery: and whosoever shall marry her that is divorced, committeth adultery.

1 Cor. vi. 18. Flee fornication. Every sin that a man doeth, is without the body; but he that committeth fornication, sinneth against his own body.

1 Cor. vi. 19. What! know ye not that your body is the temple of the Holy Ghost *which is* in you, which ye have of God, and ye are not your own?

89. What do you understand by this commandment?

That we should so fear and love God, as to live chaste, and undefiled in words and deeds, and each to love and honor his wife or her husband.

90. What is required in this commandment?

The sixth commandment requires chastity by both married and unmarried persons.

Heb. xiii. 4. Marriage *is* honorable in all, and the bed undefiled: but whoremongers and adulterers God will judge.

91. *What is the design of this commandment?*

The design of the sixth commandment is,

 1. The preservation of the sanctity of the married relation;
 2. The mutual aid and happiness of married persons;
 3. The propagation of the human race;
 4. The building up of the kingdom of God through christian nurture of children.

92. *When and by whom was marriage instituted?*

Marriage was instituted by God in Paradise, when he said, "It is not good for man to be alone, I will make a help meet for him."

93. *What is marriage?*

Marriage is a covenant between one man and one woman, in which they are bound by God's ordinance and by their own personal vows, to love and faithfulness until separated by death.

94. *What is forbidden in this commandment?*

In the sixth commandment all things which tend to its violation are forbidden, such as

 1. Evil, sensual thoughts;
 2. Obscene or impure pictures;
 3. Bad or unclean books or papers;
 4. Lewd stories and jokes;
 5. Worldly dancing;
 6. Attendance at theatres.

95. *In what ways is this commandment violated?*

The sixth commandment may be violated

 1. Internally and
 2. Externally.

96. How may this commandment be violated internally?

The sixth commandment may be violated internally, or in the heart by unchaste desires.

Matthew v. 28. But I say unto you, That whosoever looketh on a woman to lust after her, hath committed adultery with her already in his heart.

97. How may this commandment be violated externally?

The sixth commandment may be violated externally

1. By shameless or impudent behavior, as in unchaste dances or plays, improper clothing or exposure;

2. By indecent words, unchaste songs or stories;

3. By actual commission of adultery or fornication, or secret impurity.

PRACTICAL REFLECTIONS.

THOU SHALT NOT COMMIT ADULTERY.

This commandment forbids every form of sensuality in act or thought.

I. The most fearful denunciations of Scripture are against sensuality.
II. Nature protests against it.
III. It breaks down the moral principles.
IV. It does violence to the virtues.
V. It ruins others; it involves other persons in guilt.
VI. It leads to every other sin.
VII. It frustrates the great end of human life.

CONCLUSION.

I. Beware of beginnings.
II. Give this passion no allowance in your thought.
III. Be watchful against the least temptation.
IV. Avoid bad associates.
V. Avoid every incentive to vice in dress, in fashion.
VI. Attend to the words of wisdom.
VII. Give your hearts to Christ.—*Warren.*

98. By what means do we preserve chastity in ourselves?

We preserve chastity in ourselves

1. By constant thoughts of God and reflections on his attributes, such as the Omniscience, Omnipresence and Holiness of God and Christ.

Psalm xxxvii. 4. Delight thyself also in the Lord; and he shall give thee the desires of thy heart.

2. By prayer.

Ps. li. 12. Restore unto me the joy of thy salvation; and uphold me *with thy* free Spirit.

3. By watchfulness over ourselves.

Mark xiii. 13. And ye shall be hated of all *men* for my name's sake: but he that shall endure unto the end, the same shall be saved.

4. By temperance in eating and drinking.

Rom. xiii. 4. For he is the minister of God to thee for good. But if thou do that which is evil, be afraid; for he beareth not the sword in vain: for he is the minister of God, a revenger to *execute* wrath upon him that doeth evil.

5. By industry in a proper employment.

1 Timothy iv. 10. For therefore, we both labor and suffer reproach, because we trust in the living God, who is the Savior of all men, especially of those that believe.

6. By avoiding temptations, such as bad company, bad books, indecent pictures, impure songs or unchaste conversation.

99. What motives should urge us to the keeping of this commandment?

The motives for the observance of the sixth commandment are

1. The punishment threatened in the Scriptures on its violators.

Leviticus xx. 10. And the man that committeth adultery with *another* man's wife, *even he* that committeth adultery with his neighbor's wife, the adulterer and the adulteress shall surely be put to death.

Ezekiel xxiii. 46. For thus saith the Lord God; I will bring up a company upon them, and will give them to be removed and spoiled.

Ezekiel xxiii. 48. Thus will I cause lewdness to cease out of the land, that all women may be taught not to do after your lewdness.

2. The reward of chastity. Joseph became ruler of Egypt by faithfulness to this commandment.

1 Cor. vi. 17. But he that is joined unto the Lord is one spirit.

Gen. xli. 43. And he made him to ride in the second chariot which he had: and they cried before him, Bow the knee: and he made him *ruler* over all the land of Egypt.

3. Also that our body and spirit are not our own, but God's.

1 Cor. vi. 19. What! know ye not that your body is the temple of the Holy Ghost *which is* in you, which ye have of God, and ye are not your own.

ANECDOTES AND ILLUSTRATIONS.

Scriptural Examples. *We should be chaste and pure in words and deeds.* Noah and Ham, Gen. ix. 20-22. Shem and Japhet, verse 23. Lot and the Sodomites, Gen. xix. Joseph and Potiphar's wife, Gen. ix. Boaz, Ruth iii. 17, 18.

Loving and honoring his wife—her husband. Adam and Eve, Gen. ii. 18-24. Abraham, Gen. xxiv. 3. The Pharisees and divorce, Matt xix. 3-9. The disciples, verse 10-12. Joseph and Mary, Matt. ii. 14-23. Pilate's wife, Matt. xxvii. 19. Job's wife, Job ii. 9. Michal, 2 Sam. vi. 16.

This commandment is of great importance to the welfare of society and of the individual.

I. It requires a pure heart. This is to be gotten and kept by the grace of God's Spirit, and by obeying the will of God.

II. It requires chaste speech and behavior. The moral tone of God's Word is the best influence in human speech. Purity of life is promoted by temperance, self-restraint, and by prudent marriage.

III. It requires us to preserve the chastity of others in these things as much as we can. This can be done by good example, in looks, words and behavior; by avoiding temptations to sin; by counsel and warning when necessary; and by preventing public temptations to sin. It can be aided by keeping early hours at night.—*Steel.*

I. This commandment forbiddeth all unchaste thoughts. Thoughts stir up desires, and act like a spark in powder.

II. Unchaste words. Immodest expressions are polluting, and are sinful. We must give an account to God for our words: Matt. xii. 36, 37.

III. Unchaste actions These make the sin still greater, destroy character, and promote many evils.

IV. Whatsoever tends to unchastity is condemned. Immodest manner of dress, the reading of books descriptive of immodesty, the breach of marriage vows, or making rash vows of celibacy, should be guarded against.—*R. Steel.*

LESSONS.

1. Walking in the Spirit prevents the lusts of the flesh.
2. The body should be made a temple of the Holy Ghost.

The Scriptures give the law regarding behavior of the sexes to each other, and regarding marriage. When these laws are transgressed society always suffers. Young people cannot be too particular in modesty, as there are so many temptations to sin.—*R. Steel.*

A notorious adulterer had received fatal injuries by a fall. His wife asked him where he felt most pain, and he answered, "In my soul I feel most pain, for already I feel the eternal torment."

A young woman found a gold ring and rejoiced very much. But as she examined it closer, she found to her regret that the jewel or diamond had been lost out of it. "My child," said her mother, "this gold ring without its jewel is like youth and beauty when honor and virtue are lost.

The daughter of a christian man in Wittenberg was engaged to marry a physician of that city. A fire consumed the house, everything was lost and the family narrowly escaped with their lives. Some one asked the daughter, what she could now bring to her bridegroom. "Every thing," she replied, "that he sought in me, namely a pure body, a willing heart and a faithful mind."

Young married people should regard their engagement vows like Ruth, "Whither thou goest, I will go; and where thou lodgest, I will lodge; thy people shall be my people, and thy God my God; Where thou diest, will I die, and there will I be buried. The Lord do so to me, and more, if aught but death part thee and me." Ruth i. 16, 17.

When a suitor paid attention to Sybilla, daughter of Paul Richter, she entered into her closet and prayed thus, "My dear Father in heaven, grant me a companion, who loves thy word, then I am sure he will for thy sake also love me." Her prayer was heard and answered, for she became the wife of Johann Matthesius.

The husband shall love his wife like Christ loves the church; namely, with an entire, exclusive, constant and protective love.

The wife shall love her husband like the church loves Christ; namely, with an entire, exclusive, constant and dutiful love.

Man and wife shall be to each other like the two eyes in our head; namely they shall together look about or around, and they shall together look upwards namely to heaven, and when the one is injured the other weeps.

When Emperor Conrad declared war against Welf, Duke of Bavaria, the Duke entrenched himself with all his army in the city of Weinsberg. The Emperor besieged the city so long, that the Duke and his people were on the verge of starvation, and they were compelled to tender their unconditional surrender. But before this was done the good wives of the city sent a petition to the Emperor, beseeching him that he would permit them to leave the city and take with them as much of their most valuable possessions as each one could carry. The Emperor granted their petition, supposing that they meant their jewelry and clothing. But each one carried her husband on her back, and led her little children by the hand, and thus they marched out of the city. The Emperor's officers murmured mightily, contending that this was not the intention of the permission. But the Emperor was so much pleased with this display of the love and faithfulness of the Weinsberg wives, that he kept his word and invited the wives together with their husbands to a sumptuous feast, and concluded a lasting peace with the city.

Once upon a time, it is related, a pious man prayed to God that he would let him know how he could keep house and live happy in the married life. Then there was shown him a vision of three angels. The first angel knelt and prayed, "I lift up mine eyes to the hills whence cometh my help." The other angel had a hoe with which he dug in the ground and sought for roots and vegetables, saying, "In the sweat of thy face shalt thou eat thy bread." The third angel gathered the roots and vegetables, that had been dug up and said, "That which we save by economy increases," and then carried them into the cottage in which the three angels all dwelt together. This is beautiful and signifies, we should 1. pray, 2. work, 3. economize, and 4. live together in angelic love and unity.

Mr. Newton, as a commander of a slave ship, had a number of women under his absolute command; and knowing the danger of his situation on that account, he resolved to abstain from flesh in his food, and to drink nothing stronger than water during the voyage; that by abstemiousness he might subdue every improper emotion. Upon his setting sail, the sight of a certain point of land, was the signal for his beginning a rule which he was enabled to keep.

Dr. Hugh Latimer, one of the primitive reformers, was made Bishop of Worcester in the reign of Henry VIII. It was the custom of those times for each of the bishops to make presents to the king on new year's day. Bishop Latimer went with the rest of his brethren, to make the usual offering; but instead of a purse of gold, he presented the king with a New Testament, in which was a leaf doubled down to this passage:

"Whoremongers and adulterers God will judge."

A lady of suspected chastity, and who was tinctured with infidel principles, conversing with a minister of the gospel, objected to the Scriptures on account of their obscurity, and the great difficulty of understanding them. The minister wisely and smartly replied— "Why, madam, what can be easier to understand than the commandment, *Thou sha't not commit adultery.*

Anthony William Boehm, a German divine, once preached from Exod. xx. 14. "Thou shalt not commit adultery." A Chevalier, who was one of his hearers, felt himself so much offended and insulted, that he challenged Boehm to fight a duel, because he thought his sermon designed entirely to offend him. Boehm accepted the challenge, and appeared in his robes, but instead of a pistol, he had the Bible in his hand, and spoke to him in the following manner: "I am sorry you were so much offended when I preached against that destructive vice; at the time I did not even think of you: here I appear with the sword of the Spirit, and if your conscience condemns you, I beseech you for your own salvation, to repent of your sins, and lead a new life. If you will, then fire at me immediately: for I would willingly lose my life, if that might be the means of saving your soul." The Chevalier was so struck with this language, that he embraced him, and solicited his friendship.

It is said that Henry the Great, of France, took much pleasure in conversing with an honest and religious man of low situation in life, who used great freedom with his majesty. One day he said to the king, "Sire, I always take your part when I hear any man speaking evil of you; I know that you excel in justice and generosity, and that many worthy things have been done by you. But you have one vice for which God will condemn you if you do not repent, I mean the unlawful love of women." The king, it is said, was too magnanimous to resent this reproof, but he long felt it like an arrow in his bosom; and sometimes said, that the most eloquent discourses of the doctors of the Sorbonne had never made such an impression on his soul, as this honest reproof from his humble friend.

THE SEVENTH COMMANDMENT.

100. What is the seventh commandment?

" Thou shalt not steal."

Lev. xix. 11. Ye shall not steal, neither deal falsely, neither lie one to another.

1 Thess. iv. 6. That no *man* go beyond and defraud his brother in *any* matter : because that the Lord *is* the avenger of all such, as we also have forewarned you and testified.

Ephes. iv. 28. Let him that stole, steal no more : but rather let him labor, working with *his* hands the thing which is good, that he may have to give to him that needeth

1 Tim. vi. 6. But godliness with contentment is great gain.

1 Tim. vi. 10. For the love of money is a root of all evil : which while some coveted after, they have erred from the faith, and pierced themselves through with many sorrows.

101. What is meant by this commandment?

That we should so fear and love God, as not to rob our neighbor of his property, or bring it into our possession by unfair dealing or fraudulent means; but help him to augment and protect it.

102. What is forbidden in this commandment?

In the seventh commandment is forbidden all means of obtaining property in a dishonest way, such as theft or robbery, which is taking the property of our neighbor unrighteously and without his knowledge or consent.

103. In what ways can this commandment be violated?

The seventh commandment can be violated
1. Openly and
2. Secretly.

104. How is this commandment violated openly?

The seventh commandment is violated openly

1. By violence which is called robbery, and consists in violently or forcibly taking our neighbor's money or goods and compelling him to surrender them.

2. By withholding just wages from persons who have labored for us.

Deut. xxiv. 14. Thou shalt not oppress an hired servant *that is* poor and needy, *whether he be* of thy brethren, or of thy strangers that *are* in thy land within thy gates.

James v. 4. Behold, the hire of the laborers who have reaped down your fields, which is of you kept back by fraud, crieth: and the cries of them which have reaped are entered into the ears of the Lord of sabaoth.

105. How is this commandment violated secretly?

The seventh commandment is violated secretly

1. By taking our neighbors goods or money without his knowledge or consent.

2. By permitting the property of our neighbor to be ruined or lost, when it is in our power to prevent such ruin or loss.

3. By taking wages for work which we have poorly or improperly performed.

Titus. ii. 9. *Exhort* servants to be obedient unto their own masters, *and* to please *them* well in all *things*; not answering again.

Titus. ii. 10. Not purloining, but shewing all good fidelity; that they may adorn the doctrine of God our Savior in all things.

4. By deceit or the mere appearance of right.

Prov. xi. 1. A false balance *is* abomination to the Lord: but a just weight *is* his delight.

5. By gambling, whereby we gain our neighbor's money without giving him an equivalent for it.

6. By usury or exorbitant interest, whereby we take advantage of our neighbor's trouble or perplexity.

7. By begging when we are not in want, or can supply our wants ourselves. 2 Kings v. 19-27.

8. By borrowing without intention to return money or goods borrowed.

9. By false measure, or weight, in buying or selling.

10. By selling adulterated, or inferior goods at the prices of genuine articles.

11. Misrepresentation in trading, selling or buying, by which means the seller charges more, or the buyer pays less than the articles are worth.

12. By neglecting or refusing to pay the contributions which we promise for the support of the gospel at home and abroad.

13. By neglecting or refusing to pay our subscriptions to our family or Sunday-school papers.

106. Is it possible for a man to steal from himself?

A man may steal from himself

1. By stinginess, not allowing himself what is necessary for his own health and comfort.

2. By prodigality, wasting his estate for unnecessary or injurious things.

3. By idleness, spending the time in pleasure and vanity, which has been given him to work for the glory of God and the salvation of his soul.

107. What is required in this commandment?

In general, the seventh commandment requires

1. That we leave our neighbor in the peaceable possession of his own, and

2. That we help him to preserve and improve his property.

108. What does this commandment more especially require?

The seventh commandment requires more especially

1. That heads of families should properly provide for their household.

2. That we should labor in body or mind and avoid idleness.

2 Thess. iii. 7. For yourselves know how ye ought to follow us: for we behaved not ourselves disorderly among you.

2 Thess. iii. 8. Neither did we eat any man's bread for nought; but wrought with labor and travail night and day, that we might not be chargeable to any of you.

2 Thess. iii. 10. For even when we were with you, this we commanded you, that if any would not work, neither should he eat.

3. That we should faithfully render the service which we have agreed to perform, and for which we demand compensation.

4. That we should be content with what God has bestowed upon us.

1 Tim. vi. 6. But godliness with contentment is great gain.

Luke iii. 13. And he said unto them, Exact no more than that which is appointed you.

Luke iii. 14. And the soldiers likewise demanded of him, saying, And what shall we do? And he said unto them, Do violence to no man, neither accuse *any* falsely; and be content with your wages.

109. How many kinds of thieves are there?

1. The highway thief, or robber;
2. The house-thief, who steals his employer's money or goods;
3. The lawyer that under pretence of law robs his client of his property;
4. The shop-thief, who uses false weights and measures, or puts excessive prices on his commodities;
5. The usurer, who, taking advantage of others' necessities, extorts excessive interest;
6. The trustee, who appropriates the property committed to him to his own use;
7. The borrower, who never intends to pay;
8. The receiver of goods which he knows were stolen;
9. The receiver of pay for work which he has not performed.

Note 1. No one can afford to be dishonest. It never pays in the end. 2. Be careful of the beginnings of dishonesty—the smallest taint. 3. Restore what you have gained dishonestly. There is no true repentance of this sin without restitution, where it is possible. 4. A pure conscience is worth more than all the world. A man was once asked why he was so very particular to give good measure—overgood—and he replied, "God has given me but one journey through this world; and, when I am gone, I cannot return to correct mistakes.

110. What are the motives for the observance of this commandment?

The motives for the observance of the seventh commandment are,

1. The divine curse resting upon theft, robbery and all kinds of dishonesty.

1 Cor. vi. 10. Nor thieves, nor covetous, nor drunkards, nor revilers, nor extortioners, shall inherit the kingdom of God.

2. The blessedness of dealing honestly.

Psalm cxxviii. 1. Blessed *is* every one that feareth the Lord; that walketh in his ways.

Psalm cxxviii. 2. For thou shalt eat the labor of thine hands: happy *shalt* thou *be*, and *it shall be* well with thee.

Acts xx. 34. Yea, ye yourselves know, that these hands have ministered unto my necessities, and to them that were with me.

3. The ability to assist others.

Levit. xix. 9. And when ye reap the harvest of your land, thou shalt not wholly reap the corners of thy field, neither shalt thou gather the gleanings of thy harvest.

Levit. xix. 10. And thou shalt not glean thy vineyard, neither shalt thou gather *every* grape of thy vineyard; thou shalt leave them for the poor and stranger: I *am* the Lord your God.

4. The possession of a good conscience.

Eph. iv. 28. Let him that stole steal no more: but rather let him labor, working with *his* hands the thing which is good, that he may have to give to him that needeth.

ANECDOTES AND ILLUSTRATIONS.

Scriptural Examples. Achan, Jos. vii. 19-26; Ziba, 2 Saml. xvi. 1, etc; Ahab, 1 Kings xxi; Judas Iscariot, John xii. 6; Ananias and Sapphira, Acts v. 1-3; Laban, Gen. xxxi. 41; Jacob, Gen. xxvii; lxii. 12; Gehazi, 2 Kings v. 20; Zacchæus, Luke xix. 8-10; Abraham, Gen. xiv. 14; Boaz, Ruth ii; Job, xxix. 16.

Examples of Industry. Jesus, John iv. 34; Matt. viii. 2; Peter, Luke v. 1-11; Paul, Acts xviii. 1-4; xx. 23, 24; Of economy: Joseph, Gen. lxi; Ruth i-iv; Jesus, John vi. 12; Contentment: John the Baptist, Matt. iii. 4; Jesus, Matt. iv. 1-11; Paul, Phil iv. 11-13; Of discontent: The Israelites, Numb. xi. 4-6; Of avarice: Samuel's sons, 1 Sam. viii. 3; Felix, Acts xxiv. 26.

The right of property is founded upon nature. "By the law of nature," said Chancellor Kent, "I understand those fit and just rules of conduct which the Creator has prescribed to man as a dependent and social being, and which are to be ascertained from the deduction of right reason, though they may be more precisely known and are more explicitly declared by revelation."

I. Lawful means of procuring wealth and property for ourselves.

1. Every one should have a lawful calling. Industry was required of man in paradise.

2. Earnest industry is required to provide what is necessary and suitable to our condition in life.

3. This includes the moderate use of worldly things. Industry is the parent of thrift, aids health and happiness. God has stored the earth with an endless variety of means to meet our need. He has made these accessible to industry. "The hand of the dilligent maketh rich." Industry gives character and credit to men.

II. Lawful means of advancing the wealth and property of others. The law of God is never selfish, but philanthropic.

1. Every one should receive his due from us. Natural conscience dictates this, and God's word enjoins it Honesty advances both ourselves and others. "Honesty is the best policy."

2. We should do to others as we would that they should do to us. Men are a mutual provident society, in which one helps another.

3. Charity towards the needy fulfills this law. It blesses the poor, and does not impoverish the giver. The Christian religion especially commands this.—*Steel.*

I. This forbids what hinders our own wealth or estate.
 1. Idleness: Matt. xx. 6; Acts xx. 35; Eph. iv. 3; 1 Thess. iv. 11; 2 Thess. iii. 10–12.
 2. Prodigality: Luke xv. 11–32; John vi. 12.
 3. Sinful pursuits, as the Ephesians in Acts xix. 19. Gambling, smuggling, and all unlawful trades are condemned.

II. It forbids what hinders our neighbor's wealth or outward estate.
 1. Theft.
 2. Fraud.
 3. Neglecting to pay debts.
 4. Refusing to exercise charity.

There is a great tendency to break this commandment in all these ways. Besides direct stealing, there are false pretences in business, adulteration of goods, taking advantage of people's ignorance, misuse of public money or trust funds. Whatever is unfair is dishonest.—*Steel*.

LESSONS.

 1. He that provides not for his own house is worse than an infidel.
 2. It is better to give than to receive.
 3. Keep hands off what belongs to others.
 4. Withhold not what you can do for the good of others.—*Steel*.

A nobleman travelling in Scotland was asked for alms in the High Street of Edinburgh by a little ragged boy. He said he had no change; but the boy offered to procure it. His lordship then gave him a piece of silver, which the boy thought was to be first changed, and immediately ran away to get it. On his return he did not see his benefactor; but he watched for him for days. At length meeting him he gave him the change The nobleman was so pleased with the lad's honesty that he became his friend, placed him at school, and promised to aid in his advancement.

A clergyman in England, who had only forty pounds a year, and was often in distress for means to provide for his family, found a purse on the road one day. Carrying it home, his wife advised him to use it; but he answered, "Honesty is the best policy." After some inquiry he ascertained that the money belonged to a gentleman in the neighborhood, to whom he returned it. He received thanks; but no other reward; whereupon his wife complained of the ingratitude of the gentleman. Her husband said again, "Honesty is the best policy." A few months afterwards the clergyman was asked to dine with the gentleman, and was offered a living worth £300 a year, along with a purse of £50 to aid his present need. When he went home he said to his wife that he hoped she would now be convinced that "Honesty is the best policy."

The Rev. Samuel Kilpin, once minister in Exeter, said, "When seven years old, I was left in charge of my father's shop. A man passed, crying, 'Little lambs, all white and clean, at one penny each.' In my eagerness to get one, I lost all self-command, and taking a penny from the drawer I made the purchase. My keen-eyed mother wondered how I came by the money. I evaded the question by something like a lie. In God's sight it was a lie, as I kept back the truth. The lamb was placed on the chimney-shelf, and was much admired. To me it was a source of inexpressible anguish: continually there sounded in my ears and heart these words, 'Thou shalt not steal; thou shalt not lie.' Guilt and darkness overcame my soul, and in sore agony I went to a hay-loft—the place is now perfectly in my recollection—and there prayed and pleaded, with groanings that could not be uttered, for mercy and pardon. I entreated for Jesus' sake. With joy and transport I left the loft, from a believing application of the text, 'Thy sins, which are many, are forgiven.' I went to my mother, told her what I had done, and sought her forgiveness, and burned the lamb, while she wept over her young penitent." If such was Kilpin's misery and remorse in stealing a penny, then in justice he who steals a pound should have far more; but some steal tens and even hundreds of pounds. What must be the remorse of these when called to see their sin, or to meet with God?

Mr. Nott, the missionary at Tahiti, once preached from the text, "Let him that stole steal no more." The next morning many of the natives were seated before his dwelling. They said they could not sleep all night, thinking of all they had stolen from him and others. One showed an axe, another a chisel, another a knife, etc. They would not keep them any longer in their possession. Would it not be well that all acted like this?

Dr. Lawson of Selkirk, when preaching on this commandment, advocated restitution. Next morning the price of a pair of shoes was placed at the window of a family who had lost a pair recently.

A gentleman in Surry, some years ago, held a farm worth 200*l.* a year in his own hands, till he was obliged to sell half of it to pay his debts, and let the other half to a farmer, on a lease of 21 years. After a while, the farmer wanted to buy the land. "How is this," said the gentleman, "that I could not live upon the farm, being my own, while you have paid rent, and yet are able to purchase it?" "O," said the farmer, two words make all the difference: you said *go*, and I say *come*; you lay in bed, or took your pleasure, and sent others about your business; and I rise be-times, and see my business done myself."

One of the catechists of a Sabbath school going to visit a boy who had been absent, heard the following story related by his mother; "O mother!" exclaimed the boy as he entered the house one day, "something has killed all my rabbits." Without giving his mother time to reply, he continued, "It is a judgment of God come upon me for stealing meat for them; but," said he, "I am glad that I have none left, for they would have been temptation to make me steal again."

Mr. Samuel Fairclough, at thirteen years of age, hearing his godfather, Mr. Samuel Ward, preaching on restitution, from the instance of Zaccheus, and often repeating, that the sin was not forgiven unless what was taken was restored, was so touched with remorse for the robbing of an orchard, that, after a restless night, he went to a companion of his, who was guilty of the same crime, and told him that he was going to Mr. Jude, the owner, to carry him twelve pence for his three-penny worth of pears, of which he had wronged him. His companion, fearing whipping from his master, answered, Thou talkest like a fool, Sam, for God will forgive us ten times sooner than old Jude will forgive us once. But Sam, being of another mind, went to Jude's house, confessed the injury, and offered the money. Jude pardoned him; but would take no money. This grieved him more; upon which he made application to his spiritual father, Mr. Ward, and opened to him the whole state of his mind, who received and treated him with great kindness and attention.

Mr. Boston states in his memoirs, that having been employed, when a young man, for some time, by a notary, his employer failed to pay him for his services. Seeing a neglected book lying in the notary's chamber, he secretly took it away, thinking he might lawfully use this method of paying himself; but on farther reflection, he viewed his conduct as sinful, and inconsistent with strict justice. Impressed with this conviction, he replaced the book with the same secrecy in which he had taken it away. An amiable instance of that tenderness of conscience for which the venerable man was remarkable.

A wealthy merchant entrusted a large sum of money with a poor mechanic, whom he sometimes visited. He gave him the money without witnesses or writings, because he intended to visit a friend in a neighboring village for a few days. Before the merchant reached the house of his friend, he had the misfortune of being thrown from his horse and was fatally injured. As soon as the mechanic heard of it, he notified the relatives of the deceased, and gave them an account of the money that had been entrusted to his keeping, and which he also soon after remitted to them. One of his own relatives said to him, "You are a simpleton; why did you not keep the money? Who would have known anything about it?" "God would have known it," said the mechanic, "who knows all things, and I know it, too, and would never be able to forget it."

Some years ago the London Missionary Society held its anniversary; the collection amounted to 800 pound sterling, (about $4,000.) While the assembly were singing a hymn of praise to God, a thief entered, and—who would think it possible—stole a bag containing part of the collected money.

A young man, who had been known as notorious for his wickedness, came to Missionary Moffat in South Africa, and brought him 60 shillings, ($20.) for the mission. "What induces you to give this money to the mission?" said Moffat, "as you are known to be an enemy to the mission?" With tears in his eyes the young man confessed, that he had stolen type out of the mission printing office, cast them into bullets and shot a man with one of them. "But now," said he, "I come, like Zacchæus, to restore the theft four fold."

John Ernst Luther, a nephew of Dr. Martin Luther, was accustomed to give alms to every one that asked him, and said to each one, "I give it to you out of a sincere heart; if you take it for a sinful purpose, God will find you out."

A converted Indian asked a white man for some tobacco. The man reached into his pocket and give him a whole handful of tobacco. The next morning the Indian returned and brought him a quarter dollar, which he had found in the tobacco.

The Roman Emperor Titus counted the days of his reign by the acts of benevolence he had performed. On one occasion at an evening banquet, he remembered that on the past day he had not shown any person a kindness, and exclaimed, "My friends, I have lost this day."

A poor student came to Dr. Luther and asked him for assistance. Luther told his wife to give him something. But when she excused herself, saying, she had no money, Luther took a silver cup, squeezed it together and gave it to the student, telling him to sell it and keep the money.

Many years ago there was a great famine in England. In order to help the poor, Ethelnod, bishop of Winchester, sold the gold and silver vessels of the church, saying, It is not right that the dead temples of God should be rich, while the living themples of the Holy Ghost—the pious poor—should perish of hunger.

The sainted Prelate Hochstetter of Bebenhausen, Wurttemberg, gave the tenth of all his interests and salary to benevolent purposes, according to the words of St. Augustine, "If the Pharisees and Scribes gave the tenth, should we not be ashamed to give nothing?"

Dr. Jonas once gave alms to a poor man, and remarked, "Who knows but what God will return it," but Luther remarked, "As if God had not long ago given it in advance!"

Youth is the seed-time, old age the harvest. If we lay nothing up for old age it will be as related in the fable; namely, A cricket came to the ant, and said, "Give me something to eat." The ant asked, "What did you do in the summer?" "I whistled," said the cricket. "Then," said the ant, "if you whistled in summer while I was working, you may dance in the winter," and gave her nothing.

A very rich merchant was asked by his king, how much money he had. The merchant replied, the sum would not amount to much more than 1000 florins. When the king said, he thought the merchant was jesting, he replied, "I have, for God's sake, devoted 1000 florins to the poor, and these alone I consider mine own. All my other possessions are subject to the will of the king, the hands of thieves, the uncertainties of fortune, none of these can I regard as positively my own."

It is related of one of the kings of France, that he asked a servant how much he earned every year. "As much as the king," was the reply. When he was further asked, how much the king earned, he replied, "Food and raiment; more he can not use, and that I have, and earn it also." 1 Tim. vi. 8.

Dr. Luther was very contented with his condition. Duke John made him a present of a new mantel. Luther wrote him that he was doing too much for him, for if everything was given him in this world, what could he hope for in the next.

John Paul of Siena, was always very liberal to the poor. On his deathbed he exclaimed, "What I have kept, that have I lost, and what I have given away, that I have yet, what I have refused I now regret."

Another is reported to have said, "I have lost every thing except what I have given away."

A lady of the nobility once said to Dr. Bengel, "I understand, Dr. Bengel, that you are a prophet; will you please to tell me, will there be special seats reserved in heaven for persons belonging to the nobility?" "Certainly," replied Bengel, "there are special seats reserved for them, but I regret to say, that according to Matt. xix. 24 and 1 Cor. i. 26, you will find them very dusty."

THE EIGHTH COMMANDMENT.

111. What is the Eighth Commandment?

Thou shalt not bear false witness against thy neighbor." Matt. xv. 19; John viii. 44; Prov. xix. 5; John i. 19, 20; Zech. viii. 16, 17.

112. What is taught in this Commandment?

That we should so fear and love God, as not to belie, betray, slander, or raise injurious reports against our neighbor, but apologize for him, speak well of him, and put the most charitable construction on all his actions.

113. How does this commandment differ from the three preceding ones?

The Eighth Commandment differs from the Fifth, Sixth and Seventh, in that they refer to injuries done by actions, but the Eighth refers to wrong done by words.

114. What is it to belie our neighbor?

To belie our neighbor is, designedly to say that of him which is untrue and injurious.

115. What is it to betray our neighbor?

We betray our neighbor, when we publish something for the purpose of injuring him. Example, Doeg in 1 Sam. xxi, xxii; or reveal something which he has told us in confidence.

116. What is it to slander our neighbor?

We slander our neighbor, when we speak evil of him behind his back, which we would not do before his face.

117. In what ways can this be done?

We slander our neighbor,

1. When we repeat what some one has said about him, which is untrue and injurious to him;

2. When we make known the evil he has done, but which as yet is known to few persons, and is of no advantage to society to be known;

3. When we depreciate the merits or character and good qualities of our neighbor.

118. What is required in this commandment?

In the Eighth Commandment there are three duties toward our neighbors obligatory upon us; these are

1. That we apologize for him; that is, defend him against accusation, or mention ameliorating circumstances. Example, Nicodemus, John vii. 50.

<small>John vii. 50. Nicodemus saith unto them, (he that came to Jesus by night, being one of them.)
John vii. 51. Doth our law judge *any* man, before it hear him, and know what he doeth?</small>

2. When we cannot do this, then speak well of him; that is, present the commendable qualities of our neighbor. Example, Paul in his letter to Onesimus.

3. But if we cannot even do this, then put the most charitable construction on his actions. That is, construe his motives for good so long as we are not convinced to the contrary.

119. Under what circumstances is this commandment peculiarly binding upon us?

The Eighth Commandment is peculiarly binding upon us

1. In courts of justice, where very much depends

upon faithful witness-bearing. The law requires that we "speak the truth, the whole truth, and nothing but the truth," as in the very sight of God, and as answerable to him.

2. In public controversy. When words are weighed they should not give a doubtful meaning or a wrong impression.

3. In private life. Society is kept together by truth.

120. How may we violate this commandment in relation to ourselves?

We may violate the Eighth Commandment in relation to ourselves

1. By meanness, in which we think less worthily of ourselves than we ought to think, and betray a want of self-respect;

2. By self-conceit, in which we think more highly of ourselves than we ought to think, which leads to boasting of ourselves;

3. By prevarication, in which the truth is contorted, or partly concealed, by means of which a false impression is sought to be made;

4. By exaggeration, wherein things are represented as greater than truth and justice will warrant.

121. What are the motives for the observance of this commandment?

The motives for the observance of this commandment are,

1. That lying is disgraceful and injurious.

Ps. v. 6. Thou shalt destroy them that speak leasing: The LORD will abhor the bloody and deceitful man.

2. He who violates this commandment will not be believed, even when he speaks the truth; on the contrary by the observance of truth and uprightness we become like unto Christ.

Eph. iv. 21. If so be that ye have heard him, and have been taught by him, as the truth is in Jesus.

Ps. xv. 1. Lord, who shall abide in thy tabernacle? who shall dwell in thy holy hill?

Ps. xv. 2. He that walketh uprightly, and worketh righteousness, and speaketh the truth in his heart.

Ps. xv. 3. *He that* backbiteth not with his tongue, nor doeth evil to his neighbor, nor taketh up a reproach against his neighbor.

Ps. xv. 4. In whose eyes a vile person is contemned; but he honoreth them that fear the Lord. *He that* sweareth to *his own* hurt and changeth not.

Ps. xv. 5. *He that* putteth not out his money to usury, nor taketh reward against the innocent. He that doeth these *things* shall never be moved.

3. Truthfulness makes us more like God; falsehood makes us more like the devil.

John viii. 44. Ye are of *your* father the devil, and the lusts of your father ye will do. He was a murderer from the beginning, and abode not in the truth, because there is no truth in him. When he speaketh a lie he speaketh of his own: for he is a liar, and the father of it.

ANECDOTES AND ILLUSTRATIONS.

Scriptural Examples. Lying: the serpent, Gen. iii. 1, 4; John viii. 44; False witnesses against Naboth, 1 Kings xxi. 1-13; Against Jesus, Matt. xxvi. 60; Against Stephen, Acts vi. 13; Against Paul, Acts xxiv; Apologizing: Jonathan, 1 Sam. xix 4, 5; Abimelech, 1 Sam. xxii. 14; Faithful reproof: Nathan, 2 Sam. xii. 7; John Baptist, Mark vi. 18.

Speaking evil of others. Eli, 1 Sam. i. 13, 14; Sons of Belial, 1 Sam. x. 27; Eliab, 1 Sam. xvii. 28, 29; Michal, 2 Sam. vi. 16, 20; Job's wife, Job ii. 9; the Scribes, Matt. ix. 3, 4; John ix. 24; Judas, John xii. 4, 5.

I. To maintain and promote truth between man and man. We are required to speak, not as we think or wish, but as things really are. We are to be true ourselves. Joseph's brethren said, "We are true men:" Gen. xlii. 11. The Gibeonites were false: Josh. ix. We are always to speak the truth to others: Eph. iv. 25.

II. To maintain and promote our own and our neighbor's good name. A good name is our character or reputation. It is the most valuable possession, and most carefully to be kept. Whatever damages our character is dangerous. We should therefore be consistent with the truth. No evil report should be spread regarding our neighbor. We should speak for him if we can.

III. To maintain and promote truth in witness-bearing. This is frequently required—

1. In courts of justice, where very much depends on faithful witness bearing. The law requires that we "speak the truth, the whole truth, and nothing but the truth," as in the very sight of God, and as answerable to him.

2. In public controversy. When words are weighed they should not give a double meaning or a wrong impression.

3. In private life. Society is kept together by truth.—*Steel.*

I. This commandment forbiddeth whatsoever is prejudicial to truth This includes dissembling, hypocrisy, lying, breaking promises. It also affects witnesses, lawyers, and judges in courts, where so much depends upon truth. Ananias and Sapphira are great beacons.

II. Whatsoever injures our own good name. Boasting about ourselves; prevaricating truth respecting ourselves; frequenting suspicious company or places; thinking too highly of ourselves.

III. Whatsoever injures our neighbor's good name.

1. Unfounded suspicions.
2. Spreading false reports or insinuations against character; imputing unworthy motives.
3. Betraying secrets and bearing tales.

IV. Whatsoever tends to injure truth or reputation—as flattery, detraction, pride, foolish talk or conduct.—*Steel.*

LESSONS.

1. Young people should be very careful in speaking the truth always.
2. All are required to walk in the truth.
3. A liar cannot enter the kingdom of heaven.
4. The tongue requires a bridle.
5. Let us have great respect for a good reputation.—*Steel.*

Christ said, "I am the truth:" John xiv. 6. "To this end was I born, and for this cause came I into the world, that I should bear witness unto the truth. Every one that is of the truth heareth my voice:" John xviii. 37.

"Sacred was Lactantius, who denied the Earth's rotundity; sacred was Augustine, who admitted the Earth to be round but denied the antipodes; sacred is the learning of our moderns, who admit the smallness of the Earth but deny its motion; but to me more sacred than all is TRUTH."—*Kepler.*

"Above all, to thine own self be true;
Thou canst not then be false to any man."—*Shakespeare*.

When Petrarch resided in the house of Cardinal Colonna, a dispute arose among some members of the household. The Cardinal made each one swear on the Gospels that he would declare the whole truth. Even his own brother, the Bishop of Luna, was not excused. But when the poet came, the Cardinal laid aside the book and said, As to you, Petrarch, your word is sufficient."

The Rev. Robert Fleming once said to an intimate friend in London, "I bless God that in fifteen years' time I have not given any man's credit a thrust behind his back. When I have had grounds to speak well of any man, I have done so with faithfulness; but when I have wanted a subject that way I have kept silence."

When George Washington was a boy, a beautiful cherry tree was killed in his father's garden, by some violent hand stripping its bark. Mr. Washington said he would not have taken five guineas for the tree, and he would like to know the offender. Shortly after, seeing George with an axe in his hand, he asked him if he knew who had killed the cherry tree. George hesitated for a moment, then said, "I cannot tell a lie, father, I cannot tell a lie. I cut it with the hatchet." "Come to my arms!" said his father; "you have paid for it a thousand times." Such an act of heroism in telling the truth he valued more than a thousand cherry trees.

Dr. Samuel Johnson once said, "Above all, accustom your children constantly to tell the truth, without varying in any circumstance." A lady who heard him said, "Nay, this is too much, for a little variation in narrative must happen a thousand times a day, if one is not perpetually watching." "Well, madam," said the doctor, "you ought to be perpetually watching."

"From the Bible first engrave on your heart, then translate into your lives, and last emblason aloft on the pediment of your trade temple, this short and simple legend: 'A poor man is better than a liar.'"—*Arnot*.

An Indian came to a christian to hear the word of God. The christian read to him from Proverbs, "He that bridleth his tongue is wise." The Indian said, this was enough for one lecture; but he did not come again. The christian met him a month later and asked him the reason. "I have not yet learned my first lecture," replied the Indian. After six month he met him again, and received the same answer to his inquiry. Six years passed away and the Indian died. The christian visited him on his deathbed, but he declared he had not yet learned his first lesson, and did not wish to hear a second one.

The Duke of Bourgoyn, nephew of Louis XV. was even in his childhood an enemy of flattery. When asked, which of the servants he loved most, he replied, naming certain ones, "Because," said he, "they don't spare me, but tell me openly, when I do wrong, in order that I may do better."

George II., king of Great Brittain, on a visit to his German lands, asked the president of the court of appeals of Celle, at a banquet, "Why is it, Mr. President, that I lose nearly all my suits at the court of appeals?" The president replied, "Because your majesty is usually in the wrong."

The Roman Emperor Julian, apostasied from the Christian religion and thought he had entirely suppressed Christianity in his empire. Lebanius, who had assisted in the suppression of Christianity, met the pious Athanasius on the street in Rome, and said to him, "What is the Son of the carpenter doing now?" "He is making a coffin for your emperor," replied Athanasius, and in a few days later the report came, that Julian had been killed in a battle with the Parthians.

An ungodly sailor once said to a negro who belonged to a missionary's church, "We don't think much of the missionaries." The negro replied, "You say, you don't like the missionaries, will you give me one good reason why you don't like the missionaries, maybe I can give you a good answer." Such a challenge the sailor had not expected and remained silent.

St. Augustine said, "Two things I must have in this world; namely, a good conscience and a good name."

The Emperor Albright used to say, "Three kinds of people I esteem above all others; namely, pious ministers, courageous men, and chaste women." But three kinds of persons he detested; namely, liars, false tongues and slanderers.

The world loves the treason, but dispises the traitor. The high priests rejoiced when Judas promised to betray Jesus into their hands, but when afterwards he came to them in despair to find comfort, they said, "See thou to it."

He who takes a flatterer for his friend will be disappointed when he needs a friend. The flatterers are like the swallows, they remain as long as the weather is fair, but fly away when the cold winds come. They are like the flies that remain only so long as they find anything to devour; they are like the leech, which drops off as soon as it has sucked itself full of blood.

He who robs his neighbor of his good name, makes him poor, indeed, but does not enrich himself.

The question was asked, "Why we can see other peoples' failings sooner than our own? and why we can give advice to others easier than follow it ourselves? A sensible man asked in reply, "Why can our eyes see everything else but themselves?"

Old Esop gave an answer to the same question. He said, "A man carries a bag on his shoulder; in the forepart of the bag, which is always before his eyes, are contained the failings of his fellow men; in the hinder part of the bag, which hangs upon his back, are contained his own failings. He himself does not see them, and it requires great humility and good will to believe what others tell us about them.

Slander is like smoke, which seems at first as if it would blacken even the heavens, but it is scattered by the first blast of wind, and it vanishes away in the air, so that nobody knows what has become of it.

Luther says, "The slanderer has the devil sitting on his tongue, and he who listens to the slander has the devil in his ear. There is little difference between the two.

Alexander the Great used to turn only one ear to an accuser, but held the other ear closed, saying the latter he must reserve for the accused.

When Luther stood before the Diet of Worms, and had almost fainted from so much speaking, Duke Erich of Brunswick, sent him a refreshing drink in a silver cup. Some of his friends were suspicious, fearing that the Duke might be an enemy, and intend to poison him. But Luther took the cup and drank, saying, "*As Duke Erich has now remembered me, so may God remember him in the hour of death.*" And with joy the good Duke remembered these words of Luther on his death-bed.

When Alexander lay very seriously ill he received a letter, in which he was warned to take no medicine from his physician, because he was bribed by Darius, King of Persia, with a large sum of money, to poison him. But Alexander trusted his physician; with one hand he took the cup, and with the other hand he gave the letter to the physician, and while the physician read the letter, Alexander confidingly drank the medicine. He then fell into a long sleep and recovered from his sickness.

Eberhard Von Weihe, Chancelor of Brunswick, was once in conversation with some Italians at Florence, and these boasted among other things, that the Germans were simpletons, and that it was an easy matter for them to cheat the Germans just as they pleased. Eberhard replied, "An art like that is possessed and practiced by the devil, too, but he will never be saved by such an art."

One day there happened a tremendous storm of lightning and thunder, as Archbishop Leighton was going from Glasgow to Dunblane. He was descried, when at a distance by two men of bad character. They had not courage to rob him: but wishing to fall on some method of extorting money from him, one said, "I will lie down by the way-side as if I were dead, and you shall inform the archbishop, that I was killed by the lightning, and beg money of him to bury me." When the archbishop arrived at the spot, the wicked wretch told him the fabricated story. He sympathized with the survivor, gave him money, and proceeded on his journey. But when the man returned to his companion he found him really lifeless! Immediately he began to exclaim, "Oh! sir, he is dead! Oh! sir, he is dead!" On this the archbishop discovered the fraud, left the man with this important reflection, "It is a dangerous thing to trifle with the judgments of God."

When any one was speaking ill of another in the presence of Peter the Great, he at first listened to him attentively, and then interrupted him. "Is there not," said he, "a fair side also to the character of the person of whom you are speaking? Come, tell me what good qualities you have remarked about him?"

THE NINTH AND TENTH COMMANDMENTS.

122. What is the Ninth Commandment?

"Thou shalt not covet thy neighbor's house."

123. What is meant by this commandment?

We should so fear and love God as not to desire by craftiness to gain possession of our neighbor's inheritance or home, or to obtain it under the pretext of a legal right, but be ready to assist and serve him in the preservation of his own.

124. What is forbidden in this commandment?

In the Ninth Commandment are forbidden all actual evil desires which run counter to the law of God; especially those which are cherished with pleasure in the heart, and when opportunity is sought for their indulgence.

Micah ii. 1. Woe to them that devise iniquity, and work evil upon their beds! when the morning is light, they practise it, because it is in the power of their hand.

125. On what subjects are these evil desires directed?

The evil desires are directed

1. Upon riches, as for example, the desire to obtain unlawfully our neighbor's house or property.

Micah ii. 2. And they covet fields, and take *them* by violence; and houses, and take *them* away: so they oppress a man and his house, even a man and his heritage.

1 Kings xxi. 1. And it came to pass after these thing, *that* Naboth the Jezreelite had a vineyard, which *was* in Jezreel, hard by the palace of Ahab, king of Samaria.

1 Kings xxi. 2. And Ahab spake unto Naboth saying, Give me thy vineyard, that I may have it for a garden of herbs, because it *is* near unto my house: and I will give thee for it a better vineyard than it; *or*, if it seem good to thee, I will give thee the worth of it in money.

2. Honor or worldly fame.

Esther v. 12. Haman said moreover, Yea, Esther the queen did let no man come in with the king unto the banquet that she had prepared but myself; and to morrow am I invited unto her also with the king.

Esther v. 13. Yet all this availeth me nothing, so long as I see Mordecai the Jew sitting at the king's gate.

3. Luxury.

Luke xvi. 19. There was a certain rich man, which was clothed in purple and fine linen, and fared sumptuously every day.

126. What is required in this commandment?

The Ninth Commandment requires that we should have a desire for those things only which are good and pleasing to God.

127. What are those desires which are good and pleasing to God.

The desires which are good and pleasing to God are

1. A desire for the glory of God and a closer communion with him.

Ps. lxxiii. 24. Thou shalt guide me with thy counsel, and afterward receive me to glory.

Matt. vi. 21. For where your treasure is, there will your heart be also.

2. A desire to do and be what God has commanded, that is to have and to practice the christian virtues.

Ps. xix. 9. The fear of the LORD *is* clean, enduring for ever: the judgments of the LORD *are* true *and* righteous altogether.

Phil. iv. 8. Finally, brethren, whatsoever things are true, whatsoever things *are* honest, whatsoever things *are* just, whatsoever things *are* pure, whatsoever things *are* lovely, whatsoever things *are* of good report; if *there be* any virtue, and if *there be* any praise, think on these things.

Phil. iv. 9. Those things, which ye have both learned, and received, and heard, and seen in me, do: and the God of peace shall be with you.

128. Which are some of the christian virtues?

The following are christian virtues:

1. Contentment, which will also induce us to help our neighbor to preserve his own property.

1 Tim. vi. 6. But Godliness with contentment is great gain.

2. Humility.

James iv. 10. Humble yourselves in the sight of the Lord, and he shall lift you up.

3. Chastity.

1 Peter ii. 11. Dearly beloved, I beseech you as strangers and pilgrims, abstain from fleshly lusts, which war against the soul.

129. How should these virtues be cherished and promoted?

These virtues should be cherished and promoted,

1. By contemplation of the word and goodness of God.

Ps. ciii. 2. Bless the LORD, O my soul, and forget not all his benefits.

2. By temperance and watchfulness over our bodies and souls.

1 Peter v. 8. Be sober, be vigilant; because your adversary the devil, as a roaring lion, walketh about, seeking whom he may devour.

3. By prayer and contemplation of the things that are to come, such as

    a. Death.
    b. Judgment.
    c. The damnation of the ungodly, and
    d. The salvation of believers.

130. What are the motives for the observance of this commandment?

The motives for the observance of this commandment are

The divine punishment threatened against

  1. The avaricious.

1 Tim. vi. 9. But they that will be rich fall into temptation and a snare, and *into* many foolish and hurtful lusts, which drown men in destruction and perdition.

  2. The Proud.

Ps. cxix 21. Thou hast rebuked the proud *that are* cursed, which do err from thy commandments.

  3. The licentious.

1 Peter ii. 11. Dearly beloved, I beseech *you* as strangers and pilgrims, abstain from fleshly lusts, which war against the soul;

131. What is the Tenth Commandment?

"Thou shalt not covet thy neighbor's wife, nor his man servant, nor his maid servant, nor his ox, nor his ass, nor anything that is thy neighbor's." James i. 14, 15; Matt. v. 28; 2 Pet. i. 4; John ii. 15; Matt. xv. 19; Eph. iv. 22-24.

132. What is required in this commandment?

That we should so fear and love God, as

  1. Not even to wish to seduce our neighbor's wife,
  2. To corrupt or alienate from him his servants,
  3. Or to force away from him, or let loose his cattle,
  4. But rather use our endeavors, that they may continue with him, and discharge their duty to him.

133. What is forbidden in this commandment?

In the Tenth Commandment are forbidden the first emotions of a natural disposition to evil, which is original sin.

134. Wherein does original sin consist?

Original sin consists in

1. A destitution of goodness, and
2. A disposition to evil.

Rom. vii. 7. What shall we say then? *Is* the law sin? God forbid. Nay, I had not known sin, but by the law: for I had not known lust, except the law had said, Thou shalt not covet.

135. What are the negative effects of original sin or natural depravity on the mind?

By original sin, or depravity,

1. The understanding is destitute of the knowledge of that which is good.

Rom. iii. 11. There is none that understandeth, there is none that seeketh after God.

2. The will is destitute of love for that which is good, and

1 Cor. ii. 14. But the natural man receiveth not the things of the Spirit of God: for they are foolishness unto him: neither can he know *them*, because they are spiritually discerned.

3. The memory is destitute of power to retain that which is good.

136. How does original sin or natural depravity affect the mind positively?

Through original sin or natural depravity

1. The understanding is disposed to entertain false views of God and divine things;
2. The will is disposed to gain an aversion, a loathing and a hatred to and of that which is good, and a love for that which is evil;

Rom. vii. 21. I find then a law, that, when I would do good, evil is present with me.
Rom. vii. 22. For I delight in the law of God after the inward man:
Rom. vii. 23. But I see another law in my members, warring

against the law of my mind, and bringing me into captivity to the law of sin which is in my members.

3. The memory easily retains the evil which afterwards is recalled to the soul with pleasure. In this way original sin, or natural depravity, inclines a man sinfully to covet his neighbor's wife, servant, or any property of his neighbor.

137. What is required in this commandment?

The Tenth Commandment requires the proper constitution of the whole human nature, with all the faculties of his mind.

Eph. iv. 24. And that ye put on the new man, which after God is created in righteousness and true holiness.

138. Why does God require these qualities in man?

God requires these qualities in man, because he originally endowed him with them, when he created him in his image and likeness.

139. What moral qualities are necessary to restore the image and likeness of God in the soul?

To restore the image of God is required the presence of that which is good; namely, positively:

1. In the understanding a knowledge of God and his will;

2. In the will reverence for God and love to him, with a desire to please him;

3. In the memory the power to comprehend the truth of God and frequent delightful meditation upon it.

Col. iii. 16. Let the word of Christ dwell in you richly in all wisdom; teaching and admonishing one another in psalms and hymns and spiritual songs, singing with grace in your hearts to the Lord.

140. What moral qualities are required negatively?

The negative qualities are, aversion to all that is evil; namely,

1. False views of God and divine things.

Mal. iii. 15. And now we call the proud happy; yea, they that work wickedness are set up; yea, *they that* tempt God are even delivered.

Mal. iii. 16. Then they that feared the LORD spake often one to another: and the LORD hearkened, and heard *it*, and a book of remembrance was written before him for them that feared the LORD, and that thought upon his name.

2. Abhorrence of all ungodliness, whereby we neither desire to know the bad, nor to retain it in our memory, and are reminded of it with aversion.

1 Tim. i. 13. Who was before a blasphemer, and a persecutor, and injurious: but I obtained mercy, because I did *it* ignorantly in unbelief.

Gal. v. 7. Ye did run well; who did hinder you that ye should not obey the truth?

141. What are the motives for the observance of this commandment?

The motives for the observance of the Tenth and all other commandments are contained in the remarkable threatenings and promises connected with them.

142. What saith the Lord God concerning all these commandments?

He saith: "I the Lord thy God, am a jealous God, visiting the iniquities of the fathers upon the children to the third and fourth generation of them that hate me, and showing mercy unto thousands of them that love me and keep my commandments." Nahum i. 2; 2 Pet. ii. 4, 6; Hos. vi. 5; Ps. ciii. 17, 18; Exod. xx. 5, 6.

143. What do we learn from this declaration?

God threatens to punish all who transgress these commandments; we should, therefore, dread his displeasure, and not act contrary to his laws. But he also promises grace and every blessing to all such as obey these laws; we should, therefore, love and confide in him, and cheerfully do what he commanded us.

144. What does the Lord God show in these words?

In these words the Lord God shows both his severity and his mercy.

145. How does the Lord God show his severity?

The Lord God shows his severity in these words in that as Lord, with divine authority, he

    1. Commands us as his servants.

Mal. i. 6. A son honoreth *his* father, and a servant his master: if then I *be* a father, where *is* mine honor? and if I *be* a master, where *is* my fear? saith the LORD of hosts unto you, O priests, that despise my name. And ye say, Wherein have we despised thy name?

    2. Manifests himself as God, to whom we are indebted for all we have and are.

    3. Who, as Almighty God, is able to punish the wicked.

    4. Who, also, as a jealous God, will punish the impenitent transgressors of his law.

    5. Yea, he will also judge their wicked descendents, until the third and fourth generation.

146. How does God show his mercy upon those who love him and keep his commandments?

The Lord God shows his mercy in that he promises his blessing to them and their children both temporal and spiritual, even to the thousandths' generation.

NOTE 1. From Adam up to our time the three hundredth generation does not yet live upon the earth.

NOTE 2. The revealed will of the Lord our God is a law to us as his subjects, which binds us, either to perfect obedience or the penalty of its transgression. As long as neither of these is fulfilled we rest under the guilt, until the demands of our righteous God have been complied with, or his threatnings have been inflicted. This law is to us the school-master to drive us to Christ, who has both fulfilled the law and paid the penalty of our transgression.

Gal. iii. 13. Christ hath redeemed us from the curse of the law, being made a curse for us: for it is written, Cursed *is* every one that hangeth on a tree.

Luke xxiv. 44. And he said unto them, These *are* the words which I spake unto you, while I was yet with you, that all things must be fulfilled, which were written in the law of Moses, and *in* the prophets, and *in* the psalms, concerning me.

Luke xxiv. 45. Then opened he their understanding, that they might understand the scriptures.

Luke xxiv. 46. And said unto them, Thus it is written, and thus it behoved Christ to suffer, and to rise from the dead the third day.

Luke xxiv. 47. And that repentance and remission of sins should be preached in his name among all nations, beginning at Jerusalem.

ANECDOTES AND ILLUSTRATIONS.

Scriptural Examples. Covetousness: Eve, Gen. iii. 6; Esau, Gen. xxv; Potiphar's wife, Gen. xxxix. 7; David, 2 Sam. xi. 2; Ahab and Jezebel, 1 Kings xxi; Herod, Matt. xiv. 5; David, Ps. cxliii. 8; cxix. 40, 81, 174,; Isaiah, xvi. 9; Dan. i. 8, 11; Sergius Paulus, Acts xiii. 7.

Conclusion of the Commandments. Conviction of sin: Adam, Gen. iii. 10; Cain, Gen. iv. 14; Joseph's brethren, Gen. xliii. 18; Gen. l. 15; Gen. xlii. 21; xliv. 16; David, 2 Sam. xii; Ps. li; Jonah, i. 7, 12; Herod, Matt. xiv. 1, 2; Judas, Matt. xxvii. 3; Felix, Acts xxiv. 25.

The Ante Diluvians, Gen. vi. 3, 5; Lot's wife, Gen. xix. 26; Luke, xvii. 32; Abijam, 1 Kings xv. 3; the Scribes, Matt. ix. 4; Ananias, Acts v. 3; Simon the sorcerer, Acts viii. 13; David, Ps. xxvi. 40; li. 12.

God punishes sin. The serpent: Eve and Adam, Gen. iii. 14-19; the Ante Diluvians, Gen. vi, vii; Sodom, Gen. xix; Pharaoh, Exodus xiv; Nebuchadnezzar, Dan. iv. 24; Belshazzar, Dan. v. 30; Jerusalem, Luke xix. 41-44; Herod, Acts xii. 23; Elymas, Acts xiii. 11; the prodigal son, Luke xv. 14-17; Dives, Luke xvi. 23-27.

I. Personal contentment with our worldly position, our social advantages, and with God's dealings. St. Paul says that he had learned, in whatsoever state he was, therewith to be content. He knew all varieties of circumstances, but had this great happiness. In his case it arose from his relation to Christ: Phil. iv. 13. This does not forbid dilligence or lawful aspiration to better our circumstances. We should always realize dependence on God.

II. Charity to our neighbor.

1. This may be done by wishing him well in soul and body—as Boaz saluted his reapers, Ruth ii. 4; as the apostle, 3 John 3.

2. By respecting what belongs to him: Deut. xxii. 1.

3. By assisting his advancement as we may be able. For this there are many opportunities.

I. Discontent is forbidden. This includes murmuring at our worldly condition, as the Israelites did after they went out of Egypt; Num. xiv. 2-35; 1 Cor. x. 10. It also includes complaining against God, as Cain, Jonah, Israel.

II. Envying or grieving at the good of our neighbor. This is a very unhappy state of mind. It grudges others what they possess, because it is more or other than we have.

III. Covetous desires after what is our neighbor's—as, his house, his wife, his servants, his possessions, or any of his advantages. The command is very specific in its condemnation of covetousness. The apostle calls this "the root of all evil." It has led to meanness, deceit, fraud, theft, and murder, all for the sake of inordinate desires.

I. Man since the fall is sinful in his nature.

II. No mere man can in this life perfectly keep God's commandments. The law requires a perfect obedience; but man is a sinful being, and cannot render that. Christ, who rendered perfect obedience, was not a mere man.

III. Every mere man breaks the commandments of God.

1. This is done in thought: Gen. vi. 5. The imagination is wayward and evil.

2. In word. The tongue is an unruly evil: James iii. 8. Idle, thoughtless, hasty, and hurtful words are often used. Some use bad language, and some speak falsely.

3. The Psalmist says that his iniquities are innumerable, and are more than the hairs of his head: Ps. xl. 12.

LESSONS.

1. Contentment, with godliness, is great gain. It secures an interest in salvation and satisfaction with God's providence.

2. Personal contentment promotes charity to our neighbor.

3. Let us not set too high a value on worldly things: Col. iii. 2.

4. Let us beware of three evils of desire—the lust of the flesh, the lust of the eye, and the pride of life: 1 John ii. 15, 16.

5. These lusts are called deceitful, Eph. iv. 22; hurtful, 1 Tim. vi. 9; worldly, Titus ii. 12; warring against the soul, 1 Peter ii. 11; warring in our members, James iv. 1.

6. Let us pray, "Incline my heart unto thy testimonies, and not to covetousness:" Ps. cxix. 36.

7. How corrupt and helpless is man before God.

8. What great need there is of a Savior.

9. The nature renewed by grace will be able to keep all God's commandments in the glorified state.—*Steel.*

The Bible is very particular regarding the sin and danger of the covetous man. "It says,—(1) that he cannot enter heaven, 1 Cor. vi. 10; (2) that he is an idolater, Eph. v. 5; (3) that God abhors him, Ps. x. 3.

This commandment has a special interest, as it was the means, as St. Paul tells us, of leading him to the knowledge of sin. "I had not known lust, except the law had said, Thou shalt not covet," (Rom. vii. 7.) Most of the other commandments forbid external acts, but this forbids a state of the heart. It shows that no external obedience can fulfill the demands of the law; that God looks upon the heart; that he approves or disapproves of the secret affections and purposes of the soul; that a man may be a Pharisee, pure outwardly as a whited sepulchre, but inwardly full of dead men's bones and of all uncleanness."—*Dr. Hodge.*

In the greatest of the Greater Prophets we read of "greedy dogs, which can never have enough." Among the words of Agur, the son of Jakeh, we read of the horse-leech having two daughters, whose insatiate, insatiable cry is, "Give, give."

The Emperor Frederick II. said to Pope Gregory IX., "But thou, having nothing, yet possessing all things, art ever seeking what thou mayest devour and swallow up: the whole world connot glut the rapacity of thy maw, for the whole world sufficeth thee not."

Seneca in his Morals says of a happy life, "What matters it how far Alexander extended his conquests, if he never got to feel satisfied with what he had?" Every man wants as much as he covets, and labor lost is to pour into a vessel which never will be full.

It is said of a covetous man that if you were to make him a present of the islands of Great Britain and Ireland as a free gift, he would at once request to have the Isle of Man thrown in too, for a potato garden.

The covetous "eats all things and is hungry still. More, more! the glutten cries for something new. So rages appetite."

> " Learn not to be greedy, and when you've enough,
> Don't be anxious your bags any tighter to stuff;
> Nor turn every thought to increasing your store,
> And look always like Oliver asking for more."
>
> *Ingoldsby Legends.*

An Italian bishop struggled through great difficulties without repining, and through much opposition without impatience. A friend who admired his virtues asked if he could give the secret of his contentment. "Yes," said the old man; "it consists in nothing more than a right use of my eyes. In whatsoever state I am, I first of all look up to heaven, and remember that my principle business here is to get there; I then look down upon the earth, and call to mind how small a place I shall occupy in it when I am buried; I then look abroad upon the world, and observe what multitudes there are who are in all respects more unhappy than myself. Thus I learn where true happiness is placed, where all our cares must end, and how very little reason I have to repine or complain."

Plutarch tells us of Caius Marius, that at the age of seventy, distinguished by the unparalleled honor of seven consulships, and possessed of more than regal fortune, he died with the chagrin of an unfortunate wretch who had not obtained what he wanted.

Herodotus says that Alcmæon, when he was told by Crœsus that he might go into the treasury and take as much gold as he could carry on his person at one time, put on the largest tunic he could find and the roomiest buskins: then he first filled his boots with the gold dust, then stuffed his clothes with it, then powdered his hair with it, and lastly took a mouthful of it, and came out dragging his legs with difficulty, and looking scarcely like a human being! Crœsus was highly amused at his covetous spirit.

"The conquests of covetousness are greater than those of Alexander. There are those who think that the chief end of man is to glorify gold, and to enjoy it for ever."—*H. W. Beecher.*

Two weavers were once talking together of religious experience, and both complained of their trouble from vain and evil thoughts in the exercises of religion. Another weaver having heard them, said, "I always thought you two vile hypocrites, but now I know it from your own confession. I never had such vain and evil thoughts in my life." One of the men then took a piece of money out of his pocket and said, "This shall be yours, if, after you come from the church the next time, you can say you had not one vain thought there." A few days afterwards he came and said, "Keep your money, for I had not been five minutes in the church till I began to think how many looms could be set up in it!"

On the 18th of April, 1560, Melanchton lay on his deathbed. Dr. Peucer asked if he wished anything, and Melanchton replied, "Nothing but heaven."

Missionary Richards preached to the heathen in India about the sinful nature of the natural man, the darkness of his soul, and the hardness of his heart. One of the people said to a pundit, (one of their learned men) "Well, have you no reply to all this?" He answered, "What can I say against the truth? and how can a wax candle give light to the rays of the sun?" Then he turned to the missionary and said, "Sahib, thy words are truth."

A young monk complained to one of his older brethren of the distress which the many evil thoughts occasioned him. He replied, "When the birds fly over your head you can not prevent them, but you can keep them from building nests on your head. When evil thoughts come to you, do not harbor them; let them fly away; don't detain them, nor quarrel with them."

A missionary spoke to the natives on the commandments. On the first commandment a negro said to himself, I am guilty, and so also of the second, third and fourth, I am guilty. But when he came to the fifth, he said, I am not guilty; I have never murdered any one. "But," said the missionary, "have you never wished that such a man or such a woman might be dead?" "Oh, I am guilty, massa, I am that person. This morning before breakfast, I wished that ten certain persons were dead; I never thought I was so bad a man." Then the missionary preached Christ crucified to them, who can take all our sins away.

A dying woman in Wurtemburg was asked by her pastor, if she had anything on her heart on account of which she had called him? She answered cheerfully, "No, pastor, nothing." And when her pastor, who knew her to be a pious christian woman, asked her again, if she had nothing at all on her heart, she replied again, "No, pastor, nothing at all, except my sins, which are as the sands of the sea."

A teacher in Africa asked the children, "Have we anything that we have not received from God?" They hesitated, the most of them thought we had received everything from God, but a little Hottentot child said, "Yes, there is something we have not received from God, that is our sins."

Some one remarked that many of the great saints in the almanac are great sinners. "Yes," said Newton, "they are indeed poor saints, if they have never felt that they were great sinners."

Arius was a false teacher in the fourth century, who denied the divinity of Christ. He was to be re-installed into the church, but the pious Bishop Alexander prayed to God a whole night that he would rescue the honor of his only begotten Son. The next day Arius and his companions rode in triumph through the streets of the city, when he was suddenly taken ill and died.

After Duke Ugolino had attained the summit of his ambition by means of deceit and many evil deeds, he said to one of his attendents, "Lambardo, what more can I look for?" "The wrath of God" replied Lambardo.

The Danish missionary Hansel relates of the inhabitants of the island of Nicabar, among whom he labored, that it was difficult to convince them of the necessity of redemption, because they regarded themselves as such good people. They said, "What you say about a redeemer from sin will do very well for bad people, but not for us *who are so good.*

In the first commandment God says, "I will have *thy heart*," and in the ninth and tenth, he says, "The world with all its lusts and vanities shall not have thy heart." Thus the end corresponds with the beginning. The commandments begin with the heart and end with the heart. He who keeps the first commandment possesses the fountain of all good works and righteousness; namely, the love of God; and he who keeps the last commandment closes up the fountain of all sin; namely, the sinful desires from which all evil works proceed.

Luther used to say, the world is like a bad nut; outside it looks beautiful, but inside it is rotten. The world is like a drunken man; if you lift him into the saddle on one side of the horse, he will fall down on the other side.

Of all thine accumulated treasures, the coffin and the shroud goes with thee to the tomb; everything else must be left behind. Blessed art thou if thou hast a treasure laid up in heaven.

A man had a valuable horse that he had bought for $500. Sometime afterwards he chased a rabbit on horseback, and shot it, too; but he rode his horse to death in doing so.

So foolish do they act who run after the pleasures of this world and thereby lose their own souls.

When the world, the flesh and the devil would entice thee, then think on these four words, *Death, Judgment, Heaven, Hell.*

God sees the heart and judges it, not according to the actions, but the actions according to the heart. He looks not only on the superscription of the metal, but on the metal itself out of which the money is coined.

Death. which is the wages of sin, is of three kinds,

1 Spiritual death, which is a separation of the soul from God. Isaiah lix. 2.

2. Bodily death, which is a separation of the soul from the body. Romans v. 12 ; and

3. Eternal death, which is a separation of body and soul from God. Rev. xxi. 8.

"How does our good old school master come on?" inquired one who had returned to the village after a long absence. The reply was, "He is dead and yet liveth." Though dead, yet he speaketh. The memory of the just remaineth forever.

PART II.

THE CREED.

147. What is a Christian Creed?
A Christian Creed is
  1. A short statement of the doctrines taught in the Holy Scriptures;
  2. In which we confess our faith, and
  3. Which distinguishes us from all unchristian people.

148. Why is this called the Apostles' Creed?
It is called the Apostles' Creed, not because the Apostles' wrote it, but because it is founded on the Apostles' doctrines.

149. How was the Apostles' Creed formed?
No particular author of the Apostles' Creed is given, but it grew up gradually in the church during the second and third centuries from the confession of Peter, and the Baptismal formula.

Matt. xvi. 16. And Simon Peter answered and said, Thou art the Christ, the Son of the living God.

Matt. xxviii. 19. Go ye therefore, and teach all nations, baptizing them in the name of the Father, and of the Son, and of the Holy Ghost.

150. How is the Apostles' Creed divided?
The Apostles' Creed is divided into three articles.

151. Of what do these articles treat?
  1. The first article treats of creation.
  2. The second article treats of redemption.
  3. The third article treats of redemption and sanctification.

THE FIRST ARTICLE.

152. What is the first article of the Creed?

"I believe in God, the Father Almighty, maker of heaven and earth."

153. What is meant by this article?

1. I believe that God has created me and all that exists;

2. That he has given, and still preserves to me my body and soul, with all my limbs and senses, my reason and all the faculties of my mind, together with my raiment, food, home and family, and all my property;

3. That he daily provides me abundantly with all the necessaries of life, protects me from danger, and preserves me and guards me from evil;

4. All which he does out of pure, paternal and divine goodness and mercy, without any merit or worthiness in me.

5. For all which I am in duty bound to thank, praise, serve and obey him. This is most certainly true!

154. Of what does the first article treat?

The first article of the Creed treats

1. Of Creation, and
2. Of Preservation.

155. What do you understand by the words "Creator of Heaven and Earth?"

By these words we understand that God made all things out of nothing.

156. To whom is creation ascribed?

Creation is especially ascribed to

1. God the Father,

Gen. i. 1. In the beginning God created the heaven and the earth.

2. Yet so that God the Son is not excluded;

John i. 3 All things were made by him, and without him was not any thing made that was made.

3. And also the Holy Ghost is not excluded.

Psalm xxxiii. 6. By the word of the LORD were the heavens made: and all the host of them by the breath of his mouth.

157. Of what do the created things consist?

All created things consist of
1. Those which are visible and
2. Those which are invisible.

158. Which are the visible things of creation?

The visible things of God's creation are the Heavens and the Earth and all that they contain, of which man is the most important part.

159. Why is man the most important part of God's creation?

Man is the most important part of God's creation on earth, because God
1. Gave him a wonderful body and a rational mind.
2. Made him in his own image and likeness.

Gen. i. 26 And God said, Let us make man in our own image, after our likeness.

3. Bestowed on him the dominion over all living creatures on earth,

Gen. i 26. And God said, let us make man in our own image, after our likeness: and let them have dominion over the fish of the sea, and over the fowl of the air, and over the cattle, and over all the earth, and over every creeping thing that creepeth upon the earth.

4. And as the whole world could not redeem man, Christ shed his precious blood for him,

Matt. xxvi. 28 For this is my blood of the New Testament, which is shed for many for the remission of sins.

5 And thus purchased for him the title of a child of God and the inheritance of the kingdom of heaven.

Gal. iv. 4. But when the fulness of the time was come, God sent forth his Son, made of a woman, made under the law.
Gal. iv 5. To redeem them that were under the law, that he might receive the adoption of sons.
Gal. iv. 6. And because ye are sons, God hath sent forth the Spirit of his Son into your hearts, crying Abba, Father.
Gal. iv. 7. Wherefore thou art no more a servant, but a son; and if a son, then an heir of God through Christ.

160. Which are the invisible things of God's creation?

The invisible things of God are

1. The good angels which kept their first estate and remain good, holy and obedient, and

2. The bad angels, who kept not their first estate, but fell off from God and rebelled against him.

161. To whom are we indebted for our preservation?

We are indebted for our preservation to the Triune God, who bestows upon us the strength to do good.

Eph. iii. 10. To the intent that now unto the principalities and powers in heavenly *places* might be known by the church the manifold wisdom of God.

162. In what way is God our preserver?

God is our preserver,

1. By shielding us from danger and evil;

2. By bestowing upon us life and breath;

3. By bestowing upon us food and raiment, and all the necessaries and comforts of life.

Acts xvii. 2. For in him we live and move and have our being.

163. Does God exert his preserving power also upon evil men?

1. God, in wonderful mercy, lets his sun shine and his rain descend on evil, as well as good men.

Matt. v. 45. That ye may be the Children of your Father which is in heaven: for he maketh his sun to rise on the evil and on the good, and sendeth rain on the just and on the unjust.

2. He also sustains all living creatures, such as the beasts of the field, the birds of the air and fishes in the sea.

3. He also upholds all lifeless things, such as flowers, plants, trees, and all worlds are upheld by his power.

164. What is the object of God's preserving care?

The object of God's preserving care is

1. The honor and glory of his name, over which heartfelt gratitude causes us to rejoice;

2. The welfare of his creatures.

Rom. ii. 4. Or despisest thou the riches of his goodness and forbearance and long suffering; not knowing that the goodness of God leadeth thee to repentance?

1 Pet. ii. 9. But ye are a chosen generation, a royal priesthood, an holy nation, a peculiar people; that ye should shew forth the praises of him who hath called you out of darkness into his marvelous light.

EXPLANATORY NOTES.

The Apostles' Creed is a confession of the whole Christian church of the Triune God and his works.

"I believe on God the Father." Why do we not say "We believe on God," but "I believe on God?" Because each one must believe *for himself*, in order to be saved.

To believe on God means to accept God's word and testimony as true and certain, to place a heartfelt confidence in him and confess him with our lips.

It is therefore not enough

1. To believe that there *is a God*. Such faith even the heathen and evil spirits possess. Such faith does not help them. We must also

2. *Believe God;* that is, accept his word as true, and we must

3. *Believe in God;* that is, commit ourselves to him and devote ourselves to his service. Heb. xi. 1; Rom. x. 10.

God is one God; but he has revealed himself in three persons. They are called God the Father, God the Son and God the Holy Ghost. The faith in the Triune God only is saving faith.

The Trinity cannot be proved or understood by reason; it is a mystery. This mystery is revealed to us in the Scriptures. In the Old Testament the Trinity is indicated. Gen. i. 26; Num. vi. 24-26; Isa. vi. 3. But clearer in the New Testament. Matt. xxviii. 19; 2 Cor. xiii. 13; Rev. i. 4-6.

Man is the image of the Triune God. He consists of spirit, soul and body, and yet is but one human being. See 1 Thess. v. 23.

The works of the Triune God are; 1. Creation; 2. Redemption; 3. Sanctification. According to this the Creed is divided into three articles.

The Romanists have divided the Creed into twelve sentences and imagine that each apostle wrote one sentence.

Our confession of God, the Father, is this:

"I believe in God the Father, the Almighty, the Creator of heaven and earth." The word *Almighty* relates to the Father. The words heaven and earth indicate the *visible* and the *invisible* creatures. The word creatures means those things which God has created.

This first part of the Creed as explained by Luther, contains the three great benefits which God has bestowed upon me.
1. He has created me;
2. He provides for me;
3. He protects me.

The second part contains the two reasons of his benefits; namely,
1. The Divine Goodness;
2. The Divine Mercy.

The third contains what we owe to God; namely,
1. To thank and praise him;
2. To serve and obey him. Psalm ciii. 1-13.

The Invisible Creatures are angels, evidently created at one time for the glory of God and the service of man; but part of whom have rebelled against God and become devils.

This rebellion took place before the fall of man into sin (John viii. 44; Gen. iii. 1, 24). There are therefore *good* and *bad* angels. They have spiritual bodies. They are not little children with wings, as they are painted, but mighty powers who excel in strength. (Ps. ciii. 20; 2 Thess. i. 7). The angels are not men who have died, as the Swedenborgians teach. But they are entirely different beings from us.

The Bible says of them that they are
1. Swift messengers of God. Psalm civ. 4; Heb. i. 14.
2. Very wise;
3. They can assume human forms;
4. They can become visible and invisible;
5. They have in part wings. Isa. vi.
6. Their number is incalculable. Dan. vii. 10; Matt. xxvi. 1-5.
7. Their dwelling is in the higher heaven;
8. The evil spirits, or angels, are cast out, and are in the lower parts of the air. Eph. vi. 12;
9. These are called demons;
10. At their head stands a fallen archangel, who is called in the Bible the Old Serpent, the Dragon, or Satan, also the Prince of this world, or the Devil.

The bad angels, enemies of God and man, beyond redemption, exposed to the eternal judgment, (Matt. xxv. 41,) have great power, but can not do as they please. Under God's permitting providence they sometimes afflict even the pious with sickness and other trials. Job ii. 7; 2 Cor. xii. 7; Luke xiii. 11.

They seek to turn men's souls away from God. Luke xxii. 31. They like to take possession of the souls and bodies of the ungodly, and urge them to everything bad. Luke xi. 24. They propagate false doctrines, (Matt. xiii. 24), lay hindrances in the way of the servants of God, (2 Thess. ii. 18,) and rob the hearers of the preached word, (Luke viii. 12), and stir up persecutions against the kingdom of Christ. Rev. ii. 10. But they must finally be overruled for the wellfare of the saints in time and eternity. Psa. lxxviii. 49; Matt. xviii. 34. In our conflict with Satan and his evil spirits, we can gain the victory only when we take on the whole armor of God. Eph. vi. 12, etc. The Lord Jesus has gained the victory over the kingdom of Satan. Col. ii. 15; Heb. ii. 14. When we have Jesus with us and in us, we are stronger than Satan. 1 John v. 4.

The good angels see God, and praise his works, (Job xxxviii. 7,) especially the work of redemption, (Luke i. 26, 31; ii. 13); they rejoice when sinners repent, (Luke xv. 7, 10); they are appointed as guardians of the children, (Matt. xviii. 10; Acts xii. 15); they help the pious in every good work, and protect them in danger against the assaults of the evil spirits, (Psa. xxxiv. 8; xci. 11, etc; Dan. vi. 22; x. 13; Matt. i. 19; John v. 4; Acts x. 3, etc; they are near to the dying saints, and convey their souls to their heavenly rest. Luke xvi. 22. Finally they accompany the Savior on his return to judgment, (Matt. xxv. 31, etc,) they gather the nations to judgment, (Matt. xx. 31), separate the pious from the ungodly, (Matt. xiii. 41), bind the evil spirits and cast them with the ungodly into the burning lake, (Matt. xiii. 42, 50,) and bring the righteous to the right hand of the Lord and at last to the new earth.

The Visible Creatures, (man.) In the Holy Scriptures we have indications that the earth when first created was something different from its description in Gen. i. 1. It was perhaps the habitation of an archangel, (Jude vi.); but in consequence of the rebellion of its possessor and his adherents, was destroyed by a flood or by fire. It is possible that the petrifactions of animals and plants belong to this first world, which had a much earlier existence than the present formation of the earth. But God new-created this present earth in six days, as was revealed to Moses, and gave it to man as his habitation. Hence the jealousy and wrath of Satan against man.

Man is the noblest creature, because created in the image and likeness of God. This image and likeness was *lost* through sin; but renewed through the redemption of Christ. Eph. iv. 22-24.

The image of God consisted in the uncreated wisdom, righteousness, happiness and the royal dominion over the earth and the powers of nature.

To the body God has given eyes, ears and all its members Eyes and ears are especially mentioned, because they are the noblest members.

To the soul he has given reason and all the senses. Reason is the spirit, by which we percieve and know God. Besides the five senses we also have other powers of mind and soul; such as will, memory, imagination, etc.

By the fall into sin, the whole man, as to spirit, soul and body, has become depraved and exposed to death, (bodily, spiritual and eternal.)

The depraved human nature is called the *Old Adam*, and the sinful depravity, which is inherited by all men, is called original sin.

Preservation and Providence. Another blessing is, that God preserves and upholds us and the whole world. Psalm cxix. 90, 91; Gen. viii. 22; Heb. i. 3.

He provides us with food and raiment and all the necessaries and comforts of life. Psalm cxlv. 15, 16.

Why is God so kind to us, and what do we owe him in return? God is kind to us, not because we have deserved the least of his favors, but he does this out of pure paternal love and mercy; and we should therefore, praise, thank, serve and obey him in return for his goodness to us.

ANECDOTES AND ILLUSTRATIONS.

Scriptural Examples. I believe, this is most certainly true, Gen. i. 13-22; Heb. xi. 7; Abraham's call, Heb. xi. 8; Abraham as a stranger in Canaan, Gen. xii-xxiii; Heb. xi. 9, 10; Abraham at the promise, Gen. xv; at the sacrifice of Isaac, Gen. xxii; Heb. xi. 17-19; Isaac, Gen. xxvii. 29; Heb. xi. 20; Jacob, Gen. xlviii. 13-19; Heb. xi. 21; Joseph, Gen. l. 24; Heb. xi. 22; Moses, xi. 24-26; xi. 27; The disciples, Matt. xvii. 14-21; Zacharias, Luke i. 20; Thomas, John xx. 25-29.

An Arab was asked, "How do you know that there is a God?" He replied, "I know it by the same means, that I can tell by the footprints in the sand, whether a man or a beast has passed that way."

An infidel asked a Christian, scoffingly, whether his God was a great or a small God? "He is so great," replied the Christian, "that the heavens and the earth cannot contain him, and yet, he is so small, that he can dwell in this heart of mine."

In a Christian company, a minister said to a little boy, "I will give you an orange if you will tell me where God is." The little boy replied, "I will give you two oranges, if you will tell me where God is not"

A Hindoo declared, that God does everything in man, both the good and the bad. Other Hindoos agreed with him. But the missionary told the following story: A thief was brought before the Judge, and asked why he had stolen. The thief replied that he had not stolen; it was God in him who had stolen. The Judge sentenced him to be whipped and sent to prison, When the thief begged for mercy the Judge replied, "my friend, I did not order you to be whipped, but God in you, who has stolen." Then the people began to laugh, and said, "God can not steal, nor be whipped."

A missionary declared in his sermon that God is everywhere present, sees everything, and knows our most secret thoughts. Upon this the heathen cried out, "We don't want such a God, who sees everything; we have no use for such a God; we want to live a free life, and do not wish anyone to see and hear what we do."

Anton Musa, pastor at Rocklitz, complained to Dr. Luther, that often he could not believe all he preached. "Thank God," replied Luther, "that others have the same experience that I have. I thought I alone had this experience. Our God and his Gospel are too great for us poor creatures fully to grasp.

A minister asked the children, "What is faith?" As none of them could give the correct answer, the pastor himself tried, but could not give a correct definition. Then a farmer stepped forward and asked permission to answer the question. On permission being given by the pastor, he held his hat toward him, and told him to take it. The pastor tried to do so, but the farmer would not let the hat go. When the pastor became irritated the farmer said, "You see, this is what I call faith, when you *hold fast to what you have*, and let no enemy take it from you."

When Antonius, the distinguished Egyptian hermit, heard a heathen philosopher scoff at the Christian religion, he replied, "With all your philosophy and worldly wisdom, you have never converted a soul to heathenism, but we have by our faith converted many thousands to the Gospel."

The triune God. When Velenrio, Prof. at Wittenberg, was lying sick, some of his friends visited him and inquired about his condition, he answered cheerfully, "God, the Father, loves me, God, the Son, is my Redeemer, and God, the Holy Ghost, is my Comforter, why should I be sad."

When the preacher Hermes lay on his deathbed, some one said to him, "You have fought a good fight." He replied, "Yes, God be merciful to me, a sinner."

Faith and *love* are the two sisters, whom the Lord loveth. *Faith* is *Mary*, sitting at the feet of Jesus, and *love* is *Martha*, with her both hands full to do.

Luther says, "Faith is a living, active, mighty thing, for which it is impossible not to be continually doing good. It asks not whether there are good works to do, but before the asking it has already done them, and is constantly doing."

The first Christians used to say in times of persecution, "Our faith in the tribulation of this time is like the fish which lives in the stormy sea, but cannot be crushed or drowned by its waves."

To be satisfied with a secret faith is just as if we would say to God, "I regard thee as my Lord, but I do not tell it to the people; I love thee, but the people need not know it."

A Christian may be painted as one placed between God and man, having two hands, the hand of *faith* and the hand of *love*. With the hand of *faith* he reaches up toward heaven, and receives divine blessings; with the hand of *love* he reaches downward toward his neighbor and imparts blessings upon him.

He who sees no evidence of the existence of God in nature is blind, as the beast that sees the heavens, but does not know and does not think who dwells there.

To admire the beauties of nature is like a child that enjoys the gilding and engravings of a book, without concerning itself about its contents.

John Frederick, the Elector of Saxony, when a sudden storm of thunder and lightning arose, stretched out his right hand toward heaven and exclaimed, "O thou eternal, almighty God! Thou lettest thyself be heard, that thou still livest."

St. Augustine says, "God gave man two books, which he wishes him to study; namely, the *Book* of *Nature*, and the *Book* of the *Holy Scriptures*. As the first book is somewhat hard to understand, as we see in the case of the heathen and their foolish superstition; therefore the second one, the Holy Scriptures, was added."

Man is the noblest of God's creatures, because he was created in the image and likeness of God. This image consisted in the wisdom or reason, righteousness and holiness in which he was created. To this also was added immortality, freedom and dominion over the earth, and all animated nature.

CREATION AND PROVIDENCE.

God has created and preserves me and all creatures.

Scriptural Examples. Creation, Gen. i. 1, 2; The Israelites, Ex. xvi. 4, 13, 14; xvii. 6, 7; Elijah, 1 Kings xvii. 19; The feeding of the 5000 and 4000, Matt. xiv. 17, 19; xv. 33, 34; Noah, Gen. vi, vii; Lot, Gen. xix; Joseph, Gen. xxxvii.-li.; Moses, Ex. ii. 1-9; Daniel vi; Jonah ii; The child Jesus, Matt. ii. 12; Peter, Acts xii. 11; Paul, Acts xxvii.

To the question, what God was doing before heaven and earth were created, St. Augustine replied, "He built a hell for such over-inquisitive persons who are not satisfied with his word."

Dr. Luther gave a similar answer to one who asked him, what God was doing during the long eternity before he created the world. Luther replied, "He was in the woods cutting switches to scourge impertinent questioners."

A philosopher asked the hermit Antonius, "Dear father, how can you content yourself here in the wilderness without books?" Antonius replied, "My book is the whole, great world and all creatures in it; I have not far to go to find it, as oft as I wish to read the word of God."

Justus Jonas once placed a branch full of ripe cherries over his table in memory of the creation and the blessings which God bestowed upon us. Luther said to him, "Why do you not consider this much more in regard to your children, which far surpass all other creatures and fruits of the trees?"

Missionary Ziegenbalg translated the New Testament into the Malabar language with the assistance of one of the natives. When they came to 1 John iii. 1, "Behold, what manner of love the Father hath bestowed upon us, that we should be called the sons of God," the assistant was unwilling to translate the passage literally, he said, "No! that is too high, that is too much, that God should call *us* his children. Instead of that I will translate, that we should be permitted to kiss his feet; that would be glory enough."

When Dr. Luther saw the cattle in the pasture, he said, "There are our preachers, the milk-carriers, the butter-carriers, the cheese-carriers, the wool-carriers, who daily preach to us faith in God, that we shall trust him as our Father, who cares for us, and will nourish us.

Dr. Lushington was asked whether he believed in a special providence of God? "Yes," said he, "in the great events of life." "How unphilosophical and unscriptural," replied Wilberforce, "Are not the small links and members of a chain just as necessary to keep the whole together as the great ones? Small and great has relation only to our smallness, but with God there is nothing great and nothing small."

During a great flood in the Netherlands in 1571, in which 20,000 people lost their lives, an infant was found in its cradle, which had floated away and lodged upon a hill. A cat was lying beside the child and kept it warm. The child was sleeping.

In the Parochial Church in Berlin, the minister stood upon the pulpit at three o'clock in the afternoon, when he was struck by a streak of lightning. This did not kill him, however, but healed his left ear, which had been deaf for a long time.

When the storm destroyed the so-called invincible armada of Philip II, king of Spain, Queen Elizabeth of England had a coin struck, with this inscription, "God caused his wind to blow upon them and they were sunk to the bottom of the sea."

Luther says, Moses built the tabernacle with three divisions. The first was called the Holy of Holies, wherein God dwelt; the second was the Holy Place, wherein was the golden candlestick with seven lamps; the third was the Court, which was open to the light of heaven. Thus also is man. His spirit is the Holy of Holies, in which God dwells; his soul is the Holy Place, wherein are seven lamps; namely, his intellect, his knowledge of material and visible things; his body is the Court, open and visible to everybody, that we can see what he does and how he lives.

James Grunams was asked, how old he was. He expressed it in this way, "On such a day of such a year I began to sin"

Chrisostom says, the devil is like a hungry dog, that sneaks in to a company sitting at the dinner table. If you give him a piece of bread or a bone, he will constantly come again and hold on to you. But if you will give him nothing, he will forsake you, and try somewhere else.

It is said of the lion, that he cannot endure firelight, or torches, but will flee from them. Mark this fact, when the roaring lion, the devil, attacks you; take the light of the word of God, and hold it before you, and he will certainly flee from you.

God protects and upholds us not because we deserve any favor from him, but purely from paternal love and mercy. This imposes a two-fold duty upon us; namely, gratitude and praise, and service and obedience.

It is related of an Arab, that being on the point of perishing in the wilderness, of hunger and thirst—he came to a well and quenched his thirst. As he was going on he saw a sack lying in the sand: he took it up and felt that it contained small grains, "These are grains of wheat," said he, "now I shall also be saved from starvation." He hastily opened the sack, but when he looked in, he saw that they were pearls. In sadness he threw them away, exclaiming, "Alas, they are only pearls."

The Elector, John Frederick of Saxony, reviewed his army on one occasion, and a nobleman said to him, "Your majesty, these are the protectors of your land and people." But the pious Elector replied, "O they are poor protectors, when God does not defend us!"

Why should mortal man be proud? As to his body, it is taken from the earth, and must return to dust and ashes; as to his soul, he is a sinner; as to his life, he is a stranger and a so-journer on earth.

Pope Hadrian VI. had two cities painted on a tablet; the one was Utrecht, where he was born; the other was Lyons, where he received his education. Beneath them stood the likeness of the Emperor, Charles V. Then the inscription followed: "I was planted at Utrecht, watered at Lyons, and the Emperor gave the increase." Some one wrote with chalk below: "Here God has done nothing!"

Abraham Bachholzer said, "I have found five things to commend in St. Paul. He gloried in his weakness, in the cross of Christ, in his good conscience, in tribulation and the hope of eternal life."

Melchior Adam was asked, for what purpose man was created? He replied, Luther has taught that in the first article of the Creed; namely, to thank, praise, serve and obey God. When asked, how we can in this life have a fortaste of heaven? he replied, "By praising God and loving our neighbor; for that is all we shall do in the blessed life to come."

The people murmured, because it rained in the harvest time, while there had been a long drought before. Then said Luther, "That is the way in which the world thanks God. If the Lord had not spared the world for the sake of a few faithful ones, it would long ago have been destroyed."

After Melanchton's beloved daughter had died, Luther and some friends came to console him; but he seemed inconsolable, and kept on walking back and forth in his room. At last he stepped up to his table, and took up a book of Psalms; as he opened it his eye fell upon Psalm c. 3, "Know ye not that the Lord, he is God; it is he that hath made us, and not we ourselves." Then he felt himself reproved and comforted, and turning to his friends he said, "If God has made us, why should we not be resigned to his will?"

The sainted Deiterich of Elberfeld, once traveled with some of his friends in a wagon, when the conversation was about the many troubles with which we are beset in this world. He rode backwards on wagon. Then he said to his friends, "You must do as I do on this ride, *you must ride backwards*. From your seats you look only forwards, and see every stone, obstacle, deep rut, or precipice, by which you have to pass, and you trouble yourselves with the dangers you apprehend. But I see all these things only after we have safely passed them, and every stone and every difficulty is to me only a reason for praise and thanksgiving to God, that we have safely passed them, whereas they cause you only anxiety and fear."

Lewis Choguet, an evangelical colporteur in Lille, France, was by mistake sent to prison in Calais. Calmly and tired he lay down in the afternoon and fell asleep, until a peculiar noise waked him. He looked up and saw a man, who had in the meantime been brought into prison and had hanged himself. Choguet quickly released him, and spoke to the unfortunate man about his horrible deed. The Lord blest his words to the comfort and good of the man. Now the pious colporteur understood the misunderstanding, and thanked God that he had permitted him to be imprisoned.

The Elector Frederick, and his brother Duke Hans came by ship on the river Elb from Torgau to Wittenberg at a time when the ice broke up and beat against the ship from every side. Scarcely had they landed at Wittenberg, when the ship parted and the pieces sank to the bottom. Then the Elector said to his brother, "We must confess that God has preserved us. Let us thank God, who has delivered us from this and many other dangers."

Dr. Hutton, Bishop of Durham, being once on a journey, suddenly dismounted and gave his horse to the care of a servant. He then went a short distance from the highway, knelt down and remained some time in prayer. On his return one of the company asked him the cause of this action. The Bishop replied, "When I was a poor boy, without shoes or stockings, I came to this place on a frosty morning, being very cold, I drove up a cow that was lying on the ground, and lay down in her place to warm my cold limbs."

A North American Indian once came to the great Niagara Falls, and was deeply impressed by the wonderful sight. He stood for some time in adoration of the Great Spirit. At last he took what he regarded as his best and most beautiful treasure—his smoke-pipe, and cast it into the surging waters, as a sacrifice to the Great Spirit.

An eminent minister, after having been silent in a company for a considerable time, and being asked the reason, signified, that the powers of his mind had been solemnly absorbed with the thought of eternal happiness. ."O my friends," he said with energy that surprised all present, "consider what it is, to be forever with the Lord—forever, forever, forever!"

THE SECOND ARTICLE.

165. What is the second article of the Creed?
1. And on Jesus Christ his only begotten Son;
2. Who was conceived by the Holy Ghost;
3. Born of the Virgin Mary;
4. Suffered under Pontius Pilate;
5. Was crucified, dead and buried;
6. Decended into hell;
   (Place of departed spirits, Hades.)
7. On the third day rose from the dead;
8. Ascended up to heaven;
9. Sitteth on the right hand of God, the Almighty Father;
10. Whence he will come again to judge the living and the dead.

166. What is the meaning of this article?
1. I believe that Jesus Christ, true God, begotten of the Father from eternity, and also true man, born of the Virgin Mary, is my Lord,
2. Who has redeemed me, a lost and condemned sinner.
3. Secured and delivered me from all sins, from death and the power of the devil.
4. Not with silver and gold, but with his holy and precious blood, and with his innocent sufferings and death.
5. In order that I might be his, live under him in his

kingdom, and serve him in everlasting righteousness, innocence and blessedness.

6. Even as he is risen from the dead, aud lives and reigns to all eternity. This is most certainly true.

167. *Of what does the second article of the Apostles' Creed treat?*

The second article of the Apostles' Creed treats of Christ; namely,

1. Of his person;
2. Of his offices, and
3. Of his two states.

168. *What does this article teach in regard to his person?*

In regard to the person of Christ, the second article of the Creed teaches that he is true *God* and *Man.*

169. *How do you show that Christ is true God?*

The Scriptures represent Christ as true God, in that they not only speak of him as,

1. The "only begotten Son of God;"

John i. 14. And the Word was made flesh, and dwelt amcng us, (and we beheld his glory, the glory as of the only begotten of the Father,) full of grace and truth.

Psalms ii. 7. I will declare the decree: the Lord bath said unto me, Thou *art* my Son; this day have I begotten thee.

Galatians ii. 9. And when James, Cephas and John, who seemed to be pillars, perceived the grace that was given unto me, they gave to me and Barnabas the right hands of fellowship; that we *should go* unto the heathen, and they unto the circumcision.

2. But also apply divine names to him;

1 John v. 20. And we know that the Son of God is come, and hath given us an understanding, that we may know him that is true, and we are in him that is true, *even* in his Son Jesus Christ. This is the true God, and eternal life.

3. Divine attributes are attributed to him;

Matthew xxviii. 20. Teaching them to observe all things whatsoever I have commanded you: and, lo, I am with you alway, *even* unto the end of the world. Amen.

John xxi. 17. He saith unto him the third time, Simon, *son* of Jonas, lovest thou me? Peter was grieved because he said unto him the third time, Lovest thou me? And he said unto him, Lord, thou knowest all things; thou knowest that I love thee. Jesus saith unto him, Feed my sheep.

    4. Divine works were performed by him, such as

        a. The creation of the world;

John i. 3. All things were made by him, and without him was not anything made that was made.

        b. Preservation;

Hebrew i. 3. Who being the brightness of *his* glory, and the express image of his person, and upholding all things by the word of his power, when he had by himself purged our sins, sat down on the right hand of the Majesty on high.

        c. Redemption;

    5. Divine honor is conferred upon him.

John v. 13. And he that was healed wist not who it was: for Jesus had conveyed himself away, a multitude being in that place.

John v. 21. For as the Father raiseth up the dead, and quickeneth *them*; even so the Son quickeneth whom he will.

Hebrew i. 6. And again, when he bringeth in the firstbegotten into the world, he saith, And let all the angels of God worship him.

    170. How do you show that Christ is also true man?

Christ is true man, or has a true human nature, because he took upon himself a human body and a human soul, having been born of the Virgin Mary, grown up from infancy to manhood, suffered, died and was buried.

Hebrew ii. 14. Forasmuch then as the children are partakers of flesh and blood, he also himself likewise took part of the same; that through death he might destroy him that had the power of death, that is, the devil.

Hebrew ii. 16 For verily he took not on *him the nature of* angels; but he took on *him* the seed of Abraham.

    171. Why was it necessary that Christ should be man?

It was necessary that Christ should be man,

    1. In order that he might endure sufferings, such as hunger, thirst, weariness, also, joy, sorrow; yet without sin;

Luke x. 21. In that hour Jesus rejoiced in spirit, and said, I thank thee, O Father, Lord of heaven and earth, that thou hast hid these things from the wise and prudent, and hast revealed them unto babes: even so, Father; for so it seemed good in thy sight.

Matthew xxvi. 28. For this is my blood of the new testament, which is shed for many for the remission of sins.

Hebrew iv. 15. For we have not an high priest which cannot be touched with the feeling of our infirmities; but was in all points tempted like as *we are, yet* without sin.

2. In order that he might die and make atonement for our sins.

Hebrew ii. 17. Wherefore in all things it behoved him to be made like unto *his* brethren, that he might be a merciful and faithful high priest in things *pertaining* to God, to make reconciliation for the sins of the people.

172. Why was it necessary that Christ should also be true God?

It was necessary that Christ should be divine in his nature, in order that his sufferings and death might be a perfect atonement for sin and reconciliation with God.

Romans v. 10. For if, when we were enemies, we were reconciled to God by the death of his Son, much more, being reconciled, we shall be saved by his life.

173. What does the second article of the Creed teach in regard to the offices of Christ?

Christ is presented to us in the Scriptures as our High Priest, our Prophet and our King.

174. What has Christ done for us as our High Priest?

As our High Priest Christ has redeemed us by his blood,

1. From sin and death;

Colossians ii 13. And you, being dead in your sins and the uncircumcision of your flesh, hath he quickened together with him, having forgiven you all trespasses.

Colossians ii. 14. Blotting out the handwriting of ordinances that was against us, which was contrary to us, and took it out of the way, nailing it to his cross.

Colossians ii. 15. *And* having spoiled principalities and powers, he made a shew of them openly, triumphing over them in it.

2. From the power of Satan;

Hebrew ii. 14. Forasmuch then as the children are partakers of flesh and blood, he also himself likewise took part of the same; that through death he might destroy him that had the power of death, that is, the devil.

Hebrew ii. 15. And deliver them who through fear of death were all their lifetime subject to bondage.

Hebrew ii. 17. Wherefore in all things it behoved him to be made like unto *his* brethren, that he might be a merciful and faithful high priest in things *pertaining* to God, to make reconciliation for the sins of the people.

3. Reconciled us with God;

Ephesians ii. 16. And that he might reconcile both unto God in one body by the cross, having slain the enmity thereby.

4. Purchased and delivered us out of our state of sin and wrath;

Ephesians ii. 3. Among whom also we all had our conversation in times past in the lusts of our flesh, fulfilling the desires of the flesh and of the mind; and were by nature the children of wrath, even as others.

5. Restored us into a state of grace.

175. What does Christ do for us as our Prophet?

As our Prophet he instructs us in the doctrines of the gospel, and reveals to us the council of God in our salvation. He calls upon us to believe, and declares what shall be the condition of those who remain faithful to the end, and of those who continue finally in their impenitence.

176. What does Christ do for us as our King?

As our King Christ rules in and over his believing people in the kingdom of grace on earth, and over the redeemed in the kingdom of glory in heaven.

Colossians i. 18. And he is the head of the body, the church: who is the beginning, the firstborn from the dead; that in all *things* he might have the pre eminence.

John xvii. 24. Father, I will that they also, whom thou hast given me, be with me where I am; that they may behold my glory, which thou hast given me: for thou lovedst me before the foundation of the world.

177. What does the second article of the Creed teach in regard to the two states of Christ?

The second article treats of Christ's

1. State of Humiliation, and
2. State of Exaltation.

178. Wherein did Christ's humiliation consist?
Christ's humiliation consisted
1. In his humble birth;
2. In his life of poverty;
3. In his mental and bodily sufferings;
4. In his death by crucifixion, and
5. In his burial.

Isaiah liii. 9. And he made his grave with the wicked, and with the rich in his death; because he had done no violence, neither *was any* deceit in his mouth.

179. How was the death of Christ prefigured in the Old Testament?

The death of Christ was prefigured in the Old Testament by
1. The Passover Lamb;

1 Corinthians v. 7. Purge out therefore the old leaven, that ye may be a new lump, as ye are unleavened. For even Christ our passover is sacrificed for us.

2. The Brazen Serpent;

John iii. 14. And as Moses lifted up the serpent in the wilderness, even so must the Son of man be lifted up:
John iii. 15. That whosoever believeth in him should not perish, but have eternal life.

180. In what does Christ's exaltation consist?
Christ's exaltation consists
1. In his entrance into Paradise, or place of departed spirits;
2. In his resurrection from the dead;
3. In his ascension to heaven;
4. In his sitting on the right hand of God, and
5. In his return to judgment.

181. What is the meaning of the name Christ?
The name Christ means, "The Annointed."

182. After whom are we called?
We are called Christians, after Christ, or the Annointed by the Spirit of God.

1 John ii. 20. But ye have an unction from the Holy One, and ye know all things.

183. What therefore are those who truly bear the name of Christ?

Those who worthily bear the name of Christ are

1. Spiritual priests, who offer themselves as a living sacrifice to God with soul and body;

Revelations i. 6. And hath made us kings and priests unto God and his Father; to him *be* glory and dominion for ever and ever. Amen.

Romans xii. 1. I beseech you therefore, brethren, by the mercies of God, that ye present your bodies a living sacrifice, holy, acceptable unto God, *which is* your reasonable service.

2. Prophets, that is teachers in words and deeds;

Colossians iii. 16. Let the word of Christ dwell in you richly in all wisdom; teaching and admonishing one another in psalms and hymns and spiritual songs, singing with grace in your hearts to the Lord.

3. Kings, who gain the victory over sin, the world, the flesh and the devil.

Genesis iv. 7. If thou doest well, shalt not thou be accepted? and if thou doest not well, sin lieth at the door. And unto thee *shall be* his desire and thou shalt rule over him.

Revelations iii. 21. To him that overcometh will I grant to sit with me in my throne, even as I also overcame, and am set down with my Father in his throne.

EXPLANATORY NOTES.

God the Son is the second person in the Divine Being, begotten of the Father from eternity, and he became man in the fullness of time.

The second article of the Creed is divided into two parts.

The first part contains four names of the Lord, namely: 1. Jesus; 2. Christ; 3. The Son of God; 4. Lord.

The second part embraces the life of the Lord, and this is divided into two states, namely: 1. The state of humiliation; 2. The state of exaltation. Each of these states has five steps. His humiliation consists in 1. his birth; 2. suffering; 3. crucifixion; 4. death; 5. burial. His exaltation consists in 1. his entrance into Hades, (Paradise, descent into hell); 2. resurrection; 3. ascension into heaven; 4. session at the right hand of God; 5. return to judgment.

I. **The name Jesus** means the Redeemer, or Savior. Matt. i. 21. It is the sweetest name in a true Christian's ear.

II. **The name Christ**—in Hebrew Messiah, in Greek Christ, meaning the "anointed." The word Christ does not stand for a family name, but for an official name. Jesus is therefore called Christ for three reasons; namely: because he is 1. Prophet, 2. Priest,

3. **King.** But he is anointed not merely with oil, which is a symbol of the Spirit, but he is anointed with the Holy Ghost himself. Acts x. 38. This occurred at his baptism. Matt. iii. 16. Therefore all his disciples are called Christians; that is anointed ones.

As the Christ, the Lord has been promised from the beginning of the world and since. For example to Adam, Abraham, Moses, David, Simeon, etc. Read Gen. iii. 15; Gen. xxii. 18; 2 Saml. vii. 12; 1 Saml. xii. 12.

As a Prophet he was promised to Moses. Deut. xviii. 18.

As a High Priest, he was promised in Psalm cx. 4; Isaiah liii. 4, 5.

As a King, he was promised in Gen. xlix. 10; Psalm cx. 1; Isaiah ix. 6, 7; Micah v. 1; Zachariah ix. 9.

III. **The name, Son of God.** Jesus is called the "Only Begotten Son of God," because he is the true God.

There are four proofs of the divinity of Jesus:
1. The testimony of the Father in a voice from heaven. Luke i. 35; Matt. iii. 17.
2. The testimony of Christ himself. John viii. 58; xvii. 5; Matt. xviii. 20; John xiv. 9; John ix. 37; John x. 37.
3. The testimony of the Holy Ghost. Rom. i. 4.
4. The testimony of angels and men. John the Baptist, John i. 32-36; Peter, John vi. 38; Paul, Col. ii. 9; John, 1 John v. 20; The Centurion at the cross; the angel at the tomb. His mother conceived him of the Holy Ghost, that is, God himself is his Father. Luke i. 35; Heb. vii. 26.

IV. **The name Lord** is given to Christ for two reasons, namely:
1. On account of his divine nature, because he has created us. Heb. i. 1, 2.
2. On account of his human nature, for he has redeemed us by his blood and bought us as his own.

Besides these four principal names the Lord has also many other names. For example, Redeemer, Mediator, Intercessor, Shepherd, The Vine, Corner Stone, Way, Truth, The Life, The Alpha and the Omega.

The two natures of Jesus. The Lord Jesus has a human and a divine nature. The divine nature he derives from the Holy Ghost; the human nature he derived from his mother, the Virgin Mary. Both natures are intimately united in him, but yet not intermingled. He is God and man in one person, as the "God-man." Therefore divine honor and worship are due him. Rom. ix. 5; John v. 22, 23; Rev. v. 12. See the Athanasian Creed.

The two states of Christ. The Lord Jesus passed through two states or conditions in his life, namely: the state of humiliation and the state of exaltation. Each one of these states is particularly described in Phil. ii. 5-11.

Luther's explanation of the second article of the Creed. We divide this into five questions. 1. Who is the Redeemer? 2. Whom has he redeemed? 3. From what has he redeemed? 4. Wherewith hath he redeemed? 5. Why hath he redeemed?

I. The answer to the first question, Who is the Redeemer? is, *The* Jesus, who is the true God and man, has redeemed, secured and delivered me. To redeem means to make free; for we were bound and enslaved by sin and Satan. Delivered, indicates that it cost the Lord Jesus much labor and suffering, and a severe conflict with the Prince of darkness to secure our salvation.

II. The answer to the second question, Whom has he redeemed? is, Us, lost and condemned sinners. For we are all by nature alienated from God by sin, and as we could not save ourselves we must be forever lost and condemned. But the Son of God has redeemed us out of his pure love and mercy. Luke xix. 10; 1 Tim. i. 15.

III. The answer to the third question, From what has Christ redeemed us? is, From three foes we have been freed, namely: sin, death, and Satan. We are redeemed from all sin, because the Son of God has taken away 1. the guilt, and 2. the penalty of sin. 1 John i. 7; 1 Peter ii. 24.

The guilt of sin he has taken away, because by his perfect obedience he has fulfilled the whole law, which we through our disobedience have violated. Rom. v. 19; Col ii. 13, 14.

The penalty or punishment of sin he has taken away, because he took the curse of the law upon himself. Isaiah liii. 4, 5; 2 Cor. v. 21.

Christ has delivered us from death, because by his death as our substitute he took away the power of death. Believers on Jesus now die only a bodily, but not a spiritual and eternal death. John vi. 40; John xi. 25, 26; 2 Tim. i. 10.

Christ has redeemed us from the power of the devil, because the devil, Satan, now no more has power over us or claim upon us who believe on Jesus. 1 John iii. 8; Heb. ii. 14, 15.

IV. In answer to the fourth question, Wherewith hath Christ redeemed us? we remark, that all the gold and silver in the world could not pay for the redemption of one soul, because

the soul endures forever. But the eternal is more valuable than the temporal. Neither could the wrath of God possibly be atoned with money, for our redemption cost infinitely more. The Son of God paid for our redemption a three-fold price:
1. His holy, precious blood. 1 Peter i. 18, 19;
2. His innocent sufferings;
3. His painful death.

His blood is holy, because he was without sin;

His blood is precious, because it is unrequitable, cannot be repaid;

His sufferings were innocent, because he was free from sin, and no one could find any fault in him. He therefore suffered and paid for our transgressions. 1 Peter iii. 18; 1 Peter ii. 24.

We speak of the suffering obedience and the active obedience of Jesus. By his suffering obedience he endured the penalty of our sins, and by his active obedience he took upon himself the guilt of our sins.

V. In answer to the fifth question, Why or for what purpose he hath redeemed us? we find a three-fold reply:
1. That I may be his, belong to him;
2. Live in his kingdom; and
3. Serve him in everlasting righteousness, innocence and blessedness.

I belong to Christ, not only because he has created me, but because he has redeemed and bought me by his own precious blood. Titus ii. 14; 1 Cor. vi. 20.

This is my only consolation in life and death, that I belong to Christ. John xx. 27, 28.

Therefore I live even now, not in the kingdom of darkness, but in the kingdom of Christ.

Christ's kingdom is a three-fold kingdom:
1. The kingdom of nature;
2. The kingdom of grace;
3. The kingdom of glory.

In all these three kingdoms I will serve him as my king. Col. i. 12-14.

For this purpose we need an eternally valid righteousness, innocence and blessedness. These I have not, indeed, in myself, but Christ bestows them upon me out of free grace every day, because I believe on him. Rom iv. 25.

The third article of the Creed instructs us how we may obtain this faith

ANECDOTES AND ILLUSTRATIONS.

Scriptural Examples. The Lepers, Matt. viii. 2; The Centurion, Matt. viii. 5-10; The Canaanitish woman, Matt. ix. 20-22; The disciples, John ii. 11; The Samaritans, John iv. 39, 40-42; The disciples, Matt. viii. 26; Peter, Matt. xiv. 31; The disciples, Matt. xvii. 17; Nathanael, John i. 49; Peter, Matt xvi. 16; Mark viii. 29; Thomas, John xx. 28; The Eunuch, Acts viii. 37.

In South Africa some negroes came to the missionaries and asked for those books which contained the verse, "God so loved the world, that he gave his only begotten Son, that whosoever believeth on him should not perish, but have everlasting life." John iii. 16.

In an old Indian Pagoda is found an image, which illustrates the first promise of a Savior (Gen iii. 15), which had been transmitted even to heathen nations. It represents a man, whom a large serpent encircles and stings his heel. The same man stands beside him. He has released himself from the serpent, holds its body triumphantly in his hands, and stamps with one foot upon its head.

Bishop Liberius of Rome, had been deposed, through machinations of Arius, from his office, on account of his faith in the divinity of Christ, and was unwilling to approve the persecution by the emperor Athanasius. The emperor said to him scoffingly, "Wilt thou, who art only a handful of earth, resist the whole land?" To which Liberius replied, "The fact that I now stand alone, does not affect the divine truth. Were not the three witnesses in Babylon also alone? Nevertheless they were in the right against the whole Babylonian empire."

On the day of his death, Philip Landgrave of Hessen, who had been so active in promoting the Reformation, his attendants read to him the twentieth chapter of the Gospel according to St John. When the 31 verse was read, "These are written, that ye might believe that Jesus is the Christ, the Son of God, and that believing ye might have life through his name," he struck his hand upon the table and exclaimed, "That I believe, that I hope, upon this I trust, on this faith I will die, and thus it shall stand!"

The Arians Confounded. Two of Dr. Priestly's followers, eminent men, once called on an old gentleman of the Society of Friends, to ask what was *his* opinion of the person of Christ. After a little consideration, he replied: "The apostle says, We preach Christ crucified, unto the Jews a stumbling-block, because they expected a *temporal* Messiah; to the Greeks, foolishness, because he was crucified, as a malefactor; but unto them which are called, both Jews and Greeks, Christ, the power of God and the wisdom of God. Now, if you can separate the power of God from God, and the wisdom of God from God, I will come over to your opinions." They were both struck dumb, and did not attempt to utter a single word in reply.

Two gentlemen were once disputing on the divinity of Christ. One of them, who argued against it, said, "If it were true, it certainly would have been expressed in more clear and unequivocal terms." "Well," said the other, "admitting that you believed it, were authorized to teach it, and allowed to use your own language, how would you express the doctrine to make it indubitable?" "I would say," replied he, "that Jesus Christ is the true God." "You are very happy," rejoined the other, "in the choice of your words; for you have happened to hit upon the very words of inspiration. St. John, speaking of the Son, says, 'This is the true God and eternal life.'"

I BELIEVE ON JESUS CHRIST, TRUE GOD AND MAN.

Scriptural Examples. The disciples, Matt. xiv. 33; Nathanael, John i. 49; The Samaritans, John iv. 42; Peter, John vi. 69; Matt. xvi. 16; Mark viii. 29; Thomas, John xx. 28; The Eunuch, Acts viii. 37.

As in our times many profess to believe that Christ had only a human nature, so on the other hand there were some in the first century of the Christian era, who believed that Christ had only a divine nature. To these Duke Alamandurus said, "To-day I was informed by letter that the archangel Michael had died." And when they protested that this was impossible, he replied, "How then could the Son of God have died, if he had not two natures united in his person, if not even an angel can die?"

St. Bernard of Clairvaux who had died in the year 1153 was a very pious man and exerted a very great influence on the times in which he lived, but he did not trust upon his piety or self-righteousness for salvation. He exclaimed on his deathbed, "O Lord Jesus, thou hast two kinds of rights in heaven. One, as an heir over all things, because thou art God's only begotten Son; the other, because thou hast gained heaven by thy meritorious death. Keep thou the first for thyself, the second grant unto me, then I shall be saved"

Missionary Cryer visited the city of Conjeveram in East India. He passed through the streets and read appropriate passages out of the Bible to crowds of people, and preached the Gospel to them. More than once he saw tears in the eyes of his hearers, and when he spoke of the sufferings of Christ they stretched out their hands and called out, "Give me a book that tells of the sufferings of Christ."

A missionary among the North American Indians said, that nothing affected those wild men of the forest so much as the story of the Savior. But when he told them of the love of Christ and his sufferings, tears ran down over the furrowed cheeks of those red men.

A converted Greenlander was invited by his heathen countrymen to join them in the Sun Dance in which they annually engaged, to express their joy over the return of the sun. But he replied, "I have another joy, because another sun, Jesus, has arisen in my heart. I also have no time for your dance, because I must hasten to my teachers, who are about to celebrate a great festival over the fact, that the great Creator of all things was born into the world in order to save us."

Melanchton used to say, man comes short in three points, namely: in the beginning, the middle and the end—for our birth is depraved, our life is perverse, and our death dangerous. Against these three evils Christ has provided three remedies: his birth has sanctified our birth, his life has become the rule of our life, and his death has taken the sting from our death."

Just as the sun does not lose its glory when a cloud obscures its light, but is only temporarily hidden, so the humanity which Christ assumed, did not extinguish his divinity, but could only hide, but not prevent it from visibly flashing out before men.

Many years ago, a woman had fallen into a great sin, and became very melancholy on that account. If she thought of the day of judgment, she dreaded the torments of hell, if she thought of heaven, she said, I am a sinner and cannot enter heaven, if she thought of the sufferings of Christ, she said, Yes, I have trodden his blood under my unhallowed feet. But when at Christmas she heard how the Lord Jesus had become a little child, that our hearts should realize, that we could speak with him as with a little child, she became encouraged and gained a new hope.

Godfrey, Duke of Buillon, had led the army of the Crusaders through many dangers and difficulties into Palestine, and took the city of Jerusalem by storm. When, therefore, his soldiers wished to make him king of Jerusalem, and place a golden crown upon his head, he said, "God forbid that I should wear a royal golden crown in the place where my Lord and Savior wore a crown of thorns."

A youth came to one of the Fathers and asked him what it was to be *crucified to the world?* "Go out," said the Father, "to the cemetery, call the dead, and say: 'Come forth; lovely spring is here, the sky is blue and the birds are singing.'" The youth did so, and when he returned, the Father asked, "What did the dead respond?" "Nothing," said the youth. "Go again," said the Father, "call the dead and say, 'A violent storm is brewing in the sky; arise and hasten that ye may get under shelter, for the storm is impending.'" On the youth's return the Father again asked, "What have the dead replied?" "*Nothing*," said the youth. "Then go again," said the Father, "and praise the dead, and if they will not hear you, scold them." "O my Father," replied the youth, "that will also be in vain; they will not respond to praise or blame." Then said the Father, "See my son, to be indifferent to the world's pleasures and woes, its wooings and threatnings, its praises and reproaches, that it is to be crucified to the world."

*Mr. Robert Bruce, the morning before he died, being at breakfast, having, as he used, eaten an egg, he said to his daughter, "I think I am yet hungry: you may bring me another egg." But having mused a while, he said, "*Hold, daughter, hold, my Master calls me.*" With these words his sight failed him: on which he called for the Bible, and said, "turn to the 8th chapter of the Romans and set my finger on the words,—' I am persuaded that neither death nor life, etc., shall be able to separate me from the love of God, which is in *Christ Jesus my Lord.*'" When this was done, he said, "*Now, is my finger upon them?*" Being told that it was, he added, "*Now, God be with you, my dear children: I have breakfasted with you, and shall sup with my Lord Jesus Christ this night.*" And then expired.

Addison, after a long and manly, but vain struggle with his distemper, dismissed his physicians, and with them all hopes of life. But with his hopes of life, he dismissed not his concern for the living, but sent for a youth who was nearly related, and finely accomplished. He came, and after a decent pause, the youth said, "Dear sir, you sent for me, I believe: I hope you have some commands; I shall hold them most sacred" Forcibly grasping the young man's hand, he softly said, "See, in what peace a Christian can die!" He spoke with difficulty, and soon expired.

A young girl at Portsea, who had died at nine years of age, one day in her illness, said to her aunt, with whom she lived, "When I am dead, I should like Mr. Griffin to preach a sermon to children, to persuade them to love Jesus Christ, to obey their parents, not to tell lies, but to think about dying, and going to heaven. I have been thinking," said she, "what text I should like him to preach from,— 2 Kings iv. 26. You are the Shunamite, Mr. G. is the prophet, and I am the Shunamite's child. When I am dead, I dare say you will be grieved, though you need not. The prophet will come to see you, and when he says, 'How is it with the child?" you may say, 'It is well.' I am sure it will be well with me, for I shall be in heaven, singing the praises of God. You ought to think it well too." Mr. G. accordingly fulfilled the wish of this pious child.

Luther being once in great poverty, and a considerable sum of money being sent to him unexpectedly, by a nobleman of Germany, said, "I fear God will give me my reward here; but I protest, I will not be so satisfied." A little will satisfy the saints during their journey, but it is only the enjoyment of God in heaven, that will satisfy them as a portion.

A person," says Mr. Erskine, "who had been at public worship, having returned home perhaps somewhat sooner than usual, was asked, by another of the family, who had not been there, 'Is all done?' 'No,' replied he, 'all is *said*, but all is *not done*.'"

When a gentleman lately presented a Bible to a prisoner under sentence of death, he exclaimed, "Oh, sir, if I had had this book, and studied it, I should never have committed the crime of which I am convicted." So it is said of a native Irishman, when he read for the first time in his life, a New Testament, which a gentleman had put into his hands, he said, "If I believe this, it is impossible for me to remain a rebel."

Antonio Guevaza used to say, "That heaven would be filled with such as had *done good works*, and hell with such as had *intended* to do them." A very suitable hint to those who put off their convictions, to what they think will be a more convenient season.

A poor Hindoo became concerned about the forgiveness of his sins. His priests told him he must offer sacrifices to the idols, and that would atone for his sins. He did so, but the more sacrifices he offered to the idols, the heavier the burden of his sins became. At last one of them said to him, I will tell you what will take away the burden of your sins. You get yourself shoes made with sharp nails piercing through the soles, and then take a log of wood on your shoulders and make a pilgrimage to a distant idol, and offer a sacrifice; that will surely take away your sins. He did so, for he was anxious to be relieved of the burden of his sins. But he had not gone far, before he had to stop, as he was exhausted by the pain and loss of blood from his wounded feet. But when he had regained sufficient strength he resumed his dreadful journey, for he was resolved to obtain the forgiveness of his sins, even if it cost him his life. But one day he saw a missionary in the shade of a tree and a group of people around him. He managed to get near enough to see and hear what was going on. He heard the missionary repeat his text, "The blood of Jesus Christ, the Son of God, cleanses us from all sin." When he heard this his face brightened up with faith and hope, and as the missionary farther explained the text, he stooped down and took off those tormenting shoes, threw them away, and exclaimed, "Now I know what will take away my sins; it is not the blood that flows from my wounded feet; O no, it is the blood of Christ that cleanses from sin."

The Emperor Joseph II. traveled under the assumed name of The Duke of Falkenstein, and mingled with the common people. Some of the people afterwards recognized the emperor in the capital, and were greatly astonished. To this Oberlin remarked, "the day is coming on which Christ will no longer be the Duke of Falkenstein, but the Emperor, in order to reveal himself in the fullness of his glory."

THAT I MIGHT BE HIS OWN AND SERVE HIM, ETC.

Scriptural Examples. Martha and Mary, Luke x. 38, etc; Bartimeus, Luke xviii. 43; Zacheus, Luke xix; The man who was born blind, John ix. 38; Thomas, John xi. 16; The penitent malefactor, Luke xxiii 42, 43; Stephen, Acts vii. 58, 59; The sinner, Luke vii. 37.

Zinzendorff, the founder of the Moravian Church, stopped once in a hotel on his journey, and while waiting for his dinner, being left in a room by himself, he saw the picture of Christ crucified hanging on the wall. Zinzendorff wrote these words above the picture, "This I did for thee," and beneath, "What wilt thou do for me?" The family had been careless about religion, but when they read what had been written there, they were so deeply impressed that they resolved to begin a new life, and when Zinzendorff came again they thanked him, as the instrument in the hand of God, of their conversion.

When the pious Bishop Beveridge was near his end, his memory had almost entirely forsaken him. A minister with whom he had been well acquainted, visited him, but Beveridge did not remember him; another intimate friend came in and was named, but he did not know him. Then his wife stepped up to his bed and asked, "Do you know me?" "Who are you?" he asked. "I am your wife." "I know you not," he said. Now another one said, "Beveridge, do you know the Lord Jesus Christ?" "Jesus Christ," said he, as if waked out of sleep, "O yes, during forty years I have known him—he is my Savior, O blessed Savior; thou art, and ever shalt be my Redeemer and my hope."

The pious and learned John Newton had nearly entirely lost his memory towards the close of his life, but he was accustomed to say, "If everything else should be forgotten, there are two things which I will never forget, namely : 1. That I am a great sinner, and 2. That Jesus Christ is a great Savior. These two great truths are worthy of constant remembrance."

A converted Indian once gave a similar reply. Some one asked him, derisively, "What do you ignorant Indian know about religion?" The Indian replied, "I know two things, That I am a great sinner, and Christ is a great Savior. That is enough for me to know."

A Christian servant girl brought a few shillings to the benevolent societies. When she was urged to retain some of the money, because she might need it for herself, she replied, "O that is not necessary! Only count up what I have saved through Christ, and what I have saved through Christ I must save for him."

One who had been banished on account of his faith came to Luther for help. As Luther had only one Joachims Dollar in his house which he had saved up for a long time, he exclaimed, "Come out, Joachims Dollar, the Savior is here!"

When the martyr, John Huss was led out to the stake to be burned, they placed a three-fold paper crown on his head, on which devils were painted. When Huss saw this, he said, "My Lord Jesus Christ, for my sake, wore a crown of thorns, why should not I for his sake wear this light crown, and not near as disgraceful."

Maria Emerentea of Gera, a lady of nobility, used to write her own name along side that of Jesus, whenever she found it in her prayer book, to signify that it was the comfort of her heart and her joy, to live in union with Jesus.

When Gilbert on one occasion opened his oppressed heart to his friend Cramer, the latter said to him, "He who has God for his Redeemer and Savior should not be sad; at least he should not remain so." On this he was able at once to write to one of his suffering friends, "Comfort yourself with me, for God is love; he is our Strength, our Redeemer and our Salvation."

When Duke Henry, who introduced the Reformation into the cities of Dresden and Leipsie, was lying on his deathbed, (1541,) he was asked, whether he was willing to die in the faith of Christ? He answered, "I hold that I can have no better advocate than Christ."

When Gabriel Schoenleben was asked during his last sickness, if he was afraid of death, he answered, "No! for death has lost its sting. The Lord Christ broke the sting of death."

A little girl, only 11 years old, took sick, and there was no hope of her recovery. But she knew and loved her Savior, and repeatedly called out, "O come Lord Jesus, and take me home." When her mother was weeping by her bedside, she said, "O mother, how happy am I, that I get to heaven so young."

The dying testimony of Prof. S. S. Schmucker, D. D., of Gettysburg, Pa., was, "I have lived and I die in the faith of Jesus Christ."

When the Emperor, Rudolph II. felt himself nearing his end, he was asked by his courtiers, whether he looked forward to the end of his life with a desire to go hence? he replied with the hymn of Christopher Knollius, "I know of a better life," and added, "When in my youth I was in Spain, and my father sent a messenger to bring me back to my earthly home, I could not sleep that night for joy. Why then should I not be still more joyful when my heavenly Father calls me to my eternal home, which His Son has secured for me through his own precious blood!"

THE THIRD ARTICLE.

184. What is the third article of the Creed?

1. I believe in the Holy Ghost;
2. A Holy Christian Church, which is the communion of saints;
3. The forgiveness of sins;
4. The resurrection of the body; and
5. The life everlasting.

185. What is meant by this article?

1. I believe that I cannot by my own reason or strength believe in Jesus Christ, my Lord, or come to him;
2. But the Holy Ghost has called me through the gospel, enlightened me by his gifts, and sanctified and preserved me in the true faith;
3. In like manner as he calls, gathers, enlightens and

sanctifies the whole Christian Church on earth, and preserves it in union with Jesus Christ in the true faith;

4. In which Christian Church he daily forgives abundantly all my sins, and the sins of all believers;

5. And will raise up me and all the dead, at the last day;

6. And will grant everlasting life to me, and to all who believe in Christ. This is most certainly true.

186. Of whom does the third article of the Creed treat?

The third article of the Creed treats of the Holy Ghost.

187. What does the third article teach in regard to the Holy Ghost?

The third article of the Creed teaches that the Holy Ghost is true God.

188. How do you prove that the Holy Ghost is true God?

We prove that the Holy Ghost is true God,

1. From the divine names applied to him;

Acts v. 3. But Peter said, Ananias, why hath Satan filled thine heart to lie to the Holy Ghost, and to keep back *part* of the price of the land?
Acts v. 4. Whiles it remained, was it not thine own? and after it was sold, was it not in thine own power? why hast thou conceived this thing in thine heart? thou hast not lied unto men, but unto God.

2. From the divine attributes ascribed to him;

Psalm cxxxix. 7. Whither shall I go from thy Spirit? or whither shall I flee from thy presence?
1 Corinthians ii. 4. And my speech and my preaching *was* not with enticing words of man's wisdom, but in demonstration of the Spirit and of power.

3. From the divine works which he performs, such as

   a. Creation;

Genesis i. 2. And the earth was without form and void; and darkness *was* upon the face of the deep. And the Spirit of God moved upon the face of the waters.
Psalms xxxiii. 6. By the word of the Lord were the heavens made; and all the host of them by the breath of his mouth.

b. Regeneration;

John iii. 5. Jesus answered, Verily, verily, I say unto thee, Except a man be born of water and *of* the Spirit, he cannot enter into the kingdom of God.

John iii. 6. That which is born of the flesh is flesh; and that which is born of the Spirit is spirit.

4. From the honor bestowed upon him; namely, that he is the Third Person in the Holy Trinity, proceeding from the Father and the Son.

John xv. 26. But when the Comforter is come, whom I will send unto you from the Father, *even* the Spirit of truth, which proceedeth from the Father, he shall testify of me.

189. How is the Holy Ghost distinguished from the Father and the Son?

The Holy Ghost is distinguished from the Father and the Son, not in substance, but in person, as he

1. Especially reveals himself;

Matthew iii. 16. And Jesus, when he was baptized, went up straightway out of the water: and, lo, the heavens were opened unto him, and he saw the Spirit of God descending like a dove, and lighting upon him.

Matthew iii. 17. And lo a voice from heaven, saying, This is my beloved Son, in whom I am well pleased.

2. Is separately named and enumerated;

Matthew xxviii. 19. Go ye therefore, and teach all nations, baptizing them in the name of the Father, and of the Son, and of the Holy Ghost.

1 John v. 6. This is he that came by water and blood, *even* Jesus Christ; not by water only, but by water and blood. And it is the Spirit that beareth witness, because the Spirit is truth.

3. Personal attributes and works are ascribed to him, such as being grieved.

Acts xx. 28. Take heed therefore unto yourselves, and to all the flock, over the which the Holy Ghost hath made you overseers, to feed the church of God, which he hath purchased with his own blood.

2 Peter i. 21. For the prophecy came not in old time by the will of man: but holy men of God spake *as they were* moved by the Holy Ghost.

190. What are the offices of the Holy Ghost?

The offices of the Holy Ghost are manifold, among which may be mentioned

1. His Teaching Office;
2. His Reproving Office;
3. His Exhorting Office;
4. His Consoling Office.

191. What does the Holy Ghost do in his teaching office?

By his teaching office the Holy Ghost produces within us a living, that is, an active knowledge of divine truth, and moves the will to the acceptance and actual exercise of true religion, which takes place at our calling.

2 Timothy iii. 16. All scripture is given by inspiration of God, and *is* profitable for doctrine, for reproof, for correction, for instruction in righteousness.

John xiv 26. But the Comforter, *which is* the Holy Ghost, whom the Father will send in my name, he shall teach you all things, and bring all things to your remembrance, whatsoever I have said unto you.

192. What does the Holy Ghost do in his reproving office?

By his reproving office the Holy Ghost convicts of sin through the clear exhibition of the truth to the conscience, thus producing illumination, or enlightenment.

John xvi. 8. And when he is come, he will reprove the world of sin, and of righteousness, and of judgment.

Romans ii. 14. For when the Gentiles, which have not the law, do by nature the things contained in the law, these, having not the law, are a law unto themselves.

Romans ii. 15. Which shew the work of the law written in their hearts, their conscience also bearing witness, and *their* thoughts the meanwhile accusing or else excusing one another.

Genesis vi. 3. And the Lord said, My Spirit shall not always strive with man, for that he also is flesh : yet his days shall be an hundred and twenty years.

193. What does the Holy Ghost do in his exhorting office?

By his exhorting office the Holy Ghost grants us the desire and ability to do good works, which he does by producing holy thoughts in our minds, bringing divine truth to our remembrance, and directing us to holy examples, by which means our sanctification is promoted.

Philippians ii. 13. For it is God which worketh in you both to will and to do of *his* good pleasure.

Romans viii. 14. For as many as are led by the Spirit of God, they are the sons of God.

John xiv. 26. But the Comforter, *which is* the Holy Ghost, whom the Father will send in my name, he shall teach you all things, and bring all things to your remembrance, whatsoever I have said unto you.

194. What does the Holy Ghost do in his consoling office?

By his consoling office the Holy Ghost strengthens the faithful in their sufferings by the comforting assurance that all things do work together for their good, and thus contribute to their perseverance to the end.

Romans viii. 28. And we know that all things work together for good to them that love God, to them who are the called according to *his* purpose.

2 Corinthians iv. 17. For our light affliction, which is but for a moment, worketh for us a far more exceeding *and* eternal weight of glory.

195. When will the completion of the offices of the Holy Spirit be accomplished?

The work of the Holy Spirit will be fully accomplished in the future life,

196. Wherein will this complete redemption consist?

We are, indeed, already redeemed on earth through faith and in hope, but

Romans viii. 24. For we are saved by hope; but hope that is seen is not hope: for what a man seeth, why doth he yet hope for?

Hebrew xi. 1. Now faith is the substance of things hoped for, the evidence of things not seen.

1. There we shall have been raised with glorified bodies, and

2. Enter into life eternal in the church triumphant in heaven.

Colossians ii. 14. Blotting out the handwriting of ordinances that was against us, which was contrary to us, and took it out of the way, nailing it to his cross.

Revelations vii. 9. After this I beheld, and, lo, a great multitude, which no man could number, of all nations, and kindreds, and people, and tongues, stood before the throne, and before the Lamb, clothed with white robes, and palms in their hands;

Revelations vii. 10. And cried with a loud voice, saying, Salvation to our God which sitteth upon the throne, and unto the Lamb.

197. What is the Holy Christian Church?

The church is the whole body of christian believers, among whom the Gospel is preached in its purity, and the holy sacraments are administered according to the gospel.

John x. 16. And other sheep I have, which are not of this fold; them also I must bring, and they shall hear my voice; and there shall be one fold, *and* one shepherd.

1 Corinthians xii. 12. For as the body is one, and hath many members, and all the members of that one body, being many, are one body: so also *is* Christ.

1 Corinthians xii. 13. For by one Spirit are we all baptized into one body, whether *we be* Jews or Gentiles, whether *we be* bond or free; and have been all made to drink into one Spirit.

198. How may the Christian Church be divided?

The Christian Church may be divided into

1. The visible church, and
2. The invisible church.

199. Who constitute the Visible Church?

All those who make an outward profession of the christian religion, constitute the visible church of Christ.

200. Who constitute the Invisible Church of Christ?

Those who not only make an outward profession of Christianity, but who also are regenerated by the Holy Spirit, and lead a life of faith and obedience, are members of Christ's invisible and true church on earth.

201. By what other names is the church also called?

The church is also called

1. The church militant, and
2. The church triumphant.

202. What is the church militant?

The church militant is the church on earth, where she

must contend with her foes, such as the world, the flesh and the devil.

John xvi. 33. These things I have spoken unto you, that in me ye might have peace. In the world ye shall have tribulation: but be of good cheer; I have overcome the world.

2 Timothy iii. 12. Yea, and all that will live godly in Christ Jesus shall suffer persecution.

203. What is meant by the church triumphant?

By the church triumphant is meant all the redeemed saints with Christ in his kingdom of eternal glory in heaven, having triumphed over all their foes.

EXPLANATORY NOTES.

The third article of the Creed embraces six parts, but it is usually divided into three sections:

I. The Person of the Holy Ghost;
II. The institution in which he operates, and
III. The gracious benefits which he distributes in the church.

1. **The Personality of the Holy Ghost.** The Holy Ghost is not merely a power or attribute of God, but he is a real and self-existent person, just as the Father and the Son are. This is evident from such scripture passages like the following: Matt. xxviii. 19; Eph. iv. 30. The Holy Ghost proceedeth from the Father and the Son. Divine honor and adoration are due to him. He is called The Comforter, (Paraklete, that is, advocate.) He is also called the substitute of Jesus Christ. As such he came from heaven to earth on the day of Pentecost, and founded, or ordered the Christian Church, or congregation of Jesus Christ. Since that day he lives and rules in this church. His work is sanctification, in that he enkindles faith in men and leads them to salvation.

2. **The Institution in which the Holy Ghost operates,** is the Christian church. The church is also called the temple of God in which the Spirit dwelleth, 1 Cor. iii. 16, 17; also a habitation of God, through the Spirit. Eph. ii. 22. She is also called the Kingdom of God, and the body of Christ.

She is eternal, and no power of hell can overcome her. Matt. xvi. 18.

In this article the church is called "The Communion of Saints," or the congregation of those who are called to the kingdom of grace in Christ.

The church is visible and also invisible. She is present wherever the Word of God is correctly taught, and the sacraments are administered as they were instituted by Christ. Augsb. Conf. Art. 7. The church is a spiritual building. Christ is the corner stone; her foundations are the prophets and apostles, and her walls and pillars are her faithful members. The unbelievers and infidels are rejected stones, which are thrown out. Eph. ii. 19-22.

The attributes or names of the church. The third article of the Creed gives the following attributes or names of the church.

1. She is *one* church;
2. She is a *holy* church;
3. She is a *Catholic*, that is, a *Universal* church, and
4. She is a *Christian* church.
   a. It is not correct to call the different Christian denominations, as, the Roman Catholic, the Greek Catholic, the Lutheran or the Reformed, so many churches, for they are only the different divisions of the one church of Jesus Christ; they are, as it were, different compartments in the same house, or different classes in the same school. They have, indeed, many peculiarities, but they have the chief doctrines in common. For example, they have, 1. The same Lord God and Father of Jesus Christ; 2. The same Baptism in the name of the Father, Son, and Holy Ghost; 3. The same Bible, and the same three ecumenical confessions of faith.
   b. The church is *holy*, because she was founded by the Holy Ghost.
   c. The church is *Catholic*, or *Universal*, because she is designed for all men.
   d. The church is *Christian* because Christ is her head.

But not all who are baptized are true Christians. There are many who are only so in name, hypocrites, and spiritually dead members. The Lord Jesus calls these tares amid the wheat. Matt. xiii. 24-30; foul fish, Matt. xiii. 47-50.

The true Christians, genuine children of God, are known only to God. 2 Tim. ii. 19; 1 Cor. iii. 16. They are called "the believers," or "the pious," or "the meek," or "the righteous," or "saints."

They are called holy, not as though they were absolutely perfect and without sin, but because the Lord has sanctified them by his blood, and the Holy Ghost dwells within them. They are often despised by the worldly minded, misunderstood and derided; but they are the elect of God, and heirs of his kingdom. They are scattered over the whole earth, among different denominations, and they are bound together by the Holy Ghost into one invisible holy communion, as brethren and sisters in the Lord Jesus. Matt. xii. 49, 50.

This is the communion of saints in which the Holy Ghost operates. The seed is the word, of which the Lord speaks in Luke viii. 15.

The gracious gifts of the Holy Ghost. There are three gracious gifts of the Holy Ghost; namely,

I. The forgiveness of sins;
II. The resurrection of the body, and
III. Eternal life.

God forgives my sins, that is, he declares me free from the condemnation, remits the punishment of my sins, and recieves me as his child and heir.

Whose sins does the Holy Ghost forgive? Answer, My sins, and the sins of all believers. Therefore, only through faith can we obtain the forgiveness of sins. Acts x. 45; Rom. iii. 23-26, 28.

What sins are forgiven? Answer, All sins.

How often are they forgiven? Answer, Daily and abundantly.

Where are the sins forgiven? Answer, In the whole Christian world, through the means of grace; namely, the word of God and the sacraments.

Blasphemy against the Holy Ghost. All sins can be forgiven, even the blasphemy, against God the Father and the Son. Only the blasphemy against the Holy Ghost can not be forgiven. Matt. xii. 31; Heb. vi. 4-8; 1 John v. 16.

Blasphemy is a known, conscious, malicious sin. An awakened Christian, who has the Holy Ghost dwelling in him, and yet sins designedly and presumptuously, drives the Holy Spirit away from himself. Such a one can never find forgiveness, because only the Holy Ghost can forgive sin. He also can not therefore experience any more true repentance and sorrow for his sins; but remains impudent, daring, hardened, hating God, and will be eternally lost. But he who mourns over his sins, has not blasphemed against the Holy Ghost, or committed the unpardonable sin.

The last things. Of the gracious gifts in the third article of the Creed, which the Holy Ghost will bestow upon us in the future, there are two; namely, 1. The Resurrection of the Body, and, 2. Eternal Life. But these must be preceded by two other things; namely, Death and Judgment. These four future things are called the "Last Things;" namely, 1. Death; 2. Resurrection; 3. Judgment; and 4. Eternal Life.

Death. Death is the separation of the body from the soul. We usually speak of a three-fold death: 1. The Bodily Death; 2. The Spiritual Death; and 3. The Eternal Death.

The original design was, that man should not die, but develope himself without death for eternal happiness. But through sin, death, sickness, pain, misery and ruin have come upon the world of mankind, which has affected also the world of nature. Rom. viii. 20. From this death-ruin we are redeemed through faith in the Lord Jesus. Immediately after death the faithful enter into Paradise; the unbelieving dead go to a place of torment. These places in the world of spirits are separated by an impassable gulf, Luke xvi. 26, as the account of Dives and Lazarus shows. The departed still have human forms. They recognize each other, they speak and have the same capacity of thought there, as they had here. By the permission of God, departed spirits can re-appear on earth. See 1 Sam. xxviii. 13; Isaiah xiv. 9; xxxii. 21.

The doctrine of "Soul sleeping" is to be rejected. The souls of believers "live" in happiness with the Lord, Phil. i. 23, and the unbelievers live in pain. Only the body sleeps in the grave. A further development, both in happiness and misery is probable; also different degrees of glory and pain. Dan. xii. 3; 2 Cor. ix. 6; Matt. xi. 20-24.

The torments of the wicked are internal and external, and will be indescribably terrible. Matt. iii. 12; Matt. xxv. 41, 46; Luke xvi. 24.

The Resurrection and the Judgment. The bodies of all who have died will be raised from the dead. John v. 28, 29. The wicked for judgment, the believers to eternal life and happiness. Because the Lord Jesus Christ rose bodily from the dead, we also shall be raised up bodily. Luke xxiv. 39. Only after the resurrection of the body will our salvation be complete. 1 Cor. xv. 12-22; Rom. viii. 11; John vi. 54; xi. 25, 26; 2 Cor. iv. 14.

By his almighty word, and with the operation of the Holy Spirit, Christ will create new bodies out of our corruptible bodies. The bodies of the believers will be like the glorified body of Jesus Christ; namely, they will be, 1. Incorruptible; 2. Glorious; 3. Powerful; 4. Spiritual. 1 Cor. xv. 42-44. The bodies of the wicked will have a horrible appearance, like that of the devil. Isaiah lxvi. 24.

Therefore there will be two kinds of resurrection; namely, the resurrection of the righteous to life, and the resurrection of the wicked to judgment, or damnation.

Then the wicked with the devil and all evil spirits will be driven into everlasting punishment, but the righteous will enter into life eternal. Not all men will die, but many; namely, such as shall be living on earth at the coming of Christ, will be suddenly changed, as it is written in 1 Cor. xv. 51.

The eternal life. The last gracious gift of the Holy Ghost begins already here in this life ; for he who believes on the Son of God, "hath eternal life" hidden in himself. John vi. 47 ; 1 John v. 20 ; Col. iii. 3, 4. But under the expression, "Eternal life," properly, the Scriptures mean not only the new life begun in us on earth, but the blessed state of man's resurrection life, in which we shall be entirely redeemed from all evil in body, soul and spirit. Rev. vii. 15-17. Then we shall see God, John xvii. 24, and serve him with all the saints in holy joy, John xvi. 22 ; we shall dwell in the new earth and the new heaven, Rev. xxi. 5 ; we shall live in eternal righteousness, innocence and happiness, not as mere spirits or angels, but as redeemed saints, and serve God, being endowed with the richest bodily and spiritual gifts, in unspeakable joy and eternal peace.

The Order of Salvation. The order of salvation is the order by which the Holy Ghost leads men to eternal bliss. It is described in the explanation of the third article of the Creed. Four parts belong to it ; namely,

1. The Calling ;
2. The Enlightening ;
3. The Sanctification, and
4. The Perseverance.

All these four must be wrought by the Holy Ghost, if we are to be saved. By his own reason, and strength, and power, no one can believe on Christ or come to him.

The Calling. The calling means the invitation into the kingdom of Christ. This takes place through the voice of God in the conscience, and through the divine call in the dispensations of his providence, but especially by the preaching of the Gospel. 2 Tim. i. 9 ; Matt. xi. 28, 29. Read the parable of the great marriage supper. Matt. xxii. 11-13. The Holy Ghost wills that all men should be called, but all do not obey the call.

The call, therefore, does not work irresistably. Those who accept the call have therefore no merit in themselves before God, for it is all of free grace. But he who rejects the call excludes himself from the grace of God. Acts xiii. 46. Lydia accepted the call. Acts xvi. 14. But Felix and Drusilla rejected the call. Acts xxiv. 25. But we should strive to give all men (through missions) an opportunity to hear this divine call, in order that they may decide for or against accepting it. 1 Tim. ii. 4. God will that all should be saved. I have been called, through my Baptism, Instruction, the Preaching of the Gospel, etc.

The Enlightening. Men are by nature darkened by sin. Eph. iv. 18; Eph. v. 8. We must become enlightened in our understanding, will and heart. This is done by the Holy Ghost. His light is the word of God. This word of God has two flames of light; namely, the flame of the Law and the flame of the Gospel. Psalm cxix. 105; Psalm xix. 9.

The flame of the Law shows me, 1. My sins, and 2. God's wrath against sin.

The flame of the Gospel shows me 1. God's grace, or the Savior, and 2. My redemption. Now, if I permit myself to be enlightened, then I will be awakened to a new life. To this end the Holy Ghost puts his gifts into my heart; namely, 1. Repentance; 2. Sorrow for sin; 3. Change of mind; 4. Saving faith. Saving faith is different from historical faith, or half faith, or dead faith, etc.

Saving faith requires not only assent to the truth of the Gospel, but a heartfelt confidence and trust; so that we can say, "Jesus is *mine* and what he has done, he has done for me."

Accordingly the repentance of Cain, Gen. iv. 13, and the repentance of Judas, Matt. xxvii. 3, were false and vain, because they lacked a living faith. On the other hand the repentance of David, Psalm li., of Peter, Matt. xxvi. 75, and of Zacchæus, Luke xix. 8, etc were of the right kind. Such repentance we also find described in the seven penitential Psalms vi., xxxii., xxxviii., li., cxxx., cxliii., and also in Luther's first thesis. Every evidence of true repentance and living faith we can discover in the account of the lost and returned Prodigal Son. Luke xv.

The Sanctification. The Holy Ghost sanctifies me through three operations; namely, 1. Forgiveness of sins; 2. Justification; 3. New obedience. The Holy Ghost takes away the sinful robe of my own righteousness, and clothes me with the beautiful robe of Christ's innocence. Then he imputes to me the righteousness of Christ. Rom. v. 18, 19; Isaiah lxi. 10. Read the parable of the wedding garment. Matt. xxii. 11-13. Thus I become righteous and acceptable to God. Rom. iii. 23, 24. For this reason also, I am a child and heir of God. Rom. viii. 17. At the same time he makes me competent to perform good works; that is, I can walk in new obedience, and this is often called regeneration. Good works are all those which are done in faith.

Perseverance in the Faith. He who would be saved must remain steadfast in the faith unto the end. If a man should live 60 or 80 years in the faith and then apostatize, he would be lost. Ezekiel xxxiii. 12; Matt. xxiv. 42. Our consolation is this, that the Holy

Ghost will accomplish the work which he has begun. Phil. i. 6. The intercession of our Great High Priest also consoles us. Heb. ix. 24. The following are the four stations in the order of salvation :

1. The first (our Calling,) we have all passed ;
2. The second (our Enlightning,) some have attained ;
3. The third (our Sanctification,) comparatively few have attained, and
4. The fourth (our Perseverance,) none of us have yet attained.

Yet all four of these stations are necessary, although the Holy Ghost is not bound to follow the exact succession of each of these steps. He can lead one man to salvation in a short time, and another man in a longer time. For example, the thief on the cross, and good old Simeon.

ANECDOTES AND ILLUSTRATIONS.

OF SANCTIFICATION.

Scriptural Examples. The Holy Ghost came upon Saul, 1 Saml. x. 6 ; David, 1 Saml. xvi. 13 ; 2 Saml. xxiii. 2 ; Balaam, Num. xxiv. 2 ; Filled with the Holy Ghost, Elizabeth, Luke i. 41 ; Zacharias, Luke i. 67 ; Simeon, Luke ii. 25 ; Jesus, Luke iv. 1 ; Acts x. 38 ; The disciples of the Lord, Acts ii ; Peter, Acts iv. 8 ; Stephen, Acts vii. 55 ; Paul, Acts xiii. 9 ; The hearers of Peter, Acts x. 44, 45 ; The Christians at Ephesus, Acts xix. 2 ; Compare John vii. 39.

When Queen Christina of Sweden, left her throne and so-journed in Rome to make herself acquainted with the state of religion there, she wrote to Bishop Burnet in England, "It can not be otherwise, but that the church must be ruled by the Holy Ghost; for I have now become acquainted with four popes, of whom I can swear that not one of them has sound common sense."

The seed that was sown in Wurttemberg found a good soil beyoud that of any other German province. Prayer meetings were introduced by Spener and became the salt of the earth even to the present time. Albert Bengel was especially the hand of the Lord, by which this salt was cast abroad. On one occasion he expressed himself as follows : "I do not understand, why there should be opposition to prayer meetings. Why should each one be pious and remain by himself? It is just as if people were going on a journey and I should advise them, Don't go together in company, but let each remain about a gun-shot behind the other."

The Apostle Paul traced his conversion to God when he said, "It pleased God, who . . called me by his grace, to reveal his Son in me :" Gal. i. 15, 16.

"The Spirit acts upon the mind mediately, and not immediately. He acts by the Word, and in the whole operation on the heart and understanding of men there may be no contravention to the laws of our known philosophy."—*Dr. Chalmers.*

The Rev. William Guthrie of Fenwick, in the days of the Covenant, was once benighted on a moor, and lost his way. He let his horse go as he might, and by-and-by came to a farm-house. He asked leave to sit by the fire till morning. While there a Roman Catholic priest was administering extreme unction to the farmer's wife, who was dying. After the priest had gone, Mr. Guthrie asked the woman if she had peace with God. She said she had not. He then spoke to her of the redemption purchased by Christ, and how it was applied. God blessed his words, and enabled her to understand the gospel, and to embrace the Savior. She died triumphing in Jesus Christ. Mr. Guthrie departed early, and when he reached the manse said to his wife that he had seen a great wonder during the night. "I came to a farm-house, where I found a woman in a state of nature; I saw her in a state of grace; and I left her in a state of glory!"

"I have had six children," said Mr. Elliot, a devoted man, "and I bless God for his full grace that they are all either with Christ or in Christ." O that parents and teachers could say this of their children and scholars.

"As the graft is kept in union to the stock by means of the clay which has been applied by the gardner, so is the believer united to Christ by faith, which is the gift of God. The clay cement keeps the parts together, but has no virtue in itself: so faith is the means of union to Christ, but cannot of itself save us. When the clay is removed from the tree, the graft is found united to the stock; so when faith is swallowed up in sight, then the perfect union of Christ and his people is seen."—*Dr. J. H. Balfour.*

A house was on fire. All the inmates but one had escaped. He was a boy, and found the flames coming up the staircase. He ran to a window, and appealed to his father to save him. His father was on the ground, and answered him, "Do not fear; drop down, and I will be sure to catch you." The boy crept out and hung by his hands, afraid to let go.—"Drop down, my boy," said his father. "O father, I cannot see you," said the boy.—"But I am here; trust me, I will save you." "I am afraid, father, that I shall fall."—"Let go," cried the people; "your father will be sure to catch you." The flames were coming near. He felt that if he remained he would be burned. He dropped down, and in a moment was in his father's arms. Thus drop into the arms of the Savior.

A man once went to cast a stone at the Rev. George Whitefield while that eminent evangelist was preaching at Exeter, but lacked courage as soon as he heard the text. He afterwards went to Mr. Whitefield and said, "Sir, I came to hear you this day with a view to break your head; but the Spirit of God, through your ministry, has given me a broken heart." From that day he was changed, and lived a believer in Christ.

Adam would never have sought the Lord, and called, "Lord, where art thou?" But the Lord sought him, and called, "Adam where art thou?"

No one can see the sun, unless it rises first and makes the day; without this the brightest eyes are of no use. So the grace of God must always precede us, in order to make a beginning of our faith, our good works and our knowledge and love.

A snow-flake remains a snow-flake, if God does not send the sun-light and the warm air to melt it. No truth will produce a lasting effect unless God's Spirit impresses it on the heart. Otherwise it will be like pouring medicine on a stone, or singing a lovely song to a dead man.

The word and the grace of God come sometimes like a star that rises mild and gradually up into the sky; then again, like an arrow, that suddenly pierces the heart; and again, like the refreshing rain that moistens the parched earth, and again, like a hammer that breaks the flinty rocks in pieces.

The calls to repentance are, The public preaching of the law and the gospel, the still, small voice of the conscience, joy and sadness, danger and death, terror and deliverance, the death of a friend (Augustine and Luther), the appearance of pious, happy Christian people, even in the midst of privation, persecution and suffering. Acts xvi. 29, 30. In Matt. xxvii. 19, it was a dream; in Matt. xxvi. 74, it was the crowing of the cock.

A king in company of his queen visited the church where his faithful pastor preached. But in the midst of the sermon the king fell asleep. Suddenly he roused himself up and asked, what the preacher had just now said? The queen repeated the words that had just been spoken in the sermon. "No," said the king, "the words sounded otherwise—the preacher said, 'The king is lost, if he does not become converted.'" When the queen related this expression to the pastor, he replied, "What I would not have dared to tell the king while he was awake, God himself told him while he was asleep."

There are sick people who do not know that they are sick; there are sick people, who do not call a physician; there are sick people, who do not take the medicine prescribed by their physician; there are sick people, who althought they take the medicine, yet will not deny themselves of that which the physician forbids. Such people can not get well.

When any one says, I will not repent and be converted now, but I will do so at some future time, that is, as if the commander of a fort would say, I will let the enemy come in for awhile, but afterwards when I feel so disposed I will drive him out again.

A scoffer once tried to embarrass a Christian Negro by saying, "How can the Holy Ghost be at the same time in you and all around you?" The Negro replied, "Oh, dat is no great puzzle; here is de poker; I will hold dat in de fire till it is red hot; den de fire is in de poker, and all around it.

Some one praised a distinguished astronomer, telling him that his science exceeded all others in importance. The astronomer replied, We can indeed find the courses of the stars in the firmament of heaven, but of our way to heaven, we know nothing by our science.

With many people it will be as it is with the mole which is blind while it lives, and of which Pliny writes: "*Oculos incipit moriendo operire.*" That is, "Only when it dies it opens its eyes." No one has ever regretted at the end of his life, that he became a Christian, but thousands have bitterly regretted at death, that they had not been converted.

Every Christian should have the assurance of his regeneration and convertion, but every one can not determine the day or the hour of his conversion. Some, indeed, can do this; namely, the inhabitants of Ninevah, Saul of Tarsus, the Prodigal Son, or such as have heard an impressive sermon, or been taken sick, or met with a great misfortune, or accident, and date their conversion from that point. But others were brought to Christ gradually, like Nicodemus, or like the Publican, who himself did not know how penitent and near to the kingdom of heaven he was. As a seed in the earth germinates and grows, as a child lives and steadily grows larger, stronger and more intelligent, so it is also with many a child of God.

Bernard says, "A Christian is like the moon; he is either on the *increase* or the *decrease*."

With regard to preaching, the history of the church is full of illustrations. God's Spirit has blessed preaching to the salvation of souls. Pentecost, the Reformation, the Puritan age, the great revival under Whitefield and Wesley, and the great movements under Moody and Sankey, are powerful testimonies to this. In every faithful ministry preaching has its effects.—*Steel.*

A minister in Illinois offered to give any impenitent man ten dollars, who would read one chapter of the Bible on his knees, every morning for three months, commencing with the prayer, "O God, send thy Holy Spirit to convict me of sin, and to lead me in the way of truth." It was accepted by a boastful infidel, who attempted to do his part. He got on well for a few days; but then conviction fastened heavily upon him, then despair seized him. He then sent for the minister to pray for him; and after a night's pleading he found peace.—*Steel.*

Life of the church. As a ship in the midst of the sea goeth not toward the haven, unless it have a prosperous gale of wind, even so the church of God goeth not to its wished-for haven, unless it be blown by the Spirit of God, and directed and set on by the same Spirit.

Need of the Spirit. In vain do the inhabitants of London go to their conduits (hydrants) for supplies, unless the man who has the master-key turns the water on; and in vain do we think to quench our spiritual thirst at ordinances, unless God communicates the living water of his Spirit.—*Salter.*

Lesson of Spiritual mindedness. If you will go to the banks of a little stream, and watch the flies that come to bathe in it, you will notice, that while they plunge their bodies into the water, they keep their wings high out of the water; and after swimming about for a little while, they fly away with their wings unwet through the sunny air. Now, that is a lesson for us. Here we are immersed in the cares and business of the world; but let us keep the wings of our souls, our faith and our love, out of the world, that, with these unclogged, we may be ready to take our flight to heaven.

A HOLY CHRISTIAN CHURCH.

Scriptural Examples. Christ and Peter, Matt. xvi. 15-19; Peter, Acts xi. 1-8; xv. 7-11; Paul, 1 Cor. i. 10-13; The church prefigured in Noah's ark, Gen. viii. 6-8; Heb. xi. 7; 1 Peter iii. 20, 21; The church in Salem, Gen. xiv. 18; Heb. vii. 1-3; In Zoar, Gen. xix. 19-22; In Jerusalem, Gal. iv. 26; Heb. xii. 22; In Zion, Rom. ix. 33; 1 Peter ii. 6; Heb. xii. 22.

The church is like the sun. She has many rays, but only one light; she seems to eclipse herself, and yet she does not eclipse herself; she can be covered and obscured by clouds, but she does not decrease, and continually breaks forth and shines again.

The church with the confession, which Peter once made, that Jesus is "the Christ, the Son of the living God," has always been like a palm tree. The more a palm tree is loaded down, the higher it grows, and the more fruit it bears. The church is like a diamond which shines the brighter the more it is ground and cut. The church is like the burning bush which Moses saw in the desert; it stood in the midst of the flame, and yet was not consumed. The church is like Noah's ark; the higher the waters of the flood rose, the nearer it was borne up toward heaven.

When Frederick, the wise Elector of Saxony began to favor the doctrines preached by Luther, a good friend wrote to him, advising him not to provoke the pope to become his enemy, for he was very powerful. The Elector replied, Is the pope God, as some of his adherents profess? then we do not fear him, because we try to promote the doctrines of God. But if he is only a man, then we have courage enough to defend ourselves against him. But if he is the devil we care not for his enmity, but would rather have him as our enemy than our friend, because we can not be the friends of Christ, without being the enemies of the devil. If the pope will make war upon us, then we have Christ upon our side, and we will gain the victory, and in life and death we will magnify the glory of God. Therefore we do not fear his enmity in any case.

After the Augsburg Confession had been published and the opponents of the Reformation confessed that thy could not confute it from the holy scriptures, the Catholic Duke of Bavaria remarked, "Well then, the Lutherans stand on the Bible, but we Catholics stand outside of it."

A minister of the Gospel, in excusing himself and his church for not exerting themselves to instruct and gather in the multitudes around them, said, "It is impossible for so large a church as ours, to do much for those out of our body. It takes one-third of us to watch the other two-thirds!" What a confession is this! Only one in three possessing the true spirit of Christianity, and he is prevented from being an efficient soldier of the cross by the lukewarmness and sins of his brethren.

The church above and the church below. The church of Christ, which is partly militant and partly triumphant, resembles a city built on both sides of a river. There is but the stream of death between grace and glory.—*Toplady.*

Christ's church. As the bride pertaineth to none, but to the bridegroom, so the church pertaineth to Christ only.—*Cawdray.*

The church a disturber. The church was instituted to disturb the peace of man; but often it does not perform its duty for fear of disturbing the peace of the church. What kind of artillery practice would that be, which declined to fire for fear of kicking over the gun-carriages, or waking up the sentinels asleep at their posts?—*Beecher.*

Enlargement of the church. As the army of heaven is innumerable, and the sand of the sea immeasurable; even so God will multiply his church.—*Cawdray.*

Light of the church. As the moon doth borrow her light from the sun, because, of herself she has little or none at all; even so the church, having no light of herself, doth take her light from the Son of God.—*Cawdray.*

The church militant. This is the state of the church militant; she is like the ark floating upon the waters, like a lily growing among thorns, like the bush in the desert which burned with fire, and was not consumed; so the church, or city of God is always besieged, but never ruined.—*Henry Smith.*

The church a ship. As a ship upon the sea is tossed upon the waves from one place to another, even so is the church often tossed in the sea of this world, yet never drowned, because Christ is in it, and holdeth the helm with his hand.—*Cawdray.*

The union of the church. As the different oceans, called by different names, form one body; so the different denominations of Christians form one church.

As the ark was made of many pieces of wood, and joined together in one, so the church consisteth of many members, knit together in one faith.—*Cawdray.*

Have you ever read that strange book, "The Ancient Mariners?" I dare say you thought it one of the strangest imaginations ever put together, especially that part where the old mariner represents the corpses of the dead men rising up to man the ship—dead men pulling the ropes, dead men stearing, dead men spreading the sails. I thought what a strange idea that was. But do you know that I have lived to see that time? I have seen it done. I have gone into churches, and I have seen a dead man in the pulpit, a dead man as deacon, and a dead man handling the plate, and dead men sitting in the pews.—*Spurgeon.*

THE FORGIVENESS OF SIN.

Luther says, I would not like to have my soul stand in my own hand. If my soul stood in my own hand, Satan would long ago, yea, in a moment, have snatched it away, as a hawk carries off a little chicken. But neither the devil nor any one else can tear me out of the hand of God.

The brave Sir Amos Borgius, who was once a member of parliament in Paris, was condemned to death on account of his Evangelical faith. As he was led out to execution he continued in prayer, saying, "My God, my God, forsake me not, that I may never forsake thee."

A missionary in the East Indies made the following declaration in his sermon: "Every one who has been *born only once, must die twice;* but he who has been born *twice* will die only *once.*" A man in the congregation could not comprehend these words, but afterwards when he had comprehended them, he could never forget them. And when he was born again by the power of these words, he could not help confessing the truth, and became a missionary himself.

Missionary Lupoldt described in his sermon a man who tried to enter in at the narrow gate, with a large bundle on his back, when a Hindoo called out, "That bundle must come down!" Yes, that is so.

A Hindoo said, the missionaries had in their sermons a word which was very beautiful; namely, the word *forgiveness.*

At a banquet given by Peter Waldus, one of the guests suddenly fell down dead. This made such an impression on Waldus, that he exclaimed, "What must I do to be saved?" He found the answer to this question in a Latin Bible, that he had in his library.

Our church teaches, that a man is not justified by good works, but she teaches, that the man who has obtained the forgiveness of his sins, must necessarily perform good works. "It is impossible," so she teaches, "to separate works from faith, yea, it is as impossible as it is to separate heat and light from fire."

No sick man can regain his health by rising up and walking, but when he has recovered his health he does both himself.

Faith and works are related to each other like mother and daughter; they embrace each other and can not be separated.

Luther says, Where there is no faith, the head has been taken off of good works, and all their life and goodness is worthless, just as all the members of the body derive their life and action from the head.

Mark well, that you esteem the faith so highly, as if the works were an indifferent thing; on the other hand, be so diligent in works as if faith were an indifferent thing. Therefore St Paul puts two passages so close together in the second chapter of the letter to the Philippians. The one is verse twelve, "Work out your own salvation with fear and trembling." The other is verse thirteen, "For it is God who worketh in you to will and to do of his good pleasure."

The late Mr. Reynolds of Bristol, being importuned by a friend to have his portrait painted, he at last consented, when the following dialogue took place:

Q. How would you like to be painted?
A. Sitting among books.
Q. Any book in particular?
A. The Bible.
Q. Open at any part?
A. At the fifth chapter of the Epistle to the Romans, the verse to be visible, "Therefore being justified by *faith*, we have peace with God, through our Lord Jesus Christ."

A woman, professing to be under deep conviction, went to a minister, crying aloud that she was a sinner; but when he came to examine her in what point, though he went over and explained all the Ten Commandments, she would not own that she had broken one of them.

I BELIEVE IN THE RESURRECTION OF THE BODY AND THE LIFE EVERLASTING.

Scriptural Examples. Job xix 25-27; Saints of the Old Testament, Matt. xxvii. 52, 53; Christ, Matt. xxviii. 6; 1 Cor. xv. 1, etc; Martha, John xi. 24; Paul, Acts xxiii. 6; Acts xxiv. 15, 21; Acts xxvi. 8; The Sadducees, Matt. xxii. 23, etc; Acts xxiii. 8; The Epicureans and Stoicks, Acts xvii. 18; Some of the Corinthians, 1 Cor. xv. 12; Paul, Phil. i. 21, 23; The thief on the cross, Luke xxiii. 43; Lazarus, Luke xvi. 22; Stephen, Acts vii. 58, 59; Dives, Luke xvi. 22-31; Judas, Acts i. 25.

When St. Bernard lay in his last sickness, his brethren prayed to God for him. But he said, "Why will you detain a poor sinner any longer on earth? Have pity on me and let me go to the Father."

When Frances I. was taken prisoner by Charles V. at Pavia, he wrote on the door of his prison, "To-day me, to-morrow thee." Charles wrote beneath, "I am a man, and I believe that every thing human may befall me."

A mother who had lost three children by death, was asked, how many children she had, replied, "Six, three are with me, three are with God."

When Œcolampadius, the Swiss Reformer was near to his end, a friend visited him to inquire about his condition, Œcolampadius asked him, "What is the news?" "Nothing," said his friend. "Well, then," said he, "I will tell you the news: *I will soon be with Christ, my Lord.*"

When Cing-Mars was condemned to death, on account of a conspiracy against Lewis XIV., he was asked by the minister, whether he was afraid of death, and replied, "No; the only thing I fear, is my sins."

When Francis Von Sickingen was lying on his death bed, the Elector of Trier and the Duke of Hessen stepped in and reproached him for the war which he had waged against them. His only reply was, "I have now to render an account to a greater Master."

Valerius Herberger wrote in his book, *The Heavenly Jerusalem*, I once knew a remarkable preacher who had singular ideas. When he spoke of the life in heaven, he said, "When the learned men use their greatest art in describing the heavenly blessedness, they appear to me like children, who are playing in the sand and think that the mud-bake-oven, which they have made, is a grand building. Or they appear to me like children when they talk of great kings and monarchs. Or like children who have put on their grandfather's shoes and think they fit them admirably, as they scrape about in the room."

When Colonel Von Manstein learned to know a man, who did not believe in a future life, he said, Surely, this man lives like a brute, because he believes that he will remain on the earth like a brute.

When the oath of allegiance was rendered to Charles V. at Ghent, a prize question was given out; namely, "What is the best and greatest consolation of a Christian?" To solve this question many came from different places, who presented their ingenious answers on the occasion. But those from Altdorf gave this answer: "The resurrection is the best consolation." Therefore they represented the sufferings, death and resurrection of Christ, upon which our own resurrection is founded, and the prize was awarded to the Altdorfers.

A sceptic once exclaimed, "O you fools, who believe in a resurrection of the dead! Do you not see that the living die? How then can you believe that the dead shall live?" But some one answered him, "O you simpleton! Do you not believe in the creation? Well, if something lives that had never existed, why can not that which once lived, live again?"

Methodius, the missionary among the Sklaves, carried a painting about with him, on which the last judgment was represented. This made such an impression on the heathen chief of the Bulgarians, that he immediately professed Christianity and was baptized.

Gregory, the great, relates, that, Chrysaurus, an ungodly nobleman, saw on his deathbed the awaiting hellish spirits in terrible aspect around him, and therefore exclaimed in agonizing tones, "O time, only till morning! Give me time till morning!"

A young Russian nobleman availed himself of every opportunity to express derisively his doubts about eternal hell punishment. An unassuming pious man once said to him, "Well, now, but if there should after all be an eternal damnation? Mark you, If there should be an eternal damnation? Have you ever thought about this? How is it? What do you say to this?" The man began to tremble through his whole body, fell from his chair, and exclaimed, "Woe is me, I am going to ruin!" Afterwards an entire change came over him, so that he had no more need to dread the eternal hell-punishment.

On the day of his death, John Saunders stretched his right hand towards heaven and exclaimed, "Lord, do I belong to these?" Matt. xxv. 23. Then he stretched out his left hand, and said, "According to justice I belong to these; it is only by free grace that I can be saved."

The Negroes in South America once had a discussion about the judgment day. Some said, "Then we will hide ourselves in the bushes." Others said, "We will take our own lives." To this Arabini, the first convert among them, replied, "God will easily find means to find you all." "But when there are so many of us who do not believe on him," replied the Negroes, "the punishment will not be so severe." To this Arabini replied, "Well, then, all of you come and put your fingers into the fire, and we will see, whether each one of you does not feel the pain just as keenly, as if he were the only one." Silently they all departed.

The soul is in the body like a lamp in a lantern. When you take the lamp out of the lantern the light is not thereby extinguished; on the contrary it shines more brightly now than before.

In your own body you have a demonstration of the resurrection. Some time ago you were laid up with sickness, you lost your flesh and strength; but through the mercy of God you regained your blooming health, and strength. In all this you did not see how your flesh vanished away, nor how it returned.

Mr. Moffet was preaching on the resurrection, when Macoba, a notorious chief, cried out, "What are those words about the dead?—the dead arise?" "Yes," said the missionary, "all the dead shall rise."—"Will my father arise?"—"Yes," answered the missionary. "Will all the slain in battle arise?" "Yes," answered the missionary. "Will all that have been killed and eaten by lions, tigers, and crocodiles arise?"—"Yes, and come to judgment." "Hark," shouted the chief, turning to the warriors, "Ye wise men, did your ears ever hear such strange and unheard of news? Did you ever hear such news as this?" turning to an old man, the wise man of the tribe. "Never," answered the old man. The chief then turned to the missionary, and said, "Father, I love you much, but the words of a resurrection are too good for me. I do not wish to hear about the dead rising again. The dead can not rise; the dead shall not rise!" "Tell me my friend, why not," said the missionary. "I have slain my thousands; shall they arise?"

LOVE FOR THE CHURCH.

I love Thy Zion, Lord!
  The house of Thine abode;
The Church, O blest Redeemer, saved
  With Thine own precious blood.

I love Thy Church, O God!
  Her walls before Thee stand,
Dear as the apple of Thine eye,
  And graven on Thy hand.

If e'er to bless Thy sons
  My voice or hands deny,
These hands let useful skill forsake,
  This voice in silence die.

If e'er my heart forget
  Her welfare or her woe,
Let ev'ry joy this heart forsake,
  And ev'ry grief o'erflow.

For her my tears shall fall;
  For her my prayers ascend;
To her my cares and toils be given,
  Till toils and cares shall end.

PART III.

THE LORD'S PRAYER.

This prayer is very often repeated by both young and old people, but frequently merely mechanically without serious impressions as to the meaning of the words. In that case it is only a lip service, but not a heartfelt prayer. Such a prayer cannot be acceptable to God, nor be answered from the Throne of Grace.

204. What is Prayer?

In general, prayer is a conversation of the heart with God, uttered or unexpressed.

205. How should prayer be offered?

Prayer should be offered

1. In the name of Jesus, that is, in accordance with his command and promises;

2. In true faith on him;

John xvi. 23. Verily, verily, I say unto you, Whatsoever ye shall ask the Father in my name, he will give it you.

3. In sincere devotion;

4. At all times we should direct our hearts to God;

5. Which is done, when, besides the verbal prayer, we do everything as in the conscious presence of God.

Genesis xvii. 1. And when Abram was ninety years old and nine, the Lord appeared to Abram, and said unto him, I *am* the Almighty God; walk before me and be thou perfect.

206. What is the design of prayer?

The design of prayer is

1. The glorification of God's name;

2. The securing of the blessings invoked for ourselves and others.

1 Timothy ii. 1. I exhort therefore, that, first of all, supplications, prayers, intercessions, *and* giving of thanks, be made for all men.

207. *Why is this particular prayer called " The Lord's Prayer ? "*

It is so called, because at the request of his disciples, the Lord Jesus taught them this prayer, saying. "*After this manner ye shall pray.*"

Luke xi. 1. And it came to pass, that, as he was praying in a certain place, when he ceased, one of his disciples said unto him, Lord, teach us to pray, as John also taught his disciples.

Luke xi. 2. And he said unto them, When ye pray, say, Our Father which art in Heaven, Hallowed be thy name. Thy kingdom come. Thy will be done, as in heaven, so in earth.

Luke xi. 3. Give us day by day our daily bread.

Luke xi. 4. And forgive us our sins ; for we also forgive every one that is indebted to us. And lead us not into temptation ; but deliver us from evil.

Matthew vi. 9. After this manner therefore pray ye : Our Father which art in heaven, Hallowed be thy name.

Matthew vi. 10. Thy kingdom come. Thy will be done in earth, as *it is* in heaven.

Matthew vi. 11. Give us this day our daily bread.

Matthew vi 12. And forgive us our debts as we forgive our debtors.

Matthew vi. 13. And lead us not into temptation, but deliver us from evil : For thine is the kingdom, and the power, and the glory, forever. Amen.

208. *How is the Lord's Prayer divided ?*

The Lord's Prayer is divided into

1. The introduction ;
2. Seven Petitions, and
3. The conclusion.

209. *What is the import of these seven petitions in the Lord's Prayer ?*

Of the seven petitions,

1. The three first relate to the glory of God, and at the same time the salvation of our souls ;
2. The remaining four relate immediately to our own welfare ;

3. In the four first petitions we pray for the good things we need, and in the last three we pray for deliverance from the evil that we fear;

4. The first three petitions invoke spiritual, and the third bodily blessings.

PRAYER IN GENERAL.

Scriptural Examples. 1. To whom should we pray? Christ, Matt. iv. 10; Peter and Cornelius, Acts x. 25, 26; John and the angel, Rev. xix. 10; xxii. 8, 9.

2. For what should we pray? Isaac prays for his descendents, Gen. xxv. 21; Elijah prays for death, 1 Kings xix. 4; Elisha prays for victory, 2 Kings vi. 18; Hezekiah prays for recovery from sickness, Isaiah xxxvii. 15; Solomon prays for wisdom, 1 Kings iii. 9, etc; David, 2 Sam. xxiv. 10; Manasseh, 2 Chron. xxxiii. 12; The Publican prayed for the forgiveness of his sins, Luke xviii. 13.

3. How should we pray? With reverence, Abraham, Gen. xviii. 27; Daniel ix. 18; With resignation, David, 2 Sam. xv. 26; Christ, Matt. xxvi. 39; Earnestly, Jacob, Gen. xxxii. 24; Elijah, James v; xvi. 15-18.

4. When should we pray? David, Psalm lxiii. 4; Daniel vi. 10; Jesus prayed before his baptism, Luke iii. 21; Alone, Mark xiv. 35; In the presence of his disciples, Luke ix. 28; At his meals, Matt. xiv. 19; In the night, Luke vi. 12; Under the open heavens, Luke x. 21; During his sufferings, Matt. xxvi. 39.

5. Intercessory prayer, Abraham for Sodom, Gen. xviii. 23-33; Moses for Pharaoh, Ex. viii. 12, 30; For Israel, Ex. xxxii. 11; Job for his children, Job i. 5; Daniel for Jerusalem, ix. 16; Habakkuk for the afflicted ones, iii; Christ for his believers, John xvii. 9; For Peter and the other disciples, Luke xxii. 32; For his murderers, Luke xxiii. 34; Stephen for his murderers, Acts vii. 58; Paul for Israel, Rom. x. 1.

EXPLANATORY NOTES.

Prayer is an offering up of our desires to God, for things agreeable to his will, in the name of Christ, with confession of our sins, and thankful acknowledgement of his mercies.—*Shorter Catechism.*

Prayer is a conversation of the heart with God, Psalm xix. 12.—*Ernst Muehe.*

I. Prayer is an offering up of our desires unto God.
    1. God is the only object of worship: Matt. iv. 10.
    2. He only can hear and answer prayer: 1 Kings viii. 39.

  3. Prayer is more of the heart than the lips: Ps. lxii. 8; Matt. xv. 8.
II. Prayer must be offered for things agreeable to the will of God: 1 John v. 14. The promises are God's will, and may be pleaded. His will is best for our souls.
III. Prayer must be offered in the name of Christ. He himself has taught this: John xiv. 13. He is our Propitiation for sin: 1 John ii. 2. He is also our Intercessor: 1 John ii. 1. This is a very great privilege in prayer.
IV. Prayer must be accompanied by the confession of sin: Dan. ix. 4. This acknowledges our true state, as sinners by nature and by practice, and our unworthiness of God's blessing; and it also honors him as the righteous Lord. "If we confess our sins, he is faithful and just to forgive us our sins:" 1 John i. 9. This is exemplified in the case of David: Ps. xxxii.
V. Prayer must be accompanied with thanksgiving. Every favor of God deserves thanks. His mercy towards sinners especially calls for gratitude.

LESSONS.

1. Prayer is a becoming duty of all.
2. It is the cry of children to their Father in heaven.
3. A prayerless soul is a Christless soul, and a Christless soul is a graceless soul, and a graceless soul is a hopeless soul —*Steel.*

  The privilege of praying to God is one of the greatest benefits. By this we realize that the providence of God does not depend upon an unchangeable fate. God is, indeed, unchangeable in his being, but he is not unchangeable in his ways. This is evident from the interesting account of Hezekiah's sickness and recovery. Isaiah xxxviii.
  Where shall we pray? Everywhere. When shall we pray? At all times. 1 Thess v. 17. In what posture shall we pray? We may pray in any posture. Psalm xcv. 6. The saints of the Old Testament raised their hands towards heaven; we fold our hands. The main point is *how* and *what* we pray? According to the nature, the contents, and the time, prayer is divided into prayers of Petition, Penitence, Praise and Thanksgiving, Intercession, Morning and Evening, and Table Prayers.

ANECDOTES AND ILLUSTRATIONS.

  Amyntor, at a memorable period of his life, was under great distress of conscience, and harrassed by violent temptations. He made his case known to an experienced friend, who said, "Amyntor, you do not pray." Surprised at this, he replied, "I pray, if such a thing be possible, too much. I can hardly tell how many times in a day I bow my knee to God; almost to the omission of my other duties, and the neglect of my necessary studies." "You mistake my meaning, dear Amyntor, I do not refer you to the ceremony of the knee, but the devotion of the *heart*, which neglects not any business, but intermingles prayer with *all;* which in every place looks unto the Lord; and on every occasion lifts up an indigent, longing soul, for the supply of his grace. This," added he, and spoke with peculiar force, "*this* is prayer, which all the devils in hell cannot withstand."

A poor man once came to a pious minister, and said, "Mr. Carter, what will become of me? I work hard, and fare hard, and yet I cannot thrive." Mr. Carter answered, "Still you want one thing; I will tell you what you shall do: Work hard, and fare hard, and *pray* hard; and I will warrant you shall thrive."

Dr. Johnson once reproved the Rev. Dr. Maxwell for saying grace in his presence without mentioning the name of our Lord Jesus Christ; and hoped he would be more mindful in future of his apostolical injunction. A seasonable hint to many.

A Hottentot of immoral character, being under deep conviction of sin, was anxious to know how to pray. He went to his master, a Dutchman, to consult with him; but his master gave him no encouragement. A sense of his own wickedness increased, and he had no one near him to direct him. Occasionally, however, he was admitted with the family at the time of prayer. The portion of Scripture which was one day read by the master, was the parable of the Pharisee and the Publican. While the prayer of the Pharisee was read, the poor Hottentot thought within himself, "This is a *good* man; there is nothing for me;" but when his master came to the prayer of the Publican—God be merciful to me a sinner—he cried, "This suits me; now I know how to pray!" With this prayer he immediately retired, and prayed night and day for two days, and then found peace. Full of joy and gratitude, he went into the fields, and, as he had no one to whom he could speak, he exclaimed, "*Ye hills, ye rocks, ye trees, ye rivers,* hear what God has done for my soul! he has been merciful to me a sinner!"

The mother of a little boy about six years of age, some time ago went in search of a house, taking her son along with her. Having taken one of but a single apartment, the boy, on their way home, burst into tears. His mother inquired why he was weeping; "Because you have taken that house," said the child. "My dear," replied the mother, "is not that a better house than the one we at present occupy?" "Yes," said the little boy, sobbing, "but there is no closet for *prayer* in it." How few, when taking houses, look for such conveniences!

Rowland Hill was once driven by a storm into a village inn, and compelled to stay the night. When it grew late, the landlord sent a request by the waiter that the guest would go to bed. Mr. Hill replied, "I have been waiting a long time expecting to be called to family prayer." "Family prayer!" exclaimed the astonished waiter; "I don't know what you mean, sir; we never have such things here." "Indeed! then tell your master I cannot go to bed until we have had family prayer." The waiter informed his master, who, in consternation, bounded into the room occupied by the faithful minister and said, "Sir, I wish you would go to bed. I cannot go until I have seen all the lights out; I am so afraid of fire." "So am I," was the reply; "but I have been expecting every minute to be summoned to family worship." "All very good, sir; but it cannot be done at an inn." "Indeed! Then pray get me my horse. I cannot sleep in a house where there is no family prayer." The host preferred to dismiss his prejudices rather than his guest, and said, "I have no objection to have prayer, but I don't know how." "Well, then, summon your people, and let us see what can be done." The landlord obeyed, and in a few moments the astonished domestics were upon their knees, and the landlord was called upon to pray. "Sir, I never prayed in my life; I don't know how." "Ask God to teach you," was the gentle reply. The landlord folded his hands and said, "God, teach us how to pray." "That is prayer, my friend," said Mr. Hill, joyfully, "go on." "I am sure I don't know what to say now, sir." "Yes, you do; God has taught you how to pray—now thank him for it." "Thank you, God Almighty, for letting us pray to you!" "Amen! amen!" exclaimed Mr. Hill, and then prayed himself. Two years afterwards Mr. Hill found in that village a chapel and school—the result of the first effort of family prayer at the "Black Lion."

"Prayer," says the hymn, "is the soul's sincere desire, uttered or unexpressed." Phillips Brooks' definition is still better: "Prayer is a true wish sent Godward." The one who prays finds it to his advantage to put his petitions into words and whispers, but so far as the Hearer of prayer is concerned, words are unnecessary. Mutes are heard by God as well as those who say their prayers.

Prayer is the daughter of faith, but the daughter must support the mother.—*Ger. Proverb.*

Prayers answered. In the year 1812 Napoleon invaded Russia. Alexander, the Emperor of Russia, commanded that in his whole empire prayers should be offered for the aversion of the impendent danger. The people arose as one man and prayed to God for deliverance. When Napoleon heard of these prayers against him, he said, "It seems they want to overcome me with prayers. But between the emperor of Russia and me, nothing but bayonets can decide. With my 500,000 warriors I will march on to Moscow and reduce their prayers to contempt." But how God heard and answered those prayers and humbled Napoleon's pride is well known.

Luther's prayer for Melanchton. Melanchton was lying, as was supposed, on his deathbed in the year 1540 at Weimar. Luther was sent for to come immediately. He came without delay and was alarmed to find his friend unconscious, his sight, his hearing gone, and his face pale like that of a corpse. God forbid, he cried out. Then he stepped to the window and prayed most earnestly to God. Then he grasped the hand of his friend and called loudly into his ear, Be of good comfort Philip, you will not die ; I have besieged our Lord God, and have held up to him all his-promises for the answering of prayer, that I knew of in the holy Scriptures, so that he must hear and answer me. Melanchton awoke as it were from the sleep of death, he began again to draw breath, new life began to course through his veins, and he recovered his health. Melanchton said afterwards, " I would have died, if Luther, by his interceding prayer, had not snatched me from the jaws of death."

The prayers of Monika. The church father Augustine († 430) lived in his youth without God and repentance. His pious mother, Monika, prayed incessantly with tears to God, for the conversion of her son. She wept more, says Augustine himself, over her unconverted son, than other mothers mourn over the bodily death of their children. A bishop once said to her, "Be of good cheer, Monika, a son of so many tears and prayers can not be lost." And during twelve years she had prayed for her son, when her prayer was answered ; her son was converted, and the pious mother praised the grace of God. Her desire for this world was fulfilled.

Scriver's mother. Pastor Scriver of Rendsburg relates the following of his pious mother : " I often heard my dear mother pray early in the morning, before we children were up. She used to pray in a loud voice for her children, one after the other. I remember when she came to pray for me that she begged God most heartily and earnestly, that he would endow me with understanding, and knowledge, and wisdom, bless me in my studies, preserve me from the power of the devil and a wicked world, and make me an instrument through his grace, in promoting his glory, and bringing many souls to Christ, and finally make me forever blessed and happy." The prayers of this pious mother have indeed been abundantly answered, and the edifying writings of this good man are still read with great profit.

Prayer records. The pious Spener had his own list of persons for whom he prayed particularly. Those who knew this, often asked him for his intercessory prayers, just as the people had asked Samuel. Count Zinzendorf, the founder of the Moravian church had adopted the same plan.

Luther says, the best occupation of a Christian is prayer.

When man ceases to speak with heaven, then hell begins to speak with him.—*Ger. Proverb.*

It is well to select special hours for prayer, as king David did. Evening, morning, and at noon will I pray and call aloud. Psalm lv. 17. Daniel kneeled upon his knees three times a day, and prayed and gave thanks before God. Dan. vi. 10.

To some, who in the ways of the world, had no family prayers, and excused themselves by saying, that it was enough to pray in their thoughts, Dr. Schurff replied, that it was against the command of Christ, who said, When ye pray, *say,* Luke xi. 2.

In Bunslou, a country man attended a wedding where there was a large company of gay and worldly people. At the table before eating he offered a silent prayer. On this, one of the guests said, scoffingly, "I suppose in your house all pray." "Not all," said the country man, "in the dwelling house they all do; but I have a sow and her pigs in my stable, who never pray, when they come to the trough."

Themistocles was driven into exile by his own ungrateful people. He knew not whither to flee, except to king Admet, who was also his declared enemy. As he was in danger of death also from the king, he took the king's young son, whom he found in the entrance to the palace, in his arms, and said, "King Admet, I come in the name of this child whom you love, and pray for mercy. For the sake of your own son, grant me protection against mine own ungrateful people." By this means he softened the heart of the king, and obtained the promise of protection. Therefore we pray to God the Father in the name of Christ, his Son whom he loveth so much that for his sake he can not in time or eternity deny us anything that he sees good for us.

The sainted Waltersdorf was asked by some distinguished noblemen, whether it was proper to ask a blessing at the table when there was a large assembly present? He replied, I will not decide this question, but I remember seeing in Pomerania among the peasants, (farmers,) a picture on which were painted cattle and horses in a stable at the manger with these words inscribed:

> "Wer ungebetet zu Tische geht,
> Und ungebetet vom Tisch aufsteht,
> Der ist dem Rind und Eselein gleich,
> Und hat nicht Theil am Himmelreich."

Which may be rendered into English thus:
> Who goes to the table and does not pray,
> And without prayer from the table goes away,
> Makes himself with cattle and horses even,
> And has no part in the kingdom of heaven.

How God answers prayer. God always answers our prayers, when we pray aright and for what is good, but not always in the same way. He answers *outwardly* or *inwardly*, or in *both ways together*. When he sends us visible help, so that we ourselves and others can see that God has answered our prayers, then he answers *outwardly*. When after our prayer, the heart feels lighter, or a comforting word from the Bible, or a happy thought comes into our mind, then he answers *inwardly*. Sometimes consolation and help come together, then he answers *inwardly* and *outwardly* at the same time.

A man had become impatient on account of his troubles, and said, There will be no end of these troubles, prayers are useless and God does not help us. To him Livius Fink replied, "How can God hear our prayers instantly, when we, on account of wandering thoughts, often do not hear ourselves when we pray."

Luther says, If it is to be a proper prayer, then it should be in this wise, that we have *few* words, but *many* and *deep meanings* and *imports*. Few words and deep meaning is Christian; many words and little meaning is heathenish.

> Prayer is the soul's sincere desire,
>   Uttered or unexpressed;
> The motion of a hidden fire,
>   That trembles in the breast.

Read or sing the whole hymn.

A soldier who was mortally wounded, and so near to death that he could no more pray audibly, but could simply repeat these few words, "Lord, I have already told thee all before."

THE LORD'S PRAYER IN PARTICULAR.

Q. What rule hath God given for our direction in prayer?

A. The whole word of God is of use to direct us in prayer; but the special rule of direction is that form of prayer, which Christ taught his disciples, commonly called *The Lord's Prayer.—Shorter Catechism.*

EXPLANATORY NOTES.

I. We need a rule to direct us in prayer. God is so great and glorious, we know not how to approach him: Eccles. v. 2. We are so guilty, so sinful, that we need to be invited to engage in prayer, and taught how to do so: Hosea xiv. 2; Matt. vi. 9; Luke xviii. 13.

II. The rule given to direct us.
1. The whole Word of God is of use in this. It is the revelation of God's will. It contains promises and encouragements. It is full of examples of prayer: Ps. xli; Dan. ix.
2. The Lord's Prayer. This was taught the disciples by Christ himself when they asked for guidance. It is a pattern, not a liturgy. The apostles prayed freely, as Acts i. 24, 25; iv. 24-30.
3. This prayer consists of three parts, Preface, Petitions, Doxology.

LESSONS.

1. God's great goodness in teaching us how to pray.
2. The Holy Spirit is promised to aid us.
3. The sin of neglecting to pray.—*Steel.*

The Lord's Prayer is the most beautiful, the most perfect prayer; it is a model for all other prayers. It contains seven short prayers combined into one prayer. The first three have reference to God's glory; the last four have reference to our wants. In these seven petitions all possible prayers are contained, just as in the Ten Commandments all other commands of God are embraced. It is usually divided into the 1. Introduction, 2. The three first petitions, 3. The three last petitions, and 4. The Conclusion, or Doxology. In each one of these four parts the three persons in the Godhead can be recognized. It may yet be remarked, that in six petitions we pray for heavenly and only in one we pray for earthly blessings. Therefore we should pray comparatively six times for eternal and once for temporal blessings. The Lord's Prayer occurs twice in the Bible: Matt. vi. 9-13, and Luke xi. 1-4. Luke omits the Conclusion or Doxology.

ANECDOTES ON THE LORD'S PRAYER IN GENERAL.

The widow of Dr. Krapp, Prof. in Wittenberg, was in the habit of dividing the seven petitions of the Lord's Prayer among the days of the week, one petition for each day, and thus making each petition successively the basis of her prayers. One of the students came to Luther and asked directions how to pray. Luther Replied, "Go to Mrs. Dr. Krapp; she can teach you better than any of us professors; she requires a whole week for the Lord's Prayer."

Luther's Commentary on the Lord's prayer was translated into the Italian. A distinguished divine in Italy, who did not know that Luther was the author of it, declared, in reference to it: "Blessed are he *hands* that wrote this book! Blessed are the *eyes* that shall read it! And blessed are the *hearts* that pray in this manner!"

The Lord's Prayer was Archbishop Leighton's favorite prayer. "O," said he, "the spirit of this prayer would produce the most eminent Christians."

"I once," said Mr. Romaine, "uttered the Lord's Prayer without a wandering thought, and it was the worst prayer I ever offered. I was on this account as proud as the devil."

A cabinet maker in a German village was attacked by robbers at night, his house was plundered, and he himself terribly maltreated. The minister who visited him, found him near to death's door, and informed him of his situation. But the sick man grappled with despair. "God cannot permit this," he cried; "robbed of all my property, must I in addition lose my life, and leave my wife and children in poverty? It is impossible," etc. The impatience of the sick man still increased, notwithstanding all the exhortations to the contrary. In this perplexity the minister was reminded of the advice, which his sainted preceptor, Prof. Karcher, of Jena, had once given him. "If ever," said he, "you are perplexed in the discharge of your office, and unable to determine what to do, then pray the Lord's Prayer with a particular application of each petition to the difficulty in hand, and you will see what a divine power is contained in this prayer." The minister followed this advice, dwelling upon and paraphrasing each petition, so as to apply it to the case before him. When he had ended, the dying man felt encouraged and exclaimed: "Now I will gladly die; God has heard my prayer, and for Christ's sake has graciously accepted me; now I can die happy." He invoked the blessing of Heaven upon the minister, who administered the communion to him, and soon after he fell asleep in Jesus.

The prayer of all prayers is the Lord's Prayer. But says Luther, Many repeat the Lord's Prayer, perhaps several thousand times a year, and if they continued to pray as they do, they would not have tasted, or prayed a letter or tittle of it.

THE INTRODUCTION.

210. What is the Introduction to the Lord's Prayer?

"Our Father, who art in Heaven."

211. What does our Savior teach us in this preface?

The Savior teaches us that God would affectionately invite us to believe, and to be assured, that he is truly our Father, and that we are his children indeed; and therefore we should call upon him with all cheerfulness and confidence, even as beloved children entreat a kind and affectionate parent.

212. What is meant by the word "Father" in the Lord's Prayer?

By this name the Triune God is called, because we have received from him, not only

1. Our bodily life;

Acts xvii. 26. And hath made of one blood all nations of men for to dwell on all the face of the earth, and hath determined the times before appointed, and the bounds of their habitation.

Acts xvii. 27. That they should seek the Lord, if haply they might feel after him, and find him, though he be not far from every one of us.

Acts xvii. 28. For in him we live, and move, and have our being; as certain also of your own poets have said, For we also are his offspring.

2. But also our spiritual life, and
3. Our preservation,

James i. 17. Every good gift and every perfect gift is from above, and cometh down from the Father of lights, with whom is no variableness, neither shadow of turning.

4. And we also enjoy his paternal love.

Psalms ciii. 13. Like as a father pitieth *his* children, *so* the Lord pitieth them that fear him.

213. Why do we say " Our Father?"

We say *Our* Father, because God is kind to all men, both good and bad, and wishes to be worshiped by all.

214. In what respect is God Our Father?

God is our Father by creation and preservation, but still more by regeneration and adoption.

215. Why do we say " Who art in heaven?"

We say Our Father, who art in *heaven*, to express our sense of his majesty and omnipresence, and to direct our thoughts and hearts to heaven.

216. Of what should the words " us" and " our" in this prayer remind us?

Wherever the words "*us*" or "*our*" occur in the Lord's Prayer, it should remind us that we ought also to pray for others as well as for ourselves, and to assure us that others are also praying for us.

EXPLANATORY NOTES.

The preface to the Lord's Prayer (which is *Our Father which art in heaven,*) teacheth us to draw near to God with all holy reverence and confidence, as children to a father, able and ready to help us; and that we should pray with and for others.—*Shorter Catechism.*

The Lord's Prayer is the Prayer of prayers, as the Bible is the Book of books.—*Schaff.*

I. The preface itself. It points out the object of worship, and the place where he dwells.
II. What this preface teaches respecting ourselves.
    1. God is our Father in heaven. This is his most endearing name. He is our Father by creation, and still more by adoption and regeneration.
    2. We are to draw near to God with all holy reverence. He is the infinite God, far above us. He is holy, and to be had in reverence: Ps. lxxxix. 7.
    3. We are to draw near with confidence: Eph. iii. 12. He is trustworthy, and keeps all his promises.

4. We are to come as children to a father able and ready to help. He is almighty, and can help: Eph iii. 20. He is love, and therefore willing: 1 John iv. 16. Christ came to show us the Father: John xiv. 8-11.

III. What this preface teaches respecting others.
1. That we should pray with others. "Our Father" includes others in the family of God. Members of a family on earth may pray to their Father in heaven; so may friends, so may congregations, so may a nation, so may "all people that on earth do dwell."
2. That we should pray for others. They belong to the family, need blessings, and claim a share of our sympathy and effort: 1 Tim. ii. 1-3

LESSONS.

1. "Wilt thou not from this time cry unto me, My Father, thou art the guide of my youth?" Jer. iii. 4.
2. Pity the fatherless, and lead them to say, "Our Father," with you.—*Steel.*

We are permitted to call God Our Father, because his Son has accepted us as his brethren. Read Matt. xii. 49, 50. Heathen, Jews and Turks and all unbelievers or infidels have no right to call God Father. The Lord's Prayer is the Kingdom Prayer (*Reichs Gebet*) of all the children of God. Therefore we say *Our Father,* because we pray along with the other children of God. On the duty of intercessory prayer, read 1 Tim. ii. 1-6; Matt. v. 44. As true children of God we can pray to him with all trust and confidence. "For this purpose God would affectionately encourage us." Mark xi. 24.

The additional words, "who art in heaven" should induce us to humility and reverence. 1 Peter v. 5.

Consider the prayers of the Pharisee and the Publican. Luke xviii. 11, 13.

Prayer offered in the name of Jesus has the promise of an answer. That is, our prayers must be based upon the command of Jesus, and upon his promise, and merits, or in accordance with the mind of Jesus. John xvi. 23, 24.—*Ernst Muehe.*

ANECDOTES AND ILLUSTRATIONS.

"Wherever God has been acknowledged, he has been understood and worshiped as a Father. The very heathen poets so describe their gods; and their vulgar names did carry father in them, as the most popular and universal notion."—*Bishop Pearson.*

"Plato, Plutarch, and other heathen sages, speak of the Deity as 'father and maker of all.' Homer's favorite designation of Jupiter is 'father of gods and men.' Horace represents him as the "father and guardian of mankind.' And Paul in his address to the Athenians refers to two Grecian poets, Aratus and Cleanthes, as having said that 'we are the offspring of God.' "—*Dr. Crawford*.

Max Muller says that in Sanskrit, Greek, and Latin, the name of God is "Heaven-Father." Ere these languages were separated, the Aryan nation had one name for God. It was that of "Our Father which art in heaven."

"God is frequently spoken of in Scripture as the Father of the nation of Israel, and they are his sons. . . This special sonship of the national Israel was typical of the more special relation in which the spiritual Israel—they that believe on the Lord Jesus Christ—stand to God as his children. This special relationship of the believer to God rests entirely on the mediatorial work of Jesus Christ."—*Dr. L. Alexander*.

A Parsee meeting with a Jew one day, asked him what name his people gave to the Supreme Being. The Jew replied, "We call him Jehovah Adonai—the Lord, who is, and was, and is to come." "That is a grand name," said the Parsee; "but it is awful, too." A Christian who happened to be present, remarked, "*We* call him *Father*." With one accord they all raised their eyes to heaven, and said "Our Father," shook hands, and called one another brothers.

"I love sometimas in prayer to remember even the meanest stranger I have met on the public road, with whom, perhaps, I have not exchanged a word; or to be urgent in my intercessions for some common acquaintance, for whom otherwise I have never felt any interest. It is delightful to remain longer upon my bended knees, and to recall every individual, without exception, seen during the past day, and to pray for them and all connected with them, though unknown to me."—*C. B. Taylor*.

John Randolph, the eccentric, but influential statesman, once addressed himself to an intimate friend in terms something like the following:—"I used to be called a Frenchman, because I took the French side in politics; and though that was unjust, yet the truth is, I should have been a French atheist, if it had not been for one recollection, and that was the memory of the time when my departed mother used to take my little hands in hers, and cause me on my knees to say, 'Our Father which art in heaven.' "

The night before Dr. Chalmers died he went into his garden, and was overheard by one of his family, in low but very earnest tones, saying, "O Father, my heavenly Father."

In a family at Shelton, lived Mr. G., a person much given to swearing. A child, about four years of age, would often remark to her mother, with great horror, how Mr. G. swore, and wished to reprove him, but for some time durst not. One day she said to her mother, "Does Mr. G. say *Our Father?*" (a term she used to express in her prayers.) The mother replied, she could not tell; she then said, "I will watch, and if he does, I will tell him of swearing so." She did watch, and heard him say his prayers privately in bed. Soon after this, she heard him swear bitterly; upon which she said to him, "Did you not say *Our Father* this morning?—how dare you swear! Do you think he will be your Father if you swear?" He answered not a word, but seemed amazed; and well he might. He did not live long after this, but was never heard to swear again. "Out of the mouth of babes and sucklings God has ordained strength."

"Some impressions," says a young man, lately gone abroad as a missionary to the heathen, "of the importance and necessity of true religion, were made upon my mind at a very early period. The first particular one that I recollect was, I think, when I was about five years of age. There happened one day a very violent storm of thunder and lightning in our neighborhood; on which occasion a few Christian friends, who lived near us, terrified by its violence, came into my father's house. When under his roof, in a moment there came a most vivid flash, followed by a dreadful peal of thunder, which much alarmed the whole company, except my father, who turning towards my mother and our friends, with the greatest composure, repeated these words of Dr. Watts:

> "The God that rules on high,
> And thunders when he please;
> That rides upon the stormy sky,
> And manages the seas:
> This awful God is ours;
> Our Father and our Love," etc.

These words, accompanied with such circumstances, sunk deep into my heart. I thought, how safe and happy are those who have the great God for their father and friend; but, being conscious that I had sinned against him, I was afraid he was not my father, and that, instead of loving me, he was angry with me; and this, for some time after, continued to distress and grieve my mind." He then proceeds to say, that these early impressions were succeeded by others, occasioned by parental admonitions, the death of a sister, the conversation of pious friends, and the reading of useful books, which terminated in his conversion.

Luther says, When I *believe* that God, who made heaven and earth, and all creatures, and keeps them in his hand and power, is *my Father*, then I conclude most certainly, that I am also a lord of heaven and earth. Furthermore, Christ is my brother, and all his is mine; Gabriel must be my servant, Raphael must be my coachman, and all the angels must be my servants in times of need. This is conferred upon me by my *Heavenly Father*.

Inasmuch as God calls himself Our Father, he has conferred upon us his paternal oversight, care and nourishment. He will rule over us, protect us, he will have patience with our weakness, he will admonish, teach and chastise us.

THE FIRST PETITION.

217. What is the First Petition in the Lord's Prayer?

"Hallowed be thy name."

218. How is this to be understood?

God's name is indeed holy in itself; but we pray in this petition that it may also be sanctified by us.

219. When is this effected?

When the word of God is taught pure and unadulterated, and we, as the children of God, live holy lives, conformably to its precepts. To this, may the Lord our Father in heaven, incline us!

But he, whose doctrine and life are contrary to the word of God, dishonors the name of God among us. From this preserve us, O Lord, our Heavenly Father!

220. What is here meant by "Thy Name?"

By the name of God is meant God himself and everything which represents him, but here is especially meant his paternal, or Father name.

221. Who hallows God's name?

1. God hallows his own name when he reveals himself, as his name imports, as gracious, holy, just, true, etc.

Ezekiel xxxvi. 23. And I will sanctify my great name, which was profaned among the heathen, which ye have profaned in the midst of them; and the heathen shall know that I am the Lord, saith the Lord God, when I shall be sanctified in you before their eyes.

2. We human beings, who are his rational creatures, hallow God's name, when we use his attributes, his word and sacraments as he requires; for example when we trust his Omnipotence, realize his Omnipresence, and employ all the means of grace for the strengthening of our faith, in short, everything to God's glory.

222. How should we apply and improve this petition to ourselves?

1. We should be careful that among us and by us the name of God is hallowed by scriptural doctrine and holy lives.

2. We should pray God that he would shield us from desecration of his name, resulting from impure doctrine and unholy lives

223. Who pray this petition to their own condemnation?

All the ungodly pray this petition to their own condemnation, for if God shall hallow his name, that is his name of holiness and righteousness, then he must hate and punish the ungodly, and according to his truthfulness enforce his threatnings.

Psalms v. 5. The foolish shall not stand in thy sight: thou hatest all workers of iniquity.

EXPLANATORY NOTES.

In the first petition (which is *Hallowed be thy name,*) we pray, that God would enable us and others to glorify him in all that whereby he maketh himself known; and that he would dispose all things to his glory.—*Shorter Catechism.*

Luther says, The devil has no objection to have Christ pass over the tongue if only he can lie under the tongue and in the heart.

I. The first petition is, that God's name may be hallowed. To hallow is to sanctify or glorify. The name of God is that by which he maketh himself known.
II. As a prayer this implies that God would enable us and others to glorify him.
  1. All our spiritual ability comes from God : 2 Cor. iii. 5.
  2. He has promised sufficient grace for this service : 2 Cor. xii. 9.
III. We are to seek to glorify God in all that whereby he maketh himself known.
  1. In his work of creation : Ps. xix. 1-6.
  2. In his works of providence : Ps. viii ; Gen. xxxii. 10.
  3. In his works of salvation : 1 Cor. xv. 10.
IV. We pray that God would dispose all things to his own glory.
  1. This is his own great aim : Rev. iv. 11 ; Num. xiv. 21.
  2. All his intelligent and devout servants seek this. Angels : Isa. vi. 3. The redeemed : 1 Cor. vi. 20.
  3. This was the prayer of Christ : John xvii. 1.

LESSONS.

1. Man's chief end is to glorify God.
2. God will be glorified in our condemnation, if we seek not to glorify him in our salvation.—*Steel.*

The most important and holy petition is the first one. For this reason the Lord placed it first, God's name is God's being or essence. We pray that his name may be hallowed by us.

This is done, according to Luther :
1. When the Word of God is taught in its purity, unmixed with error ;
2. When we as his children live pure and holy lives.

The desecration of the name of God consist in
1. Teaching false doctrines, and
2. Living unholy, godless lives.

ANECDOTES AND ILLUSTRATIONS.

"This petition is with the utmost propriety placed first, because the name of God, and the honor and glory which belong to it, are most precious in his sight, and ought to be so in ours. If it is not our design above all things to honor the name of God, we cannot use this prayer aright ; nor can we with any propriety present unto God the other petitions."—*Patterson.*

The Honorable Robert Boyle, the natural philosopher of his time, paused always before he uttered the name of God, being impressed with solemnity.

"It is related of a little girl, who was sitting on a stranger's knee when travelling, that when he took God's name in vain nothing could induce her to retain her seat."—*Rev. J. H. Wilson.*

"My heaven is to please God, and to glorify him, and give all to him, and to be wholly devoted to his glory: that is the heaven I long for, that is my religion, and that is my happiness, and always was, ever since, I suppose, I had any true religion; and all those that are of that religion shall meet me in heaven. I do not go to heaven to be advanced, but to give honor to God. It is no matter where I shall be stationed in heaven, whether I shall have a high or a low seat there; but to love, please, and glorify God in all."—*David Brainerd.*

"It is worthy of remark and remembrance, that in teaching us to pray, in this brief summary of devotion, the same order is observed as in specifying our moral obligations in the Decalogue; that is, the duty which we owe to God takes precedence of that which is due to ourselves and to our fellow-men. Of six petitions contained in this prayer, the first three relate exclusively to God: teaching us to regard his glory as supreme, and as claiming our attention before we even mention what relates to the welfare of his creatures. It ought also to be noted, that when we pray that God would *enable* us and others to glorify him, we impliedly confess that we are *unable* to do so without his assistance."—*Dr. Ashbell Green.*

> "O ye who bear Christ's holy name,
> Give God all praise and glory;
> All ye who own his power, proclaim
> Aloud the wondrous story!
> Cast each false idol from his throne;
> The Lord is one, and he alone:
> To God all praise and glory."—*Schultz.*

In the life of Mr. Wyndham, prefixed to his speeches in parliament, it is remarked, that nothing so highly offended him as any careless or irreverent use of the name of the Creator. "I remember," says his biographer, "that, on reading a letter addressed to him, in which the words 'My God' had been made use of on a light occasion, he hastily snatched a pen, and before he could finish the letter, blotted out the misplaced exclamation."

When the Rev. Thomas Scott was speaking to Mr. Newton on a change of situation with regard to interest; Mr. N. told him the story of a nobleman who was selected as ambassador by his king, but excused himself, on the ground of his family, and urgent concerns at home; but was answered, "You must go, only do you mind my concerns heartily, and I will take care of yours." "Thus," saith Mr. Newton, "God, as it were, says to you."

One day, when the Rev. Mr. James Durham and the Rev. Mr. Andrew Gray, were to preach in the same town, as they were walking together, Mr. Durham observing multitudes throng into the church where Mr. Gray was to preach, and but one here and there dropping into the one he was to preach in, said to Mr. Gray, "Brother, I perceive you are like to have a throng church to-day." To which Mr. Gray answered, "Truly brother, they are fools to leave you, and come to me." To which Mr. Durham nobly replied. "Not so, dear brother, for a minister can receive no such honor and success in the ministry, except it be given him from heaven. I rejoice that Christ is preached and that his kingdom and interest are getting ground, and that his honor and esteem do increase, though my esteem in people's heart should decrease, and be diminished; for I am content to be any thing, so that Christ may be all in all."

When they praised Charlemagne for his great deeds, he used to praise the Lord God in these words: "Christ rules, Christ conquers, Christ triumphs."

The scoffer can injure God as little as you can defile a ray of sunlight with mud, or paint it black.—*Ger. Proverb.*

The sun loses nothing of its brightness whether we praise or blame it.—*Ger. Proverb.*

What injury is it to the diamond if you call it a pebble? or throw it under the bench? It injures only the person who does it.

Preach the Word pure. The congregation is usually the mirror in which one can see the likeness of its preacher.—*Ger. Proverb.*

A good coachman must not only know his horses but also the way. —*Ger. Proverb.*

The word "holy" is a weighty word. If you bring that which is called *holy* to your reason, then it says, I do not understand it. If you bring it to a comparison of its value, then the reply is, Here no comparison can be made. If you bring it to the estimation of your conscience, then your conscience must say, It is the most unalloyed, the purest; there is no spot or wrinkle in it, not the least. If you bring it to your consciousness that it shall give a description of that which is holy, then your consciousness will declare, It is attractive and it is re-

pulsive, it is elevating and depressing, when it comes near to me, or is within me, in the degree, that I may be pure or defiled, good or bad.
—*Claus Harm's Sermons on the Lord's Prayer.*

To the question, How is God's name hallowed? we reply with Luther. In two ways, 1. When the word of God is taught pure and unadulterated, and 2. When we ourselves live holy as the children of God.

"To this may the Lord, our Father in heaven incline us." Yes, thou art my father. This is thy glory; I am thy child, that is my glory, and my care shall be, that I do not dishonor thy and my name. *Soli Dei Gloria* means, To God be all the glory.

That we should live holy lives. Pachomius, a heathen youth, was drafted into the army by the Roman Emperor Constantine. When the recruits came into a certain city late in the evening, some men, unasked, hastened to bring some supplies to the weary and hungry soldiers, and cheer them with kind words. Surprised at this unsolicited kindness, Pachomius asked who these people were? He was told that they were Christians, who strive to do good to every one, especially to strangers. Very earnestly he sought to inform himself of their religion and silently prayed to God, "If thou wilt, enable me to understand this blessed religion of love, and deliver me out of my present distressful situation, then I will devote my whole life to thy glory and service." Soon after, Constantine obtained the victory over his adversary, and released a part of his army, among them Pachomius. He hastened to Chenoboscium, a village in Thebes, in order to receive instruction in the christian religion. Soon after he was baptized and labored with great blessing among his brethren.

In Luther's explanation it is said, "To this help us, Lord, our Heavenly Father," and "From this preserve us, O Lord, our Heavenly Father." For when God, our Heavenly Father, does not help us, we cannot abide by the pure doctrine, nor live a holy life, because by nature all men are liars, and do not love the truth.

On this subject John Pauli relates the following fable:
Once upon a time four virgins met together and talked in a friendly manner with each other and said, "O, we are so happy here together. If we wish to meet again, where shall we meet again!" Their names were *Fire, Air, Water* and *Heavenly Truth.* And they said, "Fire, where shall we find thee?" The fire answered, "In the hard flint stone; when you find it, and strike it with a steel, you will find me." Then they said to the air, "Sister, where shall we find

thee? where is thy home?" The air said, "You must look where a leaf moves and trembles on a tree, there will you find me and there is my home." Then they said to the water, "Sister, where shall we find thee? and where is thy home? The water answered, "When you find where the palm trees grow, there dig down to the roots, and you will find me; there is my home." Then they said, "Oh, thou noble daughter, heavenly, divine Truth, where shall we find thee?" And heavenly truth replied, "Oh, my dear sisters, you all have told the places where you can be found, but alas, I have no home of my own, no one will entertain me. None wish to hear tell of me, none will open where I knock, but they go away when I come; they avoid me, and where I would do them good, they regard me as an enemy, and where I would like to stay, they drive me away with hatred, lies and contradiction."

Luther used to say of Nicholas Hausman, pastor at Zwichau, "What we *teach*, Hausmann *lives*.

A teacher had told his pupils the history of Araham and Lot, and told them what a peace-loving man Abraham had been. Some days after he noticed that two of his scholars were quarreling with each other. He did not interfere, but heard the one say to the other, "Choose where you will go. If you will remain in the school-room, I will go into the yard; but, if you will go into the yard, I will stay in the school-room."

The proposition was agreed to and peace restored.

THE SECOND PETITION.

224. What is the Second Petition?

"Thy kingdom come."

225. How is this to be understood?

The kingdom of God will come, indeed, without our prayers; but, we pray, in this petition, that it may also come unto us.

226. When is this effected?

When our Heavenly Father gives us his Holy Spirit, so that by his grace we believe his holy word and live a godly life, here on earth and in heaven forever.

227. What is meant by the kingdom of God?

By the kingdom of God is meant the reign of God, as

Lord and King, and also as Father over us, as his subjects and children, who love and honor him.

228. What do we more particularly pray for in this second petition?

In this second petition we pray that
1. Satan's kingdom may be destroyed;
2. The kingdom of grace advanced;
3. Ourselves and others brought into it; and
4. The kingdom of glory hastened.

229. How may God's kingdom be classified?

God's kingdom may be classified into
1. The kingdom of nature;
2. The kingdom of grace, and
3. The kingdom of glory.

Psalm x. 16. The Lord is King forever and ever: the heathen are perished out of his land.

230. Why do we pray " thy kingdom come?

We pray thus, because it is the kingdom of the triune God, which
1. God the Father has ordained from eternity;

Ephesians i. 4. According as he hath chosen us in him before the foundation of the world, that we should be holy and without blame before him in love.

2. God the Son has purchased with his blood; and
3. God the Holy Ghost has established within us.

Luke xvii. 21. Neither shall they say, Lo, here! or, lo there! for, behold, the kingdom of God is within you.

231. What is implied in this petition?

This petition implies, that there are many yet out of the kingdom of God, and are merely in the kingdom of nature; yea, under the power and dominion of Satan, who draws them by their evil passions and the cords of sin, to become his willing slaves. These, therefore, exclude themselves from the kingdom of God.

232. When does the kingdom of God come to us personally?

The kingdom of God comes to us personally, when

1. Through the grace of the Holy Spirit, we believe and obey the word of God; and

2. Are transferred out of the state of nature and the dominion of Satan, into the kingdom of grace and holiness, and after death into the kingdom of glory.

233. Who pray this petition to their own condemnation?

All the enemies of the kingdom of God, and slaves of Satan, who seek to hinder the coming of God's kingdom and to extend the kingdom of Satan, pray this petition to their own condemnation.

EXPLANATORY NOTES.

The kingdom of God is opposed in the world; but it is, nevertheless, always coming, until it reaches its great consummation. Our Lord taught us to pray for its coming. This includes several points.

I. *That Satan's kingdom may be destroyed.*
  1. This is the grand impediment to the kingdom of God.
  2. Satan is called the "god of this world," 2 Cor. iv. 4; the "prince of this world," John xiv. 30; the "prince of the power of the air," Eph. ii. 2.
  3. He is to be overthrown: Rom xvi. 20; Rev. xx. 2, 3.

II. *That the kingdom of grace may be advanced.*
  1. There is a kingdom of grace. It is the kingdom of God which we are to seek: Matt. vi. 33.
  2. Christ is the King: John xviii. 36, 37; Eph. i. 22, 23; Col. i. 13. He is head over all.
  3. His kingdom is now in the hearts of his people: Luke xvii. 21.
  4. He rules in us by his grace, Rom. v. 21, which is the source of all our blessings, Eph. ii. 8.

III. *That ourselves and others may be brought into it, and kept in it.*
  1. We need to be delivered out of the power of darkness, and brought into the kingdom of God's dear Son: Col. i. 13.
  2. Christ has provided for this. Let us say, "Lord, remember me when thou comest into thy kingdom:" Luke xxiii. 42.

3. We should press into the kingdom of God: Luke xvi. 16.
4. We should pray and labor for others: Rom. x. 1.
5. God alone can keep us in it: Ps. xvii. 5; cxix. 117; John xvii. 15.

IV. *That the kingdom of glory may be hastened.*
1. There is a kingdom of glory: 1 Cor. xv. 50; Rev. xxii. 5.
2. It is not yet come; 1 John iii. 2.
3. It will come: Dan. ii. 44.
4. Christ will himself bring it: 2 Tim. iv. 1.
5. It is for his saints: Luke xii. 32; Dan. vii. 22.
6. We are to pray for it, Rev. xxii. 20; and to hasten its coming, 2 Peter iii. 12.

LESSONS.

1. There is no glory hereafter without grace here.
2. Every subject of Christ as King longs for the coming of his kingdom.—*Steel.*

The kingdom of God is three-fold. 1. The Kingdom of Nature, 2. The Kingdom of Grace, and 3. The Kingdom of Glory. Here we are occupied especially with the second and third, of whose coming on earth all the prophets have foretold. See for example Daniel ii. 44; Daniel vii. 23–27. By the advent of Christ it came to the earth. Since the outpouring of the Holy Ghost, it has been spread abroad. It is not *from* or *out* of this world, but it comes from above. But in the course of time it will unfold itself also externally as the glorious kingdom of Christ, and embrace all the nations of the earth. Rev. xx. 1–6. The penitent malefactor prayed for admission into this kingdom, we will also do so.

The *kingdom* of *grace* comes to us, when God gives us his Holy Spirit. But when he comes into our hearts, he works 1. that we believe the word of God, and 2. that we live a Godly life.

But we pray also, that the kingdom of Jesus may also come to the Jews, the Turks, Infidels, and heathen. It is a *Mission Prayer.* Matt. ix. 37, 38.

ANECDOTES AND ILLUSTRATIONS.

In the second petition, (which is, *Thy Kingdom Come,*) we pray that Satan's kingdom may be destroyed; and that the kingdom of grace may be advanced, ourselves and others brought into it; and that the kingdom of glory may be hastened.—*Shorter Catechism.*

A little girl sent about ten shillings to a gentleman for the purchase of some missionary tracts; and in her letter she says, "She who takes this freedom to ask so much of a stranger, began this letter with a trembling hand. She is indeed young in years and in knowledge too, and is not able to talk much with a gentleman on religion; but her mother has taught her, almost eleven years, to say, '*Thy Kingdom Come*;' and she believes she cannot be saying it sincerely if she does nothing to help it on among the heathen. This thought emboldens her to write to a stranger, almost as though he were a friend."

Melanchton, going once upon some great service for the church of Christ, and having many doubts and fears about the success of his business, was greatly relieved by a company of poor women and children, whom he found praying together for the prosperity of the church.

Dr. James Spener, some days before his death, gave orders that nothing of black should be in his coffin;—" For," said he, "I have been a sorrowful man these many years, lamenting the deplorable state of Christ's church militant upon earth; but now being upon the point of retiring into the church triumphant in heaven, I will not have the least mark of sorrow left upon me; but my body shall be wrapped up all over in white, for a testimony that I die in expectation of a better, and more glorious state of Christ's church to come, even upon earth."

"In a saving sense, Christ's kingdom is not without, but within us. Its seat is in the heart; and unless that be right, all is wrong. It does not lie in outward things. It is not meat and drink; not baptism or the communion; not sobriety, purity, honesty, and the other decencies of a common respectability. 'Except a man be born again, he cannot see the kingdom of God.' Its grace and power have their emblem in the leaven the woman lays, not on the meal, but in the meal —in the heart of the lump, where, working from within outwards, from the centre to the circumference, it sets the whole mass fermenting, changing it into its own nature. Even so the work of conversion has its origin in the heart "—*Dr. Guthrie.*

"The coming of God's kingdom towers above all other events, like the mountains above the molehills of earth. It is for that the world is kept in being; and when that event is accomplished there will be such a shout of jubilee throughout the whole universe as has never been since the world began. Anything we can do or give to bring it about is little at the best; but the King graciously permits his children to aid in bringing about what is pleasing to his fatherly heart."—*Rev. J. Wilson.*

The missionary cause is the cause of Christ's kingdom. All may aid this, by prayer, by gifts, by work.

Three resolutions were once proposed and carried at a Negro missionary meeting in the West Indies: "1. That all give something; 2. That all give as God has prospered us; 3. That all give willingly." As soon as this was passed, a leading Negro took his seat at the table with pen and ink to put down the gifts. Many came, some giving more, and some less. At length one rich old Negro came and threw down a small silver coin. "Take dat back," said the collector. "Dat may agree with de first, but not with de second resolution." The rich man went back to his seat; but feeling ashamed when he saw what others were giving, he returned and threw down a piece of gold, saying, "Dere, take dat!" "No," said the collector, "dat won't do yet It may agree with de first and second resolutions, but not with de third." The money was taken back in anger; but by-and-by, when nearly all had gone, he came up with a smile and gave a large sum. "Very well," said the Negro, "dat will do; it be according to all de resolutions!"

It does not say, "Let us come into thy kingdom," but "Let thy kingdom come" to us For we, by our own strength, are not able to enter into the kingdom of God, but it must come to us, God must bring us into his kingdom. Thus the kingdom of God comes, and no one could ever prevent its coming, but it is like the sun, which rises in its course, higher and higher, whether men will or not.

When John Huss was burnt, he called out from the midst of the flames, "To-day ye are roasting, as my name imports, a goose (in the Bohemian language Huss means a goose), but after a hundred years there shall arise out of my ashes a swan, which you will not be able to roast or burn " Luther said in regard to this, "Huss has prophesied of me, and thus it shall stand, by the will of God."

In Prague the Protestants preserved a New Testament in the Bohemian language, which was ornamented with valuable pictures. On one of these pictures could be seen Wickliff, who had attacked the Romish heresies, even before Luther, striking sparks from a flint with a steel, then Huss, lighting a match, and last Luther with a flaming torch.

One of Luthers mottoes reads as follows: "*Malo cum Christo cadere, quam cum Cœare stare.*" That is, "I would rather fall with Christ, than stand with Cæsar."

At the time of the Reformation a classical scholar found a Bible, and read in it Christ's sermon on the Mount, whereupon he exclaimed, "Either all this is not true, or we are not Christians."

The 95 theses, which Luther nailed on the Castle Church door at Wittenberg, on the 31st of Oct., 1517, were spread over all Germany in about 14 days after six weeks, they had flown over the whole of Europe, and at the beginning of the new year, a copy of them was bought by a traveller in Jerusalem.

After Luther had begun his work of the Reformation, a young nobleman came on a pilgrimage to Campostella in Spain to do penance for his sins. As he there confessed to an old monk, and told him the object for which he came, the old monk said to him, "My son, why do you run so far for that which you could find much nearer at home? I have lately seen a writing from Luther, an Augustinian monk, in which he teaches powerfully from the word of God, that man can obtain salvation by no other means, than by faith in Jesus Christ. Hold fast to this and you will be saved."

The kingdom of heaven is within you. Do you ask, how can we know that we are in the kingdom, then St. Paul gives us the answer, The kingdom of God is not meat and drink, but righteousness and peace and joy in the Holy Ghost. Rom. xiv. 17.

Do you yourself feel the blessedness of citizenship in the kingdom of heaven, then you will wish that others might also be brought into the kingdom. Paul exclaimed before Agrippa, "I would that all were such as I."

Let us enlarge the circle. "Thy kingdom come!" Alas! there are yet 600 millions heathen people on earth! What desire do you express in these words: Answer, "Thy kingdom come also to those 600 millions of benighted heathen!"

How will this be accomplished? Luther says, "When our Heavenly Father gives us his Holy Spirit." The kingdom of God could not come into the world, till the Holy Ghost was poured out upon the disciples on the day of Pentecost.

St. Paul says, 1 Cor. iii. 9. We are co-workers with God. This is the highest honor any one can enjoy in the kingdom of God.

FAITH AND A GODLY LIFE.

Scriptural Examples. Thy kingdom come. John Baptist, Matt. iii. 1, 2; Jesus and the Pharisees, Luke xvii. 20, 21; Jesus and Nicodemus, John iii. 3. The Scribe, Mark xii. 28-34; The preaching of the 70, Luke x. 9, 11; Paul, Gal. ii. 20.

In London a society was organized consisting of mothers, for the purpose of unitedly praying for the conversion of their children.

The pious pastor, John Pommer, a co-laborer with Luther, celebrated an annual anniversary of the translation of the Bible by Luther, in which, with his children and invited friends, he thanked God for the inestimable treasure of the German Bible.

When Augustine wanted to become a Christian, he asked the aged bishop Ambrosius, which book in the Bible he should read first? Ambrosius replied, he should begin with the prophet *Isaiah*, because no prophet treats so plainly of the sufferings, martyrdom, death and burial of Christ, which was most offensive to the heathen. Augustine followed this good advice, and was so much strengthened in his faith, that he said, It seems to me, that Isaiah has not written a prophecy, but a gospel.

The dutchess of Nassau heard the verse, Isaiah xliii. 25, "I, even I, am he that blotteth out thy transgressions, for mine own sake, and will not remember thy sins" She was so highly rejoiced, that she publicly exclaimed, "This verse is worth fifty dollars."

Urbanus Regius, general superintendent of Lueneburg, regarded as his favorite Scripture verse, Jeremiah xxiii. 6, "This is his name whereby he shall be called, *The Lord, our righteousness*." And he said, "I have never been so down cast, but that this verse has comforted me. I would not exchange it for a hundred worlds."

The pious minister, Seligman, persuaded an Athiest to listen to the reading of a single chapter from the Bible with earnest and close attention. The Athiest was astonished and convicted. After a few days he came again, and requested, that Seligman should read and explain another such a chapter to him. He did so, and the unbeliever was convinced of the truth of the holy Scriptures and Christianity.

THE EXTENSION OF THE KINGDOM AMONG OURSELVES, AND AMONG THE HEATHEN.

Scriptural Examples. Abraham, Gen. xviii. 19; Asa, 2 Chron. xiv. 3, 4; Joash and Zachariah, 2 Chron. xxiv.; Abraham, Gen. xvii. 13; Solomon and the queen of Sheba, 1 Kings x. 1-13; David, Psalm ix. 20; lix. 5; Daniel ii. 27; iv. 24; v. 18, etc.; Peter, Acts x. 11; Paul, Acts xiii.; Gaius, 3 John 5-8.

A Christian, who on account of his occupation was compelled to go much on journies, sought at the same time to promote the kingdom of God. He endeavored to converse with all his fellow travellers on the one thing needful. At times it was very difficult to do this. Sometimes an extraordinary dread almost overcame him at the beginning of the conversation. But then the thought came into his mind, "What a great joy it is to become the instrument in the hand of God in saving a soul from death." And this thought always inspired him with courage and zeal in this work of love.

Sophia Von Gladebach, a cotemporary with Canstein, bequeathed in her will, 1728, the sum of $500, from which every house in her estate should be supplied with two Bibles; one with large and the other with small print. These Bibles were to remain in the dwelling houses as part of the property, and when there was a change of tenants they should be given over to the new tenants. If any of them should become injured or lost, they were to be replaced, in order, as the pious lady expressed it, "That the precious word of God, as much as I can help, may be implanted in the hearts of the people."

In the year 1825, an aged widow, who was supported by charity came with great joy to pastor Kohlreiff in Moskau. She had read in the mission paper, the reports of the gospel being preached among the heathen. She had not known that anything of this kind was going on in the world. For this work, she said, she was willing to give everything she had, but that would, evidently, not help much; and this seemed evident, as she was dressed almost in rags. But after reflection; she had one precious treasure, a small gold ring; it was the most cherished and valued treasure she possessed, her wedding ring given her by her sainted husband; she gave it to the pastor for the heathen.

At a missionary meeting, a young man in the rear of the audience room arose, and with a trembling voice, said, "May I speak a few words?" All eyes were turned in the direction whence the voice proceeded. Permission was given, and amid profound silence, in the congregation, the young man began: "I am 15 years old; three years ago, I felt the need of a Savior, I sought and found him, and since that time it has been the desire of my heart to preach the gospel to the heathen. In the school I often read of the work that is done by the missionaries in Birma, and I would take great pleasure in preaching the gospel to the people of Birma. I announce this to you to-day, and if you regard me a suitable person for missionary work, I am here at your disposal." When he ended a venerable man arose and spoke as follows: "This young man is my son; for a long time I have believed that he loves the Lord, but I did not know, that such a wish possessed his heart. God forbid, that I should put any hindrances in his way; but I have no money to send him to school, in order that he may be educated and prepared for the work." Immediately after he sat down, another man rose in the assembly, and said, "I have wealth; I will pay the expense of his education, and after that, I will send him to Birma; I hope we shall meet in heaven, and together we will lay our crowns at the feet of Jesus, and adore him."

Many grains make a great heap. At a missionary meeting in the great seaport, Liverpool, in England, where a number of Welshmen, from Wales, were present, a Welsh preacher was urged to say a few words to these Welshmen, who did not understand English. He did so, and when it was observed that his address made a deep impression, the Englishmen asked him what he had said. "O," said he, "I spoke about the pennies." "About the pennies! and what did you say about the pennies?" "Well, I said, Many of you say, I can not give more for missions than a penny a week; but what will a penny help? But when I came over the mountain, on my way to Liverpool, I saw a little rivulet, and said to it, Rivulet, where are you going? Oh, I am going down to the creek. Creek, where are you going? Oh, I run into the great river, Mersey! Well, Mersey, where are you going? Oh, I am running down into Liverpool. What are you going to do in Liverpool? Oh, there I will take the ships out of the harbor, and carry them out into the ocean, and far off into strange countries; then I bring them back laden with the fruits of those countries. And so I also say now, *Pennies*, where are you going? Oh, we go to the shillings of the missionary society. And, shillings, where are you going? Oh, we go to the half and whole pounds, of the branch societies. And pounds, where are you going? Oh, we go to the Central Missionary Society, in London. And what do you wish to do in London? Well, there we take missionaries and Bibles, and carry them to the utmost parts of the earth, in order that England's God, and England's Bible may be everywhere known and loved."

John Jacobus in Church. John Jacobus attended a missionary convention, and sat along with many other good Christians in church, and listened to the sermon. The preacher divided his sermon into three parts. In the first division the preacher said, among other things, that every Christian was in duty bound to make all the money he could—honestly. John gave his neighbor, sitting next to him, a hunch, and whispered, "Hear that, neighbor?" In the second division the preacher spoke of the duty of Christians, to hold on to what they had honestly gained. At this, John Jacobus was so much overjoyed, that he turned several somersaults in his mind, and gave his neighbor another jog in the side, whispering, "Do you hear that? He is the right man in the right place!" In his third division the preacher declared, that a Christian must give up everything for Christ and his church, if it was necessary. At this, there came a remarkable expression of disappointment over the face of John Jacobus, and with downcast looks, he said to his neighbor again: "Alas! alas! now, at the end, he has spoiled everything!" But such Christians like John Jacobus will never do much mission work.

THE THIRD PETITION.

234 What is the Third Petition?

"Thy will be done on earth as it is in heaven."

235. What is meant by this petition?

The good and gracious will of God is done, indeed, without our prayer; but we pray in this petition, that it may be done by us also.

236. When is this effected?

When God prevents and destroys all evil counsels and intentions, the will of the devil, of the world, and of our own flesh, which tend to dishonor the name of God among us, and hinder the coming of his kingdom to us, and when he strengthens and preserves us steadfast in his word and faith, unto our end. This is his good and gracious will.

237. What is meant by the "will of God"?

By the "will of God" is meant his inherent and inseparable inclination to that which is good; but in this petition is meant all the good which our heavenly Father wills to us.

238. Towards what is God's will directed?

God's good and gracious will is directed towards

I. The promotion of his own glory, as is evident from
    1. The creation, especially of intelligent beings;
    2. The redemption and salvation of sinners, and
    3. The revelation of his word.

Proverbs xvi. 4. The Lord hath made all *things* for himself: yea, even the wicked for the day of evil.

Malachi i. 5. Your eyes shall see, and ye shall say, The Lord will be magnified from the border of Israel.

II. The will of God is farther directed towards the welfare of his creatures, for

    1. He wills not only our soul's salvation, for the attainment of which he has pointed out the way, but he also grants us strength to secure our salvation.

Ezekiel xxxiii. 11. Say unto them, *As* I live, saith the Lord God, I have no pleasure in the death of the wicked; but that the wicked turn from his way and live: turn ye, turn ye from your evil ways; for why will ye die, O house of Israel?

John iii. 16. For God so loved the world, that he gave his only begotten Son, that whosoever believeth in him should not perish, but have everlasting life.

Philippians ii. 13. For it is God which worketh in you both to will and to do of *his* good pleasure.

    2. In addition he also wills our bodily welfare.

Genesis i. 28. And God blessed them, and God said unto them, Be fruitful, and multiply, and replenish the earth, and subdue it: and have dominion over the fish of the sea, and over the fowl of the air, and over every living thing that moveth upon the earth.

239. Does God will that which is evil?

No, God does not approve of evil, although sometimes he permits it, because he does not compel men to do right, but then he overrules the evil for good.

Genesis l. 20. But as for you, ye thought evil against me; *but* God meant it unto good, to bring to pass, as *it is* this day, to save much people alive.

240. What do the words " thy will" include?

The words "thy will" include the will of the Triune God; namely, the will of the Father, who is our Preserver, the will of the Son, who is our Redeemer, and the will of the Holy Ghost, who is our Sanctifier.

241. What is meant by the words " thy will be done"?

By these words we pray, that we may not only

    1. Realize and learn, what is needful for the promotion of God's glory and our welfare, but also,

    2. That in all things we may strive to promote this object.

242. What is implied in the words " as in heaven, so on earth"?

These words imply,

1. That as the will of God is done in heaven, by saints and angels, in obedience, praise and thanksgiving;

2. That it might also be done in like manner by men on earth.

Psalm ciii. 1. Bless the Lord, O my soul: and all that is within me, *bless* his holy name.

Psalm ciii. 2. Bless the Lord, O my soul, and forget not all his benefits.

THE APPLICATION.

243. What is the application of this petition?

We pray in this petition, that the will of God may be done and performed not only

1. By all other rational creatures, but also

2. By ourselves, God's grace strengthening us.

Philippians iv. 13. I can do all things through Christ which strengtheneth me.

3. We pray farther that all hindrances to the fulfillment of God's will may be removed; such as the works of the devil, the world and our own flesh.

4. And farther we pray, that we may be enabled to submit our own will, entirely to the will of God, and in all things conduct ourselves according to his will.

Matthew xxvi. 39. And he went a little farther, and fell on his face, and prayed, saying, O my Father, if it be possible, let this cup pass from me: nevertheless, not as I will, but as thou *wilt.*

244. Who pray this petition to their own condemnation?

All those pray this petition to their own condemnation,

1. Who are dissatisfied with God's will and providence, and

2. Who are self-willed and obstinate even in unimportant things.

EXPLANATORY NOTES.

I. *The petition itself.* That God's will may be done on earth, as it is done in heaven.

II. *The objects desired from God.*
   1. That God would make us able and willing to know his will in all things: Eph. i. 18. (*a.*) We are ignorant by nature. (*b.*) We are unwilling to learn. (*c.*) We need God to teach us. (*d.*) God has promised this teaching: Isa. xlviii. 17. (*e.*) We have examples of prayer for this in David, Ps. xxvii. 11; Solomon, 1 Kings iii. 6-10.
   2. To obey his will in all things. (*a.*) He can renew in us a right spirit: Ps. li. 10. (*b.*) This is the great aim of the Christian: 2 Cor. x. 5. (*c.*) Divine grace is sufficient: 2 Cor. xii. 9.
   3. To submit to his will in all things. He can enable us to say, "Thy will be done." His way is best for us, and is always wise. Christ learned obedience by the things which he suffered, and can aid us: Heb. v. 8, 9.

III. *The pattern of obedience to God's will.* The angels do his will: Ps. ciii. 20. They are humble, (Isa. vi. 2,) cheerful, faithful, constant in their obedience.

LESSONS.

1. The knowledge of God's will is the most practical and useful of all inquiries.
2. The love of Christ is the best motive for obedience.—*Steel.*

God's will is gracious and good, and is always done. But we pray, that his will may also be done by us, and done just as it is done by the angels in heaven, and holy men; namely, *perfectly, willingly, promptly,* and *constantly.* Therefore, God must first suppress three evil wills; namely,
  1. The devil's will;
  2. The world's will; and
  3. The will of the flesh.

By the *world* is meant in the Scriptures, all wicked and unbelieving men. 1 John v. 19; John xv. 18, 19; 1 John iii. 13.

The *flesh* means the depraved human nature of man, with all its sinful lusts and unholy desires.

These three enemies all entertain the evil counsel and will,
  1. That God's name should not be hallowed, and
  2. That the kingdom of God should not come. But we pray that God would strengthen, and keep us in his word and faith. —*Muehe.*

ANECDOTES AND ILLUSTRATIONS.

Scriptural Examples. Abraham, Gen. xii. 1-4; xxii. 1-3; Moses, Ex. iv.; The Israelites, Ex. xxiv. 3, 7; Samuel, 1 Samuel iii.; David, 2 Samuel xi. 16; Christ, Psalm xl. 8, 9; Heb. x. 7; Matt. xxvi. 39-44; John iv. 34; v. 30; Mary, Luke i. 38.

In the third petition, (which is, *Thy will be done in earth, as it is in heaven,*) we pray, that God, by his grace, would make us able and willing to know, obey and submit to his will in all things, as the an gels do in heaven.—*Shorter Catechism.*

"Virtue is in one of its highest forms, or rather in its highest form, when the will is properly exercised in reference to the Divine Being. It is somewhat higher than mere benevolence when thus directed towards so elevated an object. We feel that God does not need our good wishes, as he does not need our help; and yet we feel that there is a holy exercise of the will due on our part, to him. Hence arises the desire to glorify God, being the highest desire which the creature can cherish, and the noblest motive by which he can be actuated. This internal exercise of the will finds its fullest and most appropriate embodiment and expression in praise and prayer. Under this feeling we say, 'Hallowed be thy name,' and earnestly long that God, as he is all-glorious, may be glorified as he ought. We say, 'Thy will be done,' and feel it to be the highest work in which we can engage to do his will, and labor also that others may know it and do it."—*Dr. M'Cosh.*

A clergyman once asked a deaf and dumb boy why he was born deaf and dumb. The boy took the chalk and wrote, "Even so, Father; for so it seemed good in thy sight."

A Scottish Lord of Session was once on the Pentland Hills, and as a mist came on, he indulged in a profane remark regarding it. A shepherd, who was standing by, said, "What ails ye at the mist? It wats the gress, it slockens the yows, and it's God's wull." It was a noble reproof, and not likely to be forgotten.

"Wish what the Holy One wishes, not from fear but affection: fear is the virtue of slaves; but the heart that loveth is willing.— *Bishop Tegner.*

A Sabbath-school teacher, instructing his class on this portion of the Lord's Prayer, said to them, "You have told me, my dear children, *what* is to be done - the will of God; and *where* it is to be done— on earth; and *how* it is to be done - as it is done in heaven. How do you think the angels and happy spirits do the will of God in heaven, as they are to be our pattern?" The first child replied, "They do it *immediately.*" The second, "They do it *diligently.*" The third, "They do it *always.*" The fourth, "They do it with *all their hearts.*" The fifth, "They do it *altogether.*" Here a pause ensued, and no child appeared to have an answer; but after some time a little girl arose and said, "They do it *without asking any questions.*"

"I am waiting for my dismission. I desire to leave the *how* and the *when* and the *where* to him who does all things well."—*Rev. John Newton.*

I have heard of a lady, who, on being visited by a friend, said, "I was just trying to learn the Lord's Prayer as you came in." "What!" said her friend, "have you never learned the Lord's Prayer?" "No," was the reply; "I have just got the length of the third petition, and I find it hard to learn. I cannot yet say, "Thy will be done!"

> " My God and Father, while I stray,
> Far from my home, in life's rough way,
> O teach me from my heart to say,
>   ' Thy will be done."
>
> " Renew my will from day to day ;
> Blend it with thine ; and take away
> All that now makes it hard to say,
>   ' Thy will be done.' "—*Elliott.*

There was a good woman, who, when she was ill, being asked, whether she was willing to live or die? answered, "Which God pleaseth." "But," said one standing by, "If God should refer it to you, whether would you choose?" "Truly," said she, "if God should refer it to me, I would even refer it to him again "

Some years ago, a Christian widow in London saw, with great alarm, her only child taken dangerously ill. As the illness increased, she became almost distracted, from a dread of losing the child; at length it became so extremely ill, and so convulsed, that she kneeled down by the bed, deeply affected, and in prayer said, "Now, Lord, thy will be done." From that hour the child began to recover, till health was perfectly restored.

"What occasions that melancholy look?" said a gentleman to one of his young favorites, one morning. He turned away his face, to hide a tear, that was ready to start from his eyes. His brother answered for him, "Mother is very angry with him," said he, "because he would not say his prayers last night; and he cried all day, because a sparrow died of which he was very fond." The little mourner hastily turned round, and looking at me, exclaimed, "I could not say, *Thy will be done*, because of my poor bird." The gentleman took him by the hand, and pointing to his school fellows, "Mark the observation," said he, "from the youngest present only six years old; for it explains the nature of prayer, of which, perhaps, some of you are ignorant. Many persons repeat words, who never prayed in their lives. My dear boy, I am very glad to find you were afraid to say to God, what you could not say truly from your heart; but you may beg of him to give you submission to his will.'"

The will of the Father must be acceptable to the children. God's will has no why. – *Ger. Proverb.*

Some one complained to Luther, "Nothing appears to be going as I wish it any more." Luther replied, "That is perfectly right. Why have you given your will over to the Lord God, and pray every day, *Thy will be done in earth, as it is in heaven?*"

A poor peasant (farmer,) was visited on his sick-bed by his pastor, who asked, how it was with him? The sick man replied, "Just as I wish it to be" "How shall I understand you," said the pastor, "do you want to be sick?" "No, but what God wills, that I will also. God wills, that I should be sick now, and that I will, too. If he wills, that I shall die, then I will that, too; if he wills that I shall get well again, then I will that, also. To him I confide all. Let him do with me as he sees best."

When in 1548, Charles V. deposed the Evangelical ministers from their churches, because they would not accept the Interim, they came to the Elector, John Frederick, of Saxony, himself a prisoner, and reported that they had not only been deposed from their services, but that his imperial majesty had also forbade them residence in the empire. On this information the Elector wept till the tears flowed down over his cheeks to the ground. Then he arose and stood by the window, but soon turned and said to them, "Has the emperor also forbid you the entrance into heaven?" "No," said they. The Elector replied, "Then, all is not lost. The kingdom must yet remain to us; therefore God will find a land wherein you can preach his word."

In the year 1537, Wolfgang, prince of Anhalt, whose name stands as one of the signers of the Augsburg Confession, was proscribed by Charles V. as an outlaw, and his possessions given to a Spanish favorite. When the letter of proscription arrived, he mounted his horse, and rode from his castle to Berleburg, and passing through the excited city, he halted in the market-place, where he sang with a clear voice, the celebrated Luther hymn, *Ein' feste Burg ist unser Gott.* "A safe, strong tower is our God," especially the last verse :

>The Word they still shall let remain,
>And not a thank have for it,
>He's by our side upon the plain,
>With his good gifts and Spirit ;
>
>Take they, then, our life,
>Goods, fame, child and wife ;
>When their worst is done,
>They yet have nothing won,
>The kingdom ours remaineth.

He then hid himself in the mill at Kaernau, disguised as a miller's servant. But in the year 1550 he was restored to his possessions by the peace of Passau, to the great joy of his friends and subjects.

God's word and *faith* are married together ; neither one shall be divorced from the other.

Cast not thy christianity away on account of many sufferings. Do not be like that monkey, who threw the whole nut away, because he tasted the bitter rind around it.

A pious man, who had encouraged a brother, weak in the faith, was asked by him, where he had obtained such a strong faith, and replied, "I have the *word*, *hand* and *seal* of my God. His *word* I have in the Holy Scriptures ; his *hand* in his works, and his *seal* in my heart, through the testimony of the Holy Spirit, that I am a child of God. Why, then, should I not believe and have full confidence?"

If you would say to a carpenter, when he cuts into the wood with his sharp axe, "Oh, how you spoil that beautiful wood ; " he would say, "Oh, you are a child, you do not understand ; this is done in order, that a more beautiful house may be made out of it." Strange beginning, glorious end.

On earth, as it is in heaven God's will is done in heaven by the holy angels and saints, for their happiness consists in doing the will of God. Bless the Lord, ye his angels that excel in strength, that do his commandments, hearkening unto the voice of his word. Bless ye the Lord, all ye, his hosts, ye ministers of his, that do his pleasure. Psalm ciii. 20, 21.

A woman in Holstein lived very happily with her husband in the married life. But her husband took sick and died. The widow was greatly distressed and wept much. She had an aged mother, who one day came to a house, where the people did not know much about religion, and they asked her, how her daughter was coming on? The old mother replied, that it was going better with her daughter now, than at first, "She has now given in her will to the death of her husband." When the old mother had gone, the people laughed at her remark, saying, "Why, she had to give her will to the death of her husband!" But what did the old mother really mean? She meant, that her daughter now submitted to God's will in this dispensation of his providence, believing, that all things work together for our good.

When Francis Xavier came, as a missionary to Japan, he found some European merchants there, who had preceded him to that country, and exclaimed, "I feel ashamed, that these merchants, for the sake of worldly gains, have come to Japan sooner than I did, for the sake of eternal gain."

In a conversation between St. Augustine and his friends, the question was asked, "Is not that person fortunate who has what he desires?" To which Monica, his mother, replied, "If he wishes and has that which is good, he is fortunate; but when he wishes that which is bad, he is miserable, even if he has it."

A savage, who hated a native Christian, by the name of Gideon, met him one day, and pointed his gun at him, saying, "Now you must die, because you are always talking of Jesus." Gideon replied, "If Jesus is not willing, you cannot kill me." The savage was deterred, took his gun down, and went away without saying a word.

WHEN GOD FRUSTRATES EVERY EVIL COUNSEL AND PURPOSE, ETC.

Scriptural Examples. The builders of the Tower of Babel, Gen. xi. 6-8; With Pharaoh, Ex. iii. 19, 20; With Israel, Ex. xvi. 28, 29; With Balaam, Num. xxii. 22-35; xxiii. 12-20; With Nebuchadnezzar, Dan. iii. 23, etc.; With the Counsellors of Darius, Dan. vi.; With the Pharisees, John ix.; With Herod, Acts xii. 3, etc.

A certain infidel had declared himself a despiser of the christian religion, and had openly attacked Christianity in his published writings. Just as he was reading one of his infidel articles to a friend, he was called away to his daughter's deathbed. His friend accompanied him to the chamber of death. As the infidel stood by the bed of his daughter, whose mother had instructed her in the christian religion, she said to him, "Father, I feel that I must die; will you please to tell me now, in which faith I shall die? Shall I die in that belief which you have taught me; or shall I die in that faith which my mother has taught me?" After a moments reflection, he replied, "Believe that which your mother has taught you!"

A chief of the Bushmans in South Africa, who had become a christian, held a prayer meeting. Just as his people were assembled and engaged in worship, a hord of wild savages entered. The chief intermitted the prayer meeting, went out to meet them, and asked what they wanted. "We want your lives or your cattle," replied the robbers. "Take our cattle," said the chief, and resumed his prayer-meeting. The robbers were amazed, drew near as they heard him pray; their hearts were impressed, and they turned away without taking a single head of his cattle.

A Hindoo, who was being instructed before baptism, related to the missionary, that he had previously, in company with other heathen people, heard him preach, and then only laughed at his words. But afterwards many misfortunes had befallen him, namely, deaths in his family, then he remembered the words which he had heard, and became very much concerned by the thought, that he might possibly, some day, by a sudden death, be called into the presence of God.

When Trouchin, the physician of the Duke of Orleans, was sent to the old scoffer, Voltaire, ordered to attend to him in his last sickness, Voltaire said to him, "Dear doctor, I wish that you could save my life; I will give you the half of my possessions, if you can add six months to the length of my life. If not, then I go to the devil, and will take you along with me."

The pious Amelia Dale learned to read, when she was sixty-six years old, in order that she might be able to read the Bible herself. And, poor as she was, she gave a little girl a shilling a week, that she should come to her cottage and teach her, until she was able to attend a school for grown people, which was established in her village.

WHEN HE STRENGTHENS US AND KEEPS US STEADFAST.

Scriptural Examples. Noah, Gen. ix. 12-17; Jacob, Gen. xxxii. 1, 2; Samuel, 1 Sam. xii. 23; Elijah, 1 Kings xix. 18; Shadrach, Meshach and Abednego, Dan. iii. 16-28; Daniel, Dan. vi. 16-22; Simeon, Luke ii. 29, 30; The Apostles, Luke xvii. 5; Luke xxii. 42, 43.

Dr. John George Knapp, Professor of Theology in Halle, who died in 1771, was in the practice of turning everything that he read in the Bible, or any other edifying book, or any subject on which he had thought, into a prayer, whereby the impressions, which the truth had made on his heart, were made more blessed and permanent.

When the news arrived at Wittenberg, that the Pope had put Luther in the ban, that is, declared him an outlaw, whom everyone was commanded to put to death, Luther went into the garden, and began to sing. He was asked, whether he had not heard the report? "That does not concern me," said Luther, "but it concerns our Lord Jesus Christ? Will he permit himself to be cast down from the right hand of God, and let his church be overthrown? *Let him see to that?* I am much too weak to defend him and his cause against the prince of this world."

Frederick II., King of Denmark, who died 1588, commanded, that at his departure from this world, the following scripture verses should be read to him: "God so loved the world, that he gave his only begotten Son, that whosoever believeth in him, should not perish, but have everlasting life." John iii. 16. Then, "Unto thee, O Lord, do I lift up my soul." Psalm xxv. 1. And finally, "Bless the Lord, O my soul, and all that is within me, bless his holy name." Psalm ciii. 1. This was done when the hour of his departure had come. The king heard these passages with great joy, and as the reader came to the verse in Psalm ciii. 13, "Like as a father pitieth his children, so the Lord pitieth them that fear him," he said, "That is true," and expired.

The Dutchess Agnes, of Witgenstein, reflected on her sickbed, on the marriage of Cana, how the Lord there had made a difference between *Mary's hour* and *his hour.* "Thus," said the sick lady, "flesh and blood prefers the *Mary's hour*, because we mortals wish that Jesus should come soon and do miracles to help us out of our troubles. But we must patiently await *Christ's hour*, and that is what I intend to do."

THE FOURTH PETITION.

245. What is the Fourth Petition?

Give us this day our daily bread.

246. What is the meaning of this petition?

God bestows, indeed, unasked, the necessaries and conveniences of life, even upon the wicked;

But in this petition we pray that he would make us sensible of his mercies, and enable us to receive them with thanksgiving.

247. *What is understood by " our daily bread" ?*

Everything necessary to the support and comfort of existence; such as

1. Food and raiment, house and land, money and goods:

2. A kind spouse, good children, faithful servants, righteous magistrates;

3. Good weather, peace, health, instruction, honor, true friends, good neighbors, and the like.

248. *What do we pray for in general in this petition ?*

In this petition we pray in general for the bestowment of all temporal blessings.

THE MEANING OF THE WORDS.

249. *What is meant by the word " bread" ?*

By the word "bread" is meant all those things which are necessary to the support of our lives, of which eating and drinking are the most essential.

250. *What is meant by " our bread" ?*

By the words " our bread " is meant,

1. That which is necessary to our preservation;

2. Which we have honestly earned, and

Genesis iii. 19. In the sweat of thy face shalt thou eat bread, till thou return unto the ground; for out of it wast thou taken: for dust thou *art*, and unto dust shalt thou return.

3. Which has not been stolen, or gained by fraud, or unnecessary begging.

1 Thessalonians iv. 11. And that ye study to be quiet, and to do your own business, and to work with your own hands, as we commanded you.

251. *What is meant by our " daily bread" ?*

By our "daily bread" is meant all things necessary to our daily wants.

252. What is meant by the words, " give us " ?

In these words is embraced the prayer that

1. God would provide for us as our true and faithful Father;

Psalm cxlv. 15. The eyes of all wait upon thee; and thou givest them their meat in due season.

Psalm cxiv. 16. Thou openest thine hand, and satisfiest the desire of every living thing.

2. Bless us in the enjoyment of his bounties;

Psalm cvii. 9. For he satisfieth the longing soul, and filleth the hungry soul with goodness.

3. Also bless our labors for their attainment;

Psalm cxxi. 1. I will lift up mine eyes unto the hills, from whence cometh my help.

Psalm cxxi. 2. My help *cometh* from the Lord, which made heaven and earth.

4. That our health may be preserved;
5. That we may be defended from injustice and fraud;
6. That our conscience may be kept pure, and
7. That we may be encouraged to benevolence.

253. What is implied in the words, " this day" ?

By these words is implied,

1. That we do not ask for God's provisions far off in the future;

2. That we should not be anxiously concerned about our future support;

3. But confidently leave all to the Providence of God, who has for so long a time provided for all our wants.

THE APPLICATION.

254. What is the application of this petition ?

The application of this petition is

1. That we recognize our daily bread as the gift of God;

1 Corinthians iv. 7 For who maketh thee to differ *from another ?* and what hast thou that thou didst not receive? now if thou didst receive *it*, why dost thou glory, as if thou hadst not received *it ?*

2. That we partake of God's bounty with thankful hearts;

3. That we devote the strength which we derive from our food and drink to his service.

255. *Who pray this petition to their own condemnation?*

1. All avaricious and miserly people, who wish to store up many goods for many years;

2. All thieves, defrauders and unnecessary beggars, who do not eat the bread which they have honestly earned, but unjustly eat the bread of their neighbors, pray this petition to their own condemnation.

EXPLANATORY NOTES.

This petition is for our daily bread, and refers to our welfare in a temporal sense. It teaches us—

I. *That temporal things are God's gifts.* 1 Chron. xxix. 14, 16.
II. *That they may be sought in prayer* Gen. xxviii. 20.
III. *That we may pray for a competent portion of the good things of this life.* This implies all that is necessary to provide for our wants. He has promised this in his Word. Isa. xxxiii. 15, 16.
IV. *That we may daily pray for this.* We are daily dependent on God's care. We are not to be over anxious of the future. We may not boast of tomorrow. Prov. xxvii. 1.
V. *That we should seek God's blessing on temporal gifts.* Prov. x. 22. God's blessing can elevate and sanctify the least temporal benefit.

LESSONS.

1. Temporal wants should lead us to God.
2. The bread of life is God's gift for our souls.—*Steele.*

The word *bread* includes everything, which man needs, or is necessary to the support or preservation of life, in order to enjoy it with pleasure and safety. For instance, good government; that is, in the family and in the country. Yet we should also think of food for the spirit and the soul; it includes all that man requires for his body, soul and spirit. But we shall pray only for *daily bread*, because we should not pray for riches, abundance or luxury, but should be satisfied with the necessaries of life. 1 Tim. vi. 6-8; Prov. xxx. 8; Prov. xvii. 1.

The word *our* signifies, that we should not eat other people's or stolen bread, but our own, honestly earned bread. 2 Thess. iii. 10-12.

The word *give*, reminds us, that we do not have our daily bread of ourselves, or obtain it through our own ingenuity, but must ask it from God. Psalm cxxvii. 1, 2; cxxviii. 2. When God permits unbelieving persons to become rich, we should not be offended. Read Ps. lxxiii. Like Dives, they receive their good things in this world. On the other hand, pious people are often poor, because in the end it is better for them. Riches are more dangerous to piety than poverty.

The word *us* indicates that we should also cheerfully help others. 1 Tim. v. 8; Heb. xiii. 16.

The words *this day* teaches us to depend upon God *every* day, and to drive away cares. Matt. vi. 34; Luke xii. 16-21.—*Muehe.*

ANECDOTES AND ILLUSTRATIONS.

WHAT IS MEANT BY DAILY BREAD?

Scriptural Examples. Hagar, Gen. xxi. 15, 16; Israel, Ex. xvii. 1-3; Ahab, 1 Kings xxi. 4-7; John, Luke vii. 33; The rich man, Luke xii. 16-21; Jesus the True Bread, John vi. 32-35; 48-58.

In the fourth petition, (which is, *give us this day our daily bread*,) we pray, that of God's free gift we may receive a competent portion of the good things of this life, and enjoy his blessing with them.—*Shorter Catechism.*

"God has so constituted his providence that man is at all times dependent on his Maker for the comforts, and the very necessaries of life. God could no doubt have placed mankind in a different constitution of things, where praise, and not prayer, would have been the befitting exercise. Situated as he is, he is constrained to feel a sense of dependence; and of that feeling prayer is a suitable expression."—*Dr. M'Cosh.*

Prayer is by some restricted to spiritual things; but Christ in his direction teaches us to seek daily bread for food. He does not teach that men should ask for it without industry or the use of means. The ordinary providence of God shows that our daily bread comes to us by toil and the proper use of means. Yet the Savior linked us to God in this by a feeling of dependence.

"This is apparently one of the smallest, yet one of the greatest, petitions.

1. Smallness of the petition. We ask what most men already possess; we ask it only for the small circle of those around our table; we ask only daily bread; we ask it only for to-day.

2. Greatness of the petition. We ask that earthly bread should be converted into heavenly manna; we ask that he would feed all those who are in want; we ask that he would meet the daily requirements of a waiting world; we ask it to-day, and ever again to-day."—*Dr. Lange.*

Lange also says, this is a grace before meals in its widest sense ; a prayer of the husbandman ; a prayer for our ordinary calling ; a prayer for our daily work ; a prayer in our distress ; and a prayer in all our earthly wants. It is also a grace before meals in its most restricted sense.

Matthew Henry says, every word here has a lesson in it :—

1. We ask for *bread*—that teaches us sobriety and temperance. We ask for *bread*, not dainties or superfluities—that which is wholesome though it be not nice.

2. We ask for *our* bread—that teaches us honesty and industry. We do not ask the bread out of other people's mouths ; not the bread of deceit, but the bread honestly gotten.

3. We ask for our *daily* bread—which teaches us not to take thought for the morrow, but constantly to depend on Divine Providence, as those that live from hand to mouth.

4. We beg of God to *give* to us, not sell it or lend it us, but give it. The greatest of men must be beholden to God for their daily bread.

5. We pray, Give it to *us*—not to me only, but to others in common with me. This teaches us charity and a passionate concern for the poor and needy. It intimates, also, that we ought to pray with our families. We and our households eat together, and therefore ought to pray together.

6. We pray that God would give it to us *this* day—which teaches us to renew the desire of our souls towards God as the wants of our bodies are renewed. As duly as the day comes we must pray to our heavenly Father, and reckon we could as well go a day without meat as without prayer.

A traveller, overtaken in a storm, sought shelter in a dilapidated and lonely dwelling. Before entering, however, he looked through one of the gaping crevices, and saw a woman seated at a table on which was placed a coarse and scanty meal. Her hands and eyes were uplifted. Her lips moved ; and as he listened he heard her say, "*All this, and Jesus Christ too !*"

Professor Francke relates that at one time all his provision was spent ; "But in addressing myself," says he, "to the Lord, I found myself deeply affected with the fourth petition of the Lord's prayer. *Give us this day our daily bread ;* and my thoughts were fixed in a more especial manner, upon the words, *this day*, because on the very same day we had great necessity for it. While I was yet praying, a friend of mine came before my door in a coach, and brought the sum of 400 crowns."

A pious woman used to say, she should never want, because her God would supply her every need. In a time of persecution, she was taken before an unjust judge, for attending a conventicle, as they styled her offense; the judge on seeing her, rejoiced over her, and tauntingly said, "I have often wished to have you in my power, and now I shall send you to prison, and then how will you be fed?" She replied, "If it be my heavenly Father's pleasure, I shall be fed from your table." And that was literally the case; for the judge's wife being present at her examination, and being greatly struck with the good woman's firmness, took care to send her victuals from her table, so that she was comfortably supplied all the while she was in confinement; and the judge's wife found her reward, for the Lord was pleased to work on her soul, to her real conversion.

> "Through each perplexing path of life
> Our wand'ring footsteps guide;
> Give us each day our daily bread,
> And raiment fit provide "—*Doddridge.*

It is something great to have the word of God and a piece of bread.—*Ger. Proverb.*

The Germans call the bread, "*das liebe Brod,*" the dear bread, and when a piece of bread falls to the ground or floor, they reverently take it up, and kissing it, say, "We must not tread the dear bread under foot."

A poor servant, who had a wife and children to support, was once reduced to such distress, that, with the concurrence of his wife, he went to his master's flock, and brought home a lamb, which was killed, and a part of it dressed, and set on the table. The next thing to be done before their hunger could be relieved, was *to ask a blessing on the food.* The poor man's heart was filled with anguish. How could he ask a blessing from God on the fruit of unrighteousness? Tears gushed from his eyes. He rose; he went directly to his master, told him what he had done and implored his forgiveness. His master knew him to be not only a sober and industrious, but an honest and well-disposed man, and, that nothing but the greatest straits, could have tempted him to be guilty of what he had done. After a suitable admonition, he assured him of his hearty forgiveness, told him that he was welcome to what he had got, and that he should not be disappointed in any future application which he might find it necessary to make to him, for the supply of his wants. The servant returned home with joy; and with his family, he ate that food which was now his own, with gladness, and praised the Lord.

Mr. C. Winter observes, that in a time when he was destitute, and knew not where to look for a supply, he received a letter, of which the following is a copy, and which he kept, as he said, to record the kind providence of the Lord. "Dear and Rev. Sir, I enclose you twenty pounds, as I suppose your purse may be low. I commend you to the grace and love of Jesus; may he long shine upon you, and bless you. My dear friend, your's affectionately, J. THORNTON."

That ye may be the children of your Father which is in heaven: for he maketh his sun to shine on the evil and on the good, and sendeth rain on the just and on the unjust. Matt. v. 45.

Luther says in one of his sermons, that he does not believe, there are as many sheaves on the harvest fields, as there are people living in the world, and yet all are fed, which is to be attributed to the power of the grace of God.

It is recorded of the emperor, Frederick III., that when he held a diet of the empire, a great multitude of people were present, and he was apprehensive, there would not be food enough to supply them all. Therefore, he gave orders that on a certain day the whole number of loaves of bread, and the whole number of persons that were present, should be counted; and there was found to be on hand for every four or five persons, one penny worth of bread. On the following day he had a very careful investigation made, whether any persons had suffered or died from hunger. On this the answer was given, that every one had enough to eat, and a good portion of provision was yet left over. From this we see, that God still works miracles, as well as thousands of years ago.

Boetius, a distinguished nobleman, noticed on one occasion that some one had arisen from the table before the meal was over, and grace had been said, and said to him, "Dear, sir, do not act like the traitor Judas, who arose from the Holy Supper as soon as he had received the sop into his mouth, and went out to sell and betray Jesus."

You may think your children are eating with you; but, behold, you are eating with them.—*Ger. Proverb.*

The ancients relate a beautiful history. They say, "At the beginning of the creation the ears of the wheat grew from the ground up to the very top, and the stem was nowhere visible. But after man had fallen into sin, God had begun to strip off the whole ear, but in consideration of the poor little children, he permitted the ears to stand at the top; and thus, we older people can eat with the children."

When God blesses a country, he gives it a wise ruler, and a long peace.—*Ger. Proverb.*

The emperor, Augustus, used to say, "The best war is like a golden fish-hook; it seldom yields as much as it costs."

A pious prince used to say, "When this snow melts," pointing to his gray hair, "I fear there will be much mud in the country." And this came true. After his death, bad times came on.

Health. Health is rightly appreciated, only when we are sick.—*Ger. Proverb.*

He that is well does not know how rich he is.—*Ger. Proverb.*

Better a healthy beggar, than a sick king.—*Ger. Proverb.*

Good friends. One enemy is too much; a thousand friends are too few.—*Ger. Proverb.*

Good neighbors. A good neighbor is a jewel.—*Ger. Proverb.*

A polish nobleman was fatally wounded in war. King Ladislaus asked him, sympathetically, whether he had much pain? He replied, "Yes, but not near as much as I often suffered at home from my bad neighbors."

The way to heaven is easier, if we have not much to drag along. *Ger. Proverb.*

He who lives in a low estate need not fear a fall from a great height.—*Ger. Proverb*

"What great reason have you to thank God?" said a rich man to his poor neighbor, who was a weaver. "Every evening you sing thanks to him, while your trade don't bring you much gain, and you have a large family; you must have scant fare sometimes." "That is true," said the weaver, "but as regards our thanksgiving, the case is as follows: For what we have we thank God, because it does us good, and for what we do not have, we also thank God, because we do not need it."

The Rabbis say, He that receives a single benefit of this world, without thankfulness, is like one who has robbed God.

My house is my castle.—*Englishman's Proverb.*

At home I am king.—*Ger. Proverb.*

Well-doing children are the staff of their parents.—*Ger. Proverb.*

He that hath pity upon the poor lendeth unto the Lord; and that which he hath given will he pay him again. Prov. xix. 17.

When Themistocles sold his residence, he proclaimed this as one of its recommendations: "It has excellent neighbors."

When Dr. Ziegler, a learned man, left the monastery, and accepted the gospel, he prayed God to give him an honorable office and about 40 dollars, in order that he might serve God and man honorably, and make an honest living. This was granted. But when he got married, this would not suffice for his support, and he prayed for 60 dollars. This also was granted. Then came a famine into the land, and he prayed for 100 dollars. God also granted him this petition. But after he became old, the amount was again insufficient. Then he came to God, and said, "My dear Father in heaven, I have read of Abraham, that for a number of times he prayed to thee, and thou didst graciously hear and answer him. This I also have done. O do thou not be angry with me, and I will speak once more. Give me what I need, and I shall have enough for all times, and I will not prescribe anything more to thee." Upon this the Lord granted him annually 150 dollars. When the noble Elector of Saxony heard, that good old Dr Ziegler had prayed thus, he said, "He shall not eat dry bread in his old age, but he shall also have a cup of comfort (*Labe Trank*)," and granted him 200 dollars in addition.

The distinguished pastor, Oberlin, had almost constantly boys in his boarding school. One of these boys, observing Oberlin's simple mode of living, remarked, boastingly, "My father lives in a different style!" Oberlin asked him, "How many coats does your father put on?" "One," was the answer. "Well, so do I," replied Oberlin. "And how long does he continue to eat?" "Until he is satisfied." "Well, I do the same, also."

A little girl 5 or 6 years old, who had a pious mother and an unbelieving father, said to him, "Father, do you pray? Father, why don't *you* pray? Mother prays, and prays for you, too, and weeps for you. Do it, father, and pray also for me." The father, who is now a pious Christian, said, later, "This was the arrow that pierced my heart, and caused me to stand still, examine my heart and seek the Savior."

A dying father caused a bundle of arrows to be handed to his sons, requesting them to try which one of them could break it. But when not one of them was found strong enough to break the combined bundle, he ordered it to be untied, and gave a single arrow to each one of his sons, and soon they were all broken in two. Then said the father, "My dear sons, there are many of you, and you are poor, but if you combine and hold together, there will be no trouble. But if you permit yourselves to be separated, then one after the other of you will easily be overcome."

A missionary in India examined the scholars in a Christian mission school on the Scripture passage, "Pray without ceasing." (1 Thess. v. 17). He asked the question: "Is there any one here who prays without ceasing?" A small Brahmin boy arose and said, "I do sir!" "Very well, what do you say, when you pray?" "I say, Lord Jesus, be merciful to me, and save my soul!"

Poor old Hugo Bourne was asked by a friend, if he were in any need. "O," said he, smiling, "I have already partaken of three meals to-day; one when I awoke this morning, another when I arose, and I have had a third one since; ought I not to be satisfied and thankful?" But he meant spiritual food; for, although it was now eleven o'clock in the forenoon, he had not yet eaten any breakfast.

OUR BREAD.

Scriptural Examples. Adam, Gen. iii. 19; The Israelites, Joshua v. 11, 12; Peter, Luke v. 5; Paul, Acts xx. 34, 35; Abraham, Gen. xviii. 1 8; Reuel, Ex. ii. 20; Boaz, Ruth ii. 8, 9, 14-17; The widow and Elijah, 1 Kings xvii. 10-16; Elisha, 2 Kings iv. 42-44; The Corinthians and the poor Christians in Jerusalem, 2 Cor. viii., ix.; The Thessalonians, 1 Thess. iv. 9-12; Nabal, 1 Sam. xxv 11.

In the town of Anklam, Pomerania, a travelling journeyman, stood at the door of a house and asked for something to eat. As no one answered his call, he entered the house and found there a sick woman, who said to him, "I have nothing that I could give you." He departed, but after a few hours he returned The woman called to him again, "I can give you nothing; I have nothing myself." But the noble youth thought, "For that very reason I have come again." He stepped up to the table, and laid much bread upon it, and many small pieces of money, which he had collected from many persons. With a smile, he said, "These are for you, poor, sick woman." Then he softly closed the door, and departed again. The woman was the widow of a military officer by the name of Laroque, but the name of that noble young man is recorded by an angel for another occasion.

A strange brother came to the aged father, Sylvanus, at the monastery of Mount Sinai, and when he saw that the brothers worked, he said, "Why labor ye for food that perishes? But Mary hath chosen the better part." On this the Superior said to one of the brothers, "Give him a book, that he may read, and take him to an empty cell, where he may remain." When it was about three o'clock in the afternoon, the stranger looked down the road, to see whether the Superior would come and call him to dinner. But the meal time passed away, and he came not." Then the stranger could endure it no longer, but went to the Superior, and asked him, "Father, did the brothers have nothing to eat to-day?" "Yes, indeed, they have eaten." "But you did not call me to dinner." "You should not think strange of this," said the Superior, "for you are a *spiritual* man, and have no need for material food, which we, who have bodies of flesh, still need, and therefore we labor. But you, who have chosen the better part, will be able to enjoy yourself the whole day with reading, without partaking of material food." Then the stranger came to himself, and said, "Pardon me, father," and Sylvanus replied, "Mary hath need of Martha, and Mary is praised on account of Martha."

GIVE US THIS DAY.

Scriptural Examples Jacob, Gen. xxviii. 20-22; The Israelites and the manna, Ex. xvi., xvii.; Samson, Judges xv. 18, 19; Elijah, 1 Kings xvii. 1-6; The people in Samaria, 2 Kings vii.; Christ feeding the 5000, Matt. xiv. 14-21; John vi. 1-7; 4000 with seven loaves, Matt. xv. 32-38; Mark viii. 1-9; Paul, 1 Cor. iii. 5, etc.; The disciples, Matt. x. 10; Mark vi. 8.

God tries, but does not forsake his people Many years ago, there lived in Bohemia a poor laboring man, who had no employment, but he had a pious, believing wife. The husband was compelled to go on a journey, and leave his wife and child alone. Soon she had nothing to eat, and yet was ashamed to beg. For a whole day she fasted with her child, and had to go to bed hungry. Also on the second day she had nothing to eat, and her child cried for bread. The mother fell upon her knees, and prayed, and was strengthened to believe, that the Lord would help. Yet the help did not come, and mother and child had again to go to bed hungry. The child cried and could not be quieted. This agonized the heart of the mother, and she importuned with God in prayer, and obtained again a comforting assurance, that the Lord would send deliverance. But again the third day, she was compelled to retire without relief. But during the night a friend had a *dream*, in which she saw the extreme distress of the mother and her child. She arose before daylight, gathered up different kinds of provisions, and hastened to the house of the poor woman, which was over a mile away, knocked at the door, and called, "Tell me, for God's sake, is it true? I dreamed, that you have nothing to eat." With an overflowing heart, and tears of joy, the believing woman was still more strengthened in her faith on the Lord, who, indeed, tries his people, but never forgets or forsakes them.

In the terrible famine during the year 1771, there lived in Coburg a widow and her son, in great destitution. The family had formerly not been considered poor, only the famine brought them into distress. No one afforded this widow any assistance, and she herself was ashamed to complain of her sad condition to her neighbors. But she knew the good Father in heaven, and she and her son prayed to him *daily*. But one day their distress had reached its greatest degree. The dinner hour had passed and there was no food yet on the table. Then the son walked outside of the town with a heavy heart in order to pour out unseen his trouble before God. And as he thus walked along the banks of the Itz, he saw several times a fish spring up out of the water, and suddenly it jumped on the shore. He quickly secured it, and found it to be a trout fish weighing several pounds. He carried it home rejoicing, to his mother. A little salt was yet found, and thus their hunger was satisfied for several days.

Fed by a raven. At the close of the 15th century, Mathias Dalanscius, one of the Bohemian brethren, was cast into prison on account of his faith in Christ, and was in danger of starvation. One day he observed a raven on the window of his cell, with a napkin in its beak. When the raven flew away, it left the napkin lay. He took it up, and found a gold coin in it, with which he induced the keepers of the prison to buy him food.

John Godlob Anger, who afterwards became owner of an ore mine in Saxony, while a child, during the remarkable famine years of 1771 and 1772, was carried by his mother daily to a bakery. Here she left him to sit for hours near the warm oven, while she went to work as a hireling, in order that he might breathe the nourishing odor of the new bread. The compassionate baker woman, who was herself very poor, gave him accasionally a few morsels of bread. Thus the child was kept alive through the winter, in which so many poor children died of hunger.

When poor Volkmar, of Eisenach, who afterwards became a preacher, came home from school at noon and in the evening, and asked for something to eat, his mother often had to say to him, "My dear Volkmar, I have not yet reeled the yarn which I have spun; when I have done this I will go out and see where I can sell it. Do you go up stairs and kneel down and *pray* to God, that I may find some one to buy my yarn." "Thus," says Volkmar, "I learned to ask God daily for my bread, and my loving Father never left me to suffer hunger.

This day. While Francke was building the orphan house in Halle, he was on one occasion in great want, and prayed the Lord's Prayer, laying particular emphasis on the words in the fourth petition, *this day,* because he needed much just then. While he was yet praying, some one brought him one hundred dollars.

The stones must turn into bread. The sainted Professor Koenig, of Bern, was remarkably beneficent. At one time he had given away so much, that his wife had to complain, that she had no more bread or flour in the house. His reply to her complaint was, "Sooner must the stones be turned into bread, than that Professor Koenig should die of starvation." This expression of the faithful friend of the poor was almost literally fulfilled. Soon after a stranger came and begged the Professor to translate a writing for him into the German language. After three hours the stranger could come and take the translation away with him. The Professor declined to accept compensation for this work. But afterwards the stranger ordered a miller to send him a bag of flour. The Professor asked the miller the name of the kind donor. The answer was, "Von Stein," (*Van Stone.*) "Do you hear," said the Professor to his wife, "Do you hear this, you unbelieving woman! The stranger's name is Van Stone! Did I not tell you, 'Sooner must the stones be turned into bread, than that Professor Koenig should die of starvation.'"

ENABLE US TO RECEIVE OUR DAILY BREAD WITH THANKSGIVING.

Scripture Examples. Jacob, Gen. xxviii. 21, 22; Christ, Mark xiv. 8; John vi. 11; Matt. xv. 36; Mark viii. 6, 7; Matt. xxvi. 26, 30; Paul, Acts xxvii. 35; The Israelites, Ex. xvi. 3, 20, 27-36; Ex. xvii. 1-6; xxxii. 6; The later Israelites, Isaiah i. 3; Jer. v. 23, 24.

On the 9th of June, 1532, Dr. Luther was walking in his garden. There had been a severe drought in the land; no rain had fallen for a long time. When he saw that all vegetation had dried up, he prayed as follows: "Oh God, thou didst say to king David, that thou art nigh to all who call upon thee, all who call upon thee with importunity. How comes it, then, that thou doest not grant us rain, although we have long been praying and crying to thee? Very well, if thou givest us no rain, thou wilt give us something better. Peace on earth and a small portion of food is still better than a fruitful year, which the enemy consumes. But dear heavenly Father, O do thou be prevailed upon, for the sake of thy dear Son, Jesus Christ, who has said, 'Verily, verily, I say unto you, Whatsoever ye shall ask the Father in my name, that will I do, that the Father may be glorified in the Son.'

Now we would have to be ashamed before thine enemies; to be continually preaching this in the churches, if thou wouldst not answer us. I know that we cry from our hearts, and long and sigh; O hear us, Good Lord!" Thus did this man talk with God in faith, and his prayer was immediately heard and answered.

A poor young man, who desired to study for the ministry, came to a place where he was a stranger, in order to attend the high school. But after he was there some time, he took sick, and was for a long time confined to his bed. His small amount of money was soon spent for doctors' bills and medicine. At last, by God's blessing, he was restored to health, and had a strong appetite. But alas, not much with which to appease his hunger. On a certain Sunday he sat in his room, at noon, without a sixpence in his pocket, and no bread, while he was suffering with an intense hunger. All at once he heard a slight noise in a corner of his room. He looked carefully in the direction whence the sound came, and behold, it was a little mouse, knawing at a crust of bread. He approached the place, the mouse crept away, but left the crust. This had lain there a long time, and was very dry; yet it was not too mean for the hungry youth. He took it hastily in his hand, but would not partake of it without prayer. He therefore laid that dry crust on the table, and prayed that God would bless this small morsel of food to the strengthening of his body, as if it were a large quantity of food. The good Lord heard his prayer, and yet in a different way from what he had thought, and gave him more food than he needed. For before he had finished his prayer, there came the servant of a nobleman, who lived in the neighborhood, and had heard of the circumstances of the poor student, and brought him three plates full of warm food. Then he rejoiced and thanked God anew, who had so mercifully helped him in his time of need.

While Captain Gambier was in Otaheite, a number of natives visited him on his ship, where he sometimes invited them to take dinner with him. When he did this the first time, through an oversight no blessing was asked at the table. To his surprise he observed, that the poor natives did not begin to eat. For a long time he did not know the reason, until he learned, that they waited till a blessing should be asked, and would not eat until this was done.

THE FIFTH PETITION.

256. *What is the Fifth Petition?*

"And forgive us our tresspasses, as we forgive those who tresspass against us."

257. How is this to be understood?

We pray in this petition

1. That our heavenly Father would not regard our sins, nor deny us our requests on account of them;

2. For we are not worthy of anything for which we pray, and have not merited it;

3. But we pray that he would grant us all things through grace, although we daily commit many sins and deserve only chastisement;

4. We will therefore, on our part, both heartily forgive, and also do good to those who may injure or offend us.

THE MEANING OF THE WORDS.

258. How do the trespasses occur?

The trespasses, of which there are many, occur when we do not obey God's commands according to the law or the gospel, for then we become debtors to God.

Psalm xl. 12. For innumerable evils have compassed me about: mine iniquities have taken hold upon me, so that I am not able to look up; they are more than the hairs of mine head: therefore my heart faileth me.

Acts xvi. 30. And brought them out, and said, Sirs, what must I do to be saved?

Acts xvi. 31. And they said, Believe on the Lord Jesus Christ, and thou shalt be saved, and thy house.

259. Wherein do these trespasses consist?

Our trespasses consist in our refusing or neglecting to do, or to suffer anything that God requires of us.

260. Why do we say " our trespasses"?

We say "our trespasses" because we ourselves have committed them, as disobedient children against their loving Father, which we cannot deny, and therefore make *ourselves* responsible for them.

Ezekiel xviii. 20. The soul that sinneth, it shall die. The son shall not bear the iniquity of the father, neither shall the father bear the iniquity of the son: the righteousness of the righteous shall be upon him, and the wickedness of the wicked shall be upon him.

261. Why do we pray "forgive us"?

By the words "forgive us," we confess, that,

1. We ourselves cannot make satisfaction for our past sins;

2. For, if we could *henceforth* perform all the duties which we owe to God, we could not make satisfaction for our past sins;

Luke xvii. 10. So likewise ye, when ye shall have done all those things which are commanded you, say, We are unprofitable servants: we have done that which was our duty to do.

3. Because we owe all our powers of body and of mind now and always to God;

4. Also we pray God to forgive us, because he does not require satisfaction for our trespasses from us, but from another; namely, the satisfaction which Christ has wrought out for us.

1 John ii. 2. And he is the propitiation for our sins: and not for our's only, but also for *the sins of* the whole world.

262. What is meant when we pray, "As we forgive those who trespass against us"?

In this petition we promise, that

1. We will heartily forgive those who have sinned against us, and not avenge ourselves, but patiently endure injuries;

Romans xii. 19 Dearly beloved, avenge not yourselves, but rather give place unto wrath: for it is written, Vengeance is mine; I will repay, saith the Lord.

2. And that God will forgive us, or treat us just as we treat our neighbor; namely, that he would forgive our sins, when we forgive those who have trespassed against us; and on the other hand, that he would not forgive, when we do not forgive.

Matthew vi. 14. For if ye forgive men their trespasses, your heavenly Father will also forgive you.

263. What is the application of this petition?

We pray in this petition, that

1. God would not look upon our sins and unworthiness, nor deny us this prayer, because we are not deserving of the least of his mercies;

<small>Genesis xxxii. 10. I am not worthy of the least of all the mercies, and of all the truth, which thou hast shewed unto thy servant; for with my staff I passed over this Jordan; and now I am two bands.</small>

2. That God would forgive our sins out of his free grace for Christ's sake;

3. That this should lead us to reconciliation with those who have injured us.

<small>Matthew xviii. 21. Then came Peter to him, and said, Lord, how oft shall my brother sin against me, and I forgive him? till seven times?
Matthew xviii. 22. Jesus saith unto him, I say not unto thee, Until seven times: but, Until seventy times seven.</small>

264. Who pray this petition to their own condemnation?

All those pray this petition to their own condemnation,

1. Who trust for salvation in their own good works;

2. Who do not acknowledge themselves to be sinners;

<small>Luke xviii. 11. The Pharisee stood and prayed thus with himself, God, I thank thee, that I am not as other men *are*, extortioners, unjust, adulterers, or even as this publican.
Luke xviii. 12. I fast twice in the week, I give tithes of all that I possess.</small>

3. Also, all revengeful and malicious people, who are unwilling to forgive others their faults.

<small>Mark xi. 25. And when ye stand praying, forgive, if ye have ought against any: that your Father also which is in heaven may forgive you your trespasses.
Mark xi. 26. But if ye do not forgive, neither will your Father which is in heaven forgive your trespasses.</small>

EXPLANATORY NOTES.

I. *Sin is a debt to the law of God.* It is one which we cannot pay. We are dependent on God's mercy for our forgiveness. God has revealed his mercy: Ex. xxxiv. 6, 7; Isa. lv. 6, 7; Micah vii. 18.

II. *This petition seeks forgiveness.*
1. We may pray for the pardon of sin, since God has offered to forgive us. He only can forgive: Luke v. 21; Rom. viii. 33.

2. We can pray for it only for Christ's sake. He is the mediator: Eph. i. 7.
3. We may pray in faith. God has pledged his word. He has sent his Son to be the propitiation for our sins: 1 John iv. 10.
4. We may pray for a free pardon. Such God gives: Rom. iii. 24.
5. We may ask a full pardon: Ps. ciii. 1-3; 1 John i. 7.

III. *This petition asserts our willingness to forgive others.* It is a duty to forgive those who sin against us.

We need grace to enable us to forgive others.

IV. *Our forgiveness of others is our encouragement to ask forgiveness for ourselves from God.*
1. God has connected these: Matt. vi. 14, 15.
2. The example of Christ enforces it: Luke xxiii. 34; 1 Peter ii. 23.
3. We cannot expect forgiveness from God if we have an unforgiving spirit to others: Matt. xviii. 24-35.

LESSONS.

1. Forgiveness of sins is essential to peace with God.
2. Let us cultivate a forgiving spirit.—*Steel.*

The forgiveness of our sins is as necessary as our daily bread Without the forgiveness of sins, God must deny us all our other petitions and leave them unanswered. But because we sin daily, we deserve only punishment. Rom. iii. 23. There are four kinds of sins:

1. Sins of thought;
2. Sins of words;
3. Sins of actions; and
4. Sins of omission.

Sins have also been divided into pardonable and unpardonable; that is, such as extinguish the spiritual life entirely, and cause eternal death.

Therefore we must pray daily for forgiveness; but God will not forgive us, unless we have a forgiving heart towards those who have tresspassed against us. If we do not forgive those who have injured us, God will not forgive us. Matt. vi. 14, 15. Read Matt. xviii. 21.—*Muehe.*

ANECDOTES AND ILLUSTRATIONS.

AND FORGIVE US—FOR WE DAILY SIN.

Scriptural Examples David, Psalm xix. 13; Psalm li.; Rehoboam, 2 Chron. xii. 12; The sinner, Luke vii. 37; The Publican, Luke xviii. 13; The wicked servant, Matt. xviii. 23-27; Cain, Gen. iv. 13; Abimelech, Judges ix 56, 57; Abraham, Gen xviii. 23-33; Moses, Ex. xxxii. 11-13; Ex. xxxiv. 9; Israel, Judges x. 10-17; Daniel ix. 5.

In the fifth petition, (which is, *And forgive us our tresspasses as we forgive those who tresspass against us,*) we pray, That God, for Christ's sake, would pardon all our sins; which we are the rather encouraged to ask, because by his grace we are enabled from our heart to forgive others. —*Shorter Catechism*

"*This is the prayer of penitence,* 'Forgive us our tresspasses.' 1. It realizes sin, and realizes it as a debt. 2. It realizes the burden of sin resting on mankind generally. 3. It realizes forgiveness as a free grace and a free gift. True penitence appears in the prayer of faith. Assurances of forgiveness call forth the prayer, "Forgive us.' Forgiveness and readiness to forgive cannot be separated.

There is a connection between the two: 1. Forgiveness makes us ready to forgive; 2. Readiness to forgive inspires us with courage to seek forgiveness; 3. The spirit of forgiveness ever joins the two more closely together.

He who cannot forgive man cannot find forgiveness with God;— (1.) because he will not believe in forgiving love; (2) because he will not act upon its directions." –*Dr. Lange.*

Dr. Cotton Mather was remarkable for the sweetness of his temper. He took some interest in the political concerns of his country, and on this account, as well as because he faithfully reproved iniquity, he had many enemies. Many abusive letters were sent, all of which he tied up in a packet, and wrote upon the cover, "Libels: Father forgive them."

A gentleman once asked Sir Eardley Wilmot, Lord Chief-Justice of the Court of Common Pleas in England, if he did not think it manly to resent an injury which he had received from a person in a high political position. "Yes," said the judge, "it will be manly to resent it, but it will be Godlike to forgive it." The gentleman felt the observation, and went home in a different temper from that in which he came.

The Marquis of Argyle, who suffered death in the reign of Charles II., on whose head he had put the crown of Scotland at Scone, was employed on the morning of the day of his execution in settling his worldly affairs. Under the influence of a sensible effusion of spiritual joy, he said to those about him, "I am now ordering my affairs, and God is sealing my charter to a better inheritance, and just now saying to me, 'Son, be of good cheer; thy sins are forgiven thee.'" Having with great cheerfulness dined with his friends, he retired a little. Upon his opening the door, the Rev. Mr. Hutchison said, "What cheer, my lord?" He replied, "Good cheer. The Lord has again confirmed, and said to me from heaven, 'Thy sins be forgiven thee.'"

> "Consider this,—
> That, in the course of justice, none of us
> Should see salvation: we do pray for mercy;
> And that same prayer doth teach us all to render
> The deeds of mercy."
> "How shalt thou hope for mercy, rendering none?"
> —*Shakespeare.*

When Tetzel was at Leipsic, and had collected a great deal of money from all ranks of people, a nobleman, who suspected the imposition, put the question to him: "Can you grant absolution for a sin which a man shall intend to commit in future?" "Yes," replied the frontless commissioner, "but on condition that the proper sum of money be actually paid down." The nobleman instantly produced the sum demanded; and in return, received a diploma, sealed and signed by Tetzel, absolving him from the unexplained crime, which he secretly intended to commit. Not long after, when Tetzel was about to leave Leipsic, the nobleman made inquiry respecting the road he would probably travel, waited for him in ambush at a convenient place, attacked and robbed him; then beat him soundly with a stick, sent him back again to Leipsic with his chest empty, and at parting said, "This is the fault I intended to commit, and for which I have your absolution."

A poor little African Negro, only ten years of age, went to hear the preaching of one of the missionaries, and became through his instrumentality, a convert to the Christian religion. His master, (an inveterate enemy to missions,) hearing of it, commanded him never to go again, and declared he would have him whipped to death if he did. The poor little boy in consequence of this mandate, was very miserable. He could scarcely refrain from going, yet he knew his death was inevitable if he did. In this critical situation, he sought direction and assistance at the throne of grace, and after having done this, he felt convinced that it was still his duty to attend, but to be careful that he should never interfere with his master's business, and, for the rest, to leave himself in the hands of God. He therefore went, and on his return, was summoned to his master's presence; and after much violent and abusive language, received five-and-twenty lashes, and then in a sarcastic tone of blasphemous ridicule, his master exclaimed, "What can Jesus Christ do for you now?" "He enables me to bear it patiently," said the poor child. "Give him five-and-twenty lashes more," said the inhuman wretch. He was obeyed. "And what can Jesus Christ do for you now?" asked the unfeeling monster. "He helps me to look forward to a future reward," replied the little sufferer. "Give him five-and-twenty lashes more," vociferated the cruel tyrant, in a transport of rage. They complied; and while he listened with savage delight to the extorted groans of his dying victim, he again demanded, "What can Jesus Christ do for you now?" The youthful martyr, with the last effort of expiring nature, meekly answered, "He enables me *to pray for you, massa.*" And instantly breathed his last!

In a school at Youghall, in the master's accidental absence, one boy having been provoked, struck another. On hearing the complaint, the master determined to punish the culprit, when the aggrieved boy entreated pardon for the offender. On being asked, why he would interpose to prevent a just example, he said, "I was reading in the New Testament lately, that Jesus Christ said, we should forgive our enemies, and I wish to forgive him, and I beg he may not be punished for my sake." This Christian plea was too powerful to be resisted. The offender was pardoned, and the parent of the poor boy was highly pleased at the circumstance.

Martin Luther and the Roll. After a time of great trial, Luther tells us, he was seeking rest in sleep; and he saw as sleep came to him —in his dream he saw—Satan standing at the foot of his bed. And Satan jeeringly said to him: "Martin, thou art a pretty Christian! Hast thou got the impudence to assume that thou art a Christian?"— "Yes," said Martin, "I am a Christian, Satan, because Christ has allowed me, as any sinner may, to come to him." "What!" said Satan, "thou a Christian? Martin! See what thou hast done!" And Satan took a roll and began to unroll it; and there at its head Martin Luther saw some sins set down that had passed away in the dim distance of childhood. He had forgotton them. Martin sank as it struck his sight, but the roll was unrolled, leaf after leaf, foot after foot, and to his horror he saw sin after sin of which he remembered nothing any more, written down there, complete in every detail—an awful list; and in his dream, he says, the sweat of mortal agony stood on his brow. He thought, "In truth, Satan has got right on his side. Can such a sinner as this be just with God?" He said, "Unroll it!" and Satan jeeringly unrolled it, and Luther thought it would never end. At last he came nearly to the end, and in desperation he cried, "Let us see the end!" But, as the last foot of the paper rolled out he caught sight of some writing red as blood, at the end, and his eye caught the words, "The blood of Jesus Christ, his Son, cleanseth us from all sin." And the vision of Satan floated away, and Luther says he went to sleep. Ah, yes, dear friends, that is it. The Savior deigns to wash away even the unknown defilements of his child's soul. "The blood of Jesus Christ, his Son, cleanseth from all sin."

The sainted John Arndt, author of the *True Christianity*, was very much slandered and persecuted on account of his earnest piety and evangelical doctrines. He had the habit of reverently uncovering his head and praying, when he heard the words in the hymn, "In thee have I put my trust," and "The world has judged me with deceit." When asked, why he did so, he replied, "When I hear these words, I am always reminded of the grace of my God, which he imparts to me by means of mine enemies and slanderers; for thereby he promotes my growth in true Christianity, inasmuch as against their own will, my piety, prayers, and devotion are increased, so that I become so much more holy and consecrated." This accords exactly with the words of Christ, "Blessed are ye, when men shall revile you and persecute you, and shall say all manner of evil against you, falsely, for my sake. Rejoice and be exceeding glad, for great is your reward in heaven; for so persecuted they the prophets which were before you." Matt. v. 11, 12.

On the *give* follows immediately the *forgive.—Ger. Proverb.*

A man without forgiveness of sins is like a man who sleeps, while his house is burning.

Over the portal of perdition stands written, "Your deserved reward;" Over the gate of heaven, "The grace and mercy of your God."

We daily sin. Abraham Buchholzer used to say, "Would to God, we were as much dissatisfied with ourselves in life, as we shall be dissatisfied with ourselves, when we come to die, then we would pray the fifth petition more deeply from the heart."

To the fifth petition we must first bring a heart filled with faith, and then also a heart filled with love.

The wise king Alphonsus, of Arragon, (1327-1361) was very angry with some of his courtiers, who had become unfaithful to him, and to whom he had shown many favors. But soon he came to reflection, and said: "O merciful Lord God, thou hast shown me much more kindness! If thou hadst been thus angry only once at my unthankful heart, what would have become of me? O give me a heart that can overlook the ingratitude of the world."

Just as a candle burns bright in the darkness, yet not without occassional smoke, but when the sun shines, is regarded as no light at all, so it is with the greatest piety of men in this life, when it is brought before the just and holy God.

A brother had sinned, and the elder in the congregation commanded him to leave the assembly, because he was not worthy hence forth to dwell among them. Then the sainted, pious church father, Besorean, arose and went out with him, saying, "I beg pardon, my brethren; '*I am also a sinner.*'"

Franciscus Vatelius, king of France, who died in the year 1547, came across the words in Psalm cxliii. 2, "O Lord, enter not into judgment with thy servant; for in thy sight shall no man living be justified." These words he repeated more than a hundred times.

Luther once heard his wife scold the servants for some mischief they had committed. Luther heard this and said to her, "Dear Katie, did you also pray the Lord's Prayer before your sermon?"

This petition lays three things upon our hearts:
1. That we regard and feel our sins as a debt, or tresspass. From this flows repentance and sorrow; and consequently follows,
2. The prayer for forgiveness. Are you assured in your heart of forgiveness,
3. Then you will *forgive*.

THEN WE WILL ALSO FORGIVE THOSE WHO HAVE TRESSPASSED AGAINST US—HEARTILY.

Scriptural Examples. Moses, Numbers xii. 13; David, 1 Samuel xxiv.; 1 Samuel xxvi.; 2 Samuel xix. 22, 23; Christ, Luke xxiii. 34; Stephen, Acts vii. 59; Paul, 2 Tim. iv. 16; Peter, Matt. xviii. 21, 22.

A young converted New Zealand woman had been slandered. When she found this out, she expressed herself as follows: "Although the Jews crucified Christ, yet the gospel was preached to them nevertheless; and thus I also hope to pray for those who slandered me, and to wish them well."

On one occasion there came a woman to Halle, who declared, that when the church spires would lie down upon the ground, then she would lay down her hatred towards her mother-in-law; for she had treated her so badly. On this, Prof. A. H. Francke said to her, "This does not surprise me, for I feel sure, you are not able to become reconciled to your mother-in-law. That can be possible to you only then, when you call on God for forgiving grace. I entreat you, therefore, most earnestly, that you promise me to pray to God for a *forgiving heart.*" The woman could not refuse to comply with this request. After a few days she came again, and said, " Now I will go and become reconciled with my mother-in-law." She did this; and when the Professor asked her, why she had not sooner sought reconciliation, she replied, " You often exhorted me to become reconciled, but you never told me how I should do it; you never instructed me that I must pray to God for a forgiving heart."

A young Monk once came to a pious Abbot, and told him, he was going to avenge himself for an injustice that had been done him. When the Abbot could not change his mind from his purpose, he said to him, "Well, then, let us kneel down and pray." Then he prayed as follows: "Eternal, Almighty God, thou art no longer worth anything to us, and especially to this, my young brother; for, as he says, we shall and must avenge *ourselves.* Vengeance does no longer belong to thee!" (Rom. xii 19.) This alarmed the young Monk, and he became penitent and reformed.

An angry nobleman once sent his neighbor, John Brune, word, that he and his people should never presume to tread upon his ground or premises. Brune sent him word in return, that if he, the nobleman, or any of his people, should wish to come upon his ground or premises, they would be heartily welcome; or if they should come into his house, he would be still better pleased. This friendly reply overcame the pride of the nobleman, and affected him to tears. He came to his nighbor and was reconciled to him.

WE MUST HEARTILY FORGIVE AND DO GOOD TO THOSE WHO INJURE US.

Scriptural Examples. Abraham, Gen. xiii. 8, 9; xiv. 14-16; Esau and Jacob, Gen. xxxiii. 1-4; Joseph, Gen. l. 19-21; Samson, Judges xv. 5-7; Peter, Matt. xxvi. 51; The wicked servant, Matt. xviii. 28-35.

A chaplain in the English Navy, going out to preach on board a ship, passed by a vessel where he overheard a quarrel between the captain and a sailor. As he did not hear them swear, he concluded, that they were Christians, and invited both to come to the preaching, and take part in the service. The captain thought he was not in the proper state of mind, but the sailor promised to come. As the chaplain arrived on board the ship, on which the service was to be held, the captain thought the assembly was yet too small, and rowing out with the boat, invited the neighboring captains and sailors, and had the satisfaction to induce many to come; so that the whole cabin was filled. Among them came also the captain who had had the quarrel. The assembly had just been seated as another man came in; it was the sailor who had been quarreling with his captain. As there was not another seat vacant, the captain arose, gave the sailor his own seat, and himself stood in a corner.

In Antioch lived a Greek Presbyter by the name of *Lapricius*, and another Christian by the name of *Nicephorus*, who had long been the most intimate friends. But on one occasion they fell into a dispute, and became so hostile to one another that they would not speak to each other. Nicephorus first came to reflection, and sent a messenger to the Presbyter with an offer for a reconciliation. But as the messenger returned for the second time without an answer, he went himself, prostrated himself at the feet of his enemy, and begged, "Forgive me, father, for the sake of the Lord." But the Presbyter remained unmoved. Not long after this a persecution broke out, in which Lapricius, who had been a firm and steadfast believer, was condemned to death. He walked with great joyfulness toward the place of his death. Nicephorus ran to meet him on the way to execution, fell down before him, and cried, "O thou witness of Christ, forgive me!" But the martyr walked silently past him. Once more Nicephorus renewed his petition, but in vain. The executioners derided him as a fool, because, they said, he begged forgiveness of a condemned criminal. Now they had arrived at the place of execution, and Nicephorus called out, "O it is written, Ask, and it shall be given you." But even the word of God made no impression on the implacable man. But just as Lapricius was told to kneel down to receive the death-stroke, he felt himself forsaken of God. "Hold on," he cried, "I will offer sacrifice to the idols!" Then Nicephorus called out to him, "O sin not, my brother, do not apostatize, cast not away the crown that shall so soon be yours." But all in vain. Then Nicephorus turned to the executioners and said, "I believe on the name of the Lord Jesus Christ, whom he has denied; therefore put me to death!" Astonished, the rude executioners bring the marvelous account to the governor. Nicephorus was beheaded, and Lapricius was brought back to offer sacrifice to the idols.

In one of the wars between Denmark and Sweden, a Danish soldier on the field of battle had with a great effort obtained a bottle of water, with which he was about to quench his thirst. But just as he was going to drink, he heard the cry of an enemy, lying near by, both of whose legs were shot off, and who made a sign, begging for a drink. The Dane stooped down to the wounded Swede, and was about to give him a drink, before even he himself had tasted it. But in that moment the treacherous Swede fired a pistol at his benefactor, which fortunately missed its aim. Quietly the Dane took the bottle back, drank it half empty, then handed it back to the dying Swede, saying, "See, now you only get half of it."

Henry VII., who became German emperor in the year 1309, was desirous of restoring the Roman empire to its original dimensions, and made an effort to regain Mailand and Florence. On his journey in his return, some of his enemies instigated a Florentine Monk to poison him by administering a poisoned wafer at the Lord's Supper. As soon as the emperor felt that the bread was poisoned, he said secretly to the Monk, "Thou hast given me the bread of life to produce my death. Flee, lest my servants arrest thee, and put thee to death! Repent of your crime; for God has no pleasure in the death of the sinner, but rather that he should turn and live."

A chamberlain of an English bishop had committed a crime, and Hale, the conscientious presiding judge, had him punished, as the law prescribed. When Hale saw that this had offended the bishop, he said to him, "Do you think, if God should ask me, why I favored this criminal, that I should answer, 'Because he is the chamberlain of a bishop?'"

THE SIXTH PETITION.

265. What is the Sixth Petition?

"And lead us not into temptation."

266. What is meant by this petition?

1. God, indeed, tempts no one to sin;

2. But we pray in this petition, that God would so guard and preserve us, that the devil, the world and our own flesh may not deceive us, nor lead us into error and unbelief, despair and other great and shameful sins;

3. And that, though we may be thus tempted, we may nevertheless finally prevail and gain the victory.

THE MEANING OF THE WORDS.

267. What is meant by "temptation"?

Temptation is the trial of a person, in order that the nature of his heart may become evident to himself and others.

Deuteronomy viii. 2. And thou shalt remember all the way which the Lord thy God led thee these forty years in the wilderness, to humble thee, and to prove thee, to know what was in thine heart, whether thou wouldest keep his commandments, or no.

268. How many kinds of temptations or trials are there?

There are two kinds of temptations or trials; namely, good and evil temptations.

269. What is a good temptation or trial?

A good temptation or trial is one that is designed for our good, as for example, when God tempts or tries us

1. By his commandments;

Psalm lxvi. 10. For thou, O God, hast proved us: thou hast tried us, as silver is tried.

2. Or by his benefits;

Romans ii. 4. Or despisest thou the riches of his goodness and forbearance and long-suffering; not knowing that the goodness of God leadeth thee to repentance?

3. Or by the hiding of his face, as in misfortune, trouble and suffering, he reveals as a loving Father, the good that is in our hearts.

2 Chronicles xxxii. 31. Howbeit in the business of the embassadors of the princes of Babylon, who sent unto him to enquire of the wonder that was done in the land, God left him, to try him, that he might know all *that was* in his heart.

270. What is an evil temptation or trial?

An evil temptation or trial is, that in which a person is influenced or induced to commit sin.

271. By what means are people influenced to commit sin?

People are tempted to sin

1. By Satan;

Matthew iv. 3. And when the tempter came to him, he said, If thou be the Son of God, command that these stones be made bread.

2. By bad people in the world, or

Proverbs i. 10. My son, if sinners entice thee, consent thou not.

3. By their own evil inclinations or passions; namely, into unbelief, impatience and other sins.

James i. 13. Let no man say when he is tempted, I am tempted of God: for God cannot be tempted with evil, neither tempteth he any man.

James i. 14. But every man is tempted, when he is drawn away of his own lust, and enticed.

272. *What is meant when we pray " lead us not into temptation " ?*

By this we mean,

1. That God would preserve us from the opportunity or occasion of falling into sin;

Luke xxii. 40. And when he was at the place, he said unto them, Pray that ye enter not into temptation.

2. That in such temptations he would preserve us from falling into sin;

Matthew xxvi. 41. Watch and pray, that ye enter not into temptation: the spirit indeed *is* willing, but the flesh *is* weak.

3. That he would grant us the power to overcome the temptations;

Ephesians vi 10. Finally, my brethren, be strong in the Lord, and in the power of his might.

1 John v. 4. For whatsoever is born of God overcometh the world: and this is the victory that overcometh the world, *even* our faith.

4. And overrule them for our good and his glory.

1 Corinthians x. 13. There hath no temptation taken you, but such as is common to man: but God *is* faithful, who will not suffer you to be tempted above that ye are able: but will with the temptation also make a way to escape, that ye may be able to bear *it*.

THE APPLICATION.

273. *What is the application of this petition?*

The application of this petition is

1. That God tempts no one to do evil;

James i. 13. Let no man say when he is tempted, I am tempted of God: for God cannot be tempted with evil, neither tempteth he any man,

2. That we should pray for the overruling for good results of our temptations.

Luke xxii. 31. And the Lord said, Simon, Simon, behold, Satan hath desired *to have* you, that he may sift you as wheat.

Luke xxii. 32. But I have prayed for thee, that thy faith fail not: and when thou art converted, strengthen thy brethren.

274. *Who pray this petition to their own condemnation?*

Those pray this petition to their own condemnation,

1. Who seek occasion to sin;

Micah ii. 1. Woe to them that devise iniquity, and work evil upon their beds! when the morning is light, they practice it, because it is in the power of their hand.

2. Who willingly permit themselves to be led into sin by others.

Psalm xxxvi. 4. He deviseth mischief upon his bed; he setteth himself in a way *that is* not good; he abhorreth not evil.

EXPLANATORY NOTES.

This petition recognizes the fact that the soul, while in this world, is in danger of sin, and needs always to be watchful, and dependent on divine grace.

I. *We are taught here to pray that God would keep us from being tempted to sin.*
   1. God cannot tempt us to sin (James i. 13), but he may permit us to be tempted, to try our faith and obedience.
   2. Satan is a tempter. He tempted our Lord: Matt. iv. 1-10. He tempts us: 1 Cor. vii. 5. He is malicious, insinuating, and persevering in effort.
   3. People tempt one another: 1 Kings xxi. 7; Gen. xxxix. 7-12.
   4. The sinful heart tempts by its own lusts: James i. 14.
   5. The world tempts us: 1 Tim. vi. 9, 10; 2 Tim. iv. 10.

II. *That God would support and deliver us when we are tempted.*
   We cannot expect to be free from temptation; but by divine grace we may overcome, and escape the evil. For this we may pray: 1 Chron. iv. 10.
   1. That we may not yield to sin.
   2. That we may be delivered from the lusts of the flesh.
   3. That we may be preserved amidst temptations from the world.
   4. That we may be delivered from the snares of the devil: Matt. xiii. 19.
   5. That our faith may be strengthened to overcome the world, the devil, and the flesh.

III. *God has promised grace to support us:* 1 Cor. x. 13.
    1. He knows how to deliver us: 2 Peter ii. 9.
    2. He has delivered his people: Ps. lvi. 13.
    3. Christ prayed that we may be kept from evil: John xvii. 15.

LESSONS.

    1. We should dread sin more than suffering.
    2. We should watch and pray, that we enter not into temptation.—*Steel.*

This petition treats of temptation to do evil. There are three enemies, who would lead us into temptation; namely, 1. The devil; 2. The world, and 3. The flesh. We have had our attention directed to them in the third petition. All three would deceive us and lead us into falsehood and unbelief and bring us into trouble. The devil does this usually in this way:
    1. He fills us with evil thoughts;
    2. He induces us to commit sin;
    3. He misleads us into unbelief;
    4. Finally he casts us into despair, shame, and crime.

Of this we have examples in Cain and Judas. We shall and can overcome the devil.

The *world* (that is worldly minded, sinful people) tempts us,
    1. By ungodly company;
    2. By evil examples;
    3. By flattering promises;
    4. By fearful threatnings. Example: Joseph, Prov. i. 10.

The *flesh* tempts us, when the sinful passions and desires of our hearts are awakened. James i. 14, 15.

Here we pray to God, that he would give us strength, to overcome and gain the victory over all those three enemies. 1 Cor. x. 13; James i. 12.

Paul has plainly described the proper weapons of our warfare against these foes. Eph. vi. 10-17.

ANECDOTES AND ILLUSTRATIONS.

In the sixth petition (which is *Lead us not into temptation, but deliver us from evil*), we pray, that God would either keep us from being tempted, or support and deliver us when we are tempted.—*Shorter Catechism.*

An old divine remarked that we may not pray to be kept from suffering, but we may always pray to be kept from sinning.

"Temptation will give oil and fuel to our lusts; incite, provoke, and make them tumultuate and rage beyond measure. Tendering a lust, a corruption, a suitable object, advantage, occasion, it heightens and exasperates it, makes it for a season wholly predominant: so dealt it with carnal fear in Peter, with pride in Hezekiah, with covetousness in Achan, with uncleanness in David, with worldliness in Demas, with ambition in Diotrephes. It will lay the reins on the neck of a lust, and put spurs to the sides of it, that it may rush forward like a horse into battle. A man knows not the pride, fury, madness of a corruption, until it meet with a suitable temptation.

"Temptation is like a knife, that may either cut the meat or the throat of a man; it may be his food or his poison, his exercise or his destruction.

"Let no man pretend to fear sin that doth not fear temptation to it. They are too nearly allied to be separated. Satan hath put them so together that it is very hard for any man to put them asunder. He hates not the fruit that delights in the root.

"What, think you, are the thoughts, and what the heart of Christ, when he sees a temptation hastening towards us, a storm rising about us, and we are fast asleep? Does it not grieve him to see us expose ourselves so to danger, after he has given us warning upon warning?"
—*Dr. Owen.*

How many have been tempted to drink, and yielding, have been ruined! How many have been tempted to take money not their own, and lost honesty and place! How many have been tempted to sin once, and have gone down the inclined plane to disgrace and misery!

The great resource in temptation is prayer and watching.

A fleet of a hundred vessels lay at anchor in a port of the Mediterranean, when a fearful storm burst upon them, and drove all save one upon the shore. The wonder was how that one could have held its anchorage. It was found that its anchor had grappled into another which lay firmly embedded in the bottom of the sea. So the soul anchored to Christ, as in the cleft of the Rock of Ages, will be able to outride all the storms of temptation.

> " Go to dark Gethsemane,
>   Ye that feel the tempter's power;
>   Your Redeemer's conflict see;
>   Watch with him one bitter hour:
>   Turn not from his griefs away;
>   Learn of Jesus Christ to pray."—*Hart.*

Dr. Pendleton and Mr. Saunders, meeting together in the beginning of Queen Mary's reign, and speaking of the persecution which would likely arise, with regard to which Mr. Saunders discovered much weakness and fear; Pendleton on the other hand, boasted of his resolution, that he would endure the severest treatment, rather than forsake Jesus Christ, and the truth which he had professed. Yet not long after, poor, feeble, faint-hearted Saunders, through the goodness of God, sealed the truth with his blood, while proud Pendleton played the apostate, and turned papist.

A plain countryman, who was effectually called by divine grace under a sermon from Zech. iii. 2, was some time afterwards accosted by a quondam companion of his drunken fits, and strongly solicited to accompany him to the ale house. But the good man strongly resisted all his arguments, saying, "I am a brand plucked out of the fire." His old companion not understanding this, he explained it thus: "Look ye," said he, "there is a great difference between a brand and a green stick; if a spark flies upon a brand that has been partly burned, it will soon catch fire again; but it is not so with a green stick. I tell you I am that brand plucked out of the fire, and I dare not venture into the way of temptation for fear of being set on fire."

One night Mr. Newton found a bill put up at St. Mary Woolnoth's, upon which he commented a great deal when he came to preach. The bill was to this effect, "A young man, having come to the possession of a very considerable fortune, desires the prayers of the congregation, that he may be preserved from the snares to which it exposes him."—"Now, if the man," said Mr. Newton, "had lost a fortune, the world would not have wondered to have seen him put up a bill, but *this* man has been better taught."

GOD TEMPTS NO ONE TO SIN, BUT ONLY FOR GOOD

Scriptural Examples. Through God's commands and directions, Adam and Eve, Gen. ii. 16, 17; Abraham, Gen. xxii. 1, 2, 12; The Israelites, Ex. xvi. 4, 5; Ex. xx 20; By kindness or misfortunes, The Israelites, Deut. viii. 2,3,15,16; The Canaanite woman, Matt. xv. 21, 22; Through opportunities for good or evil, The Corinthians, 2 Cor. viii. 8; The Israelites, Deut. xiii. 1-3; Judges ii. 21, 22; Hezekiah, 2 Chron. xxxii. 31.

Professor A. H. Francke, went one day with a heavy heart to the building of the orphan house, because he was in need of money for stone and lime. There a laborer handed him a coin, which he had found in the rubbish, upon which stood the following inscription:

"*Jehovah, Conditor, Condita Caronide Caronet.*" That is, Jehovah, the Founder, shall crown that which was founded! This was a sign from heaven for Francke. The work was begun with prayer daily, and at the end of the week was closed with prayer and an edifying address. The world, indeed, laughed, and ridiculed the builder, who had no money in his pocket, and a blasphemer even said, "When the wall is finished I will permit myself to be hanged upon it." But the right hand of the Lord, which Francke grasped by faith, obtained the victory.

With a gloomy countenance and a heart filled with fear, a poor, but pious man, in Paris, came to the metropolitan bishop, and said to him, "Father, I am a sinner; I feel that I am a sinner. Every hour I pray to God for light and faith, yet doubts arise in my mind. Certainly, if I were not cast away from God, he would not permit me to be so terribly alarmed about the salvation of my soul." The bishop comforted his deeply concerned son in this wise: The king of France has two strong castles in different parts of the country and in different conditions, and to each one he appoints a commander. The castle Montelberry is far inland, where it is not much exposed to danger, but the castle La Rochelle stands on the sea shore, where it is always in danger of hostile attacks. What think you now, which of these two commanders stands highest in the confidence of the king? The man replied, "Without doubt, the king has the most confidence, and holds in the highest esteem, the commander who has the greatest responsibility resting upon him, and is most courageous in time of danger." "You are right," said the bishop, "and now apply this to my and your position; for my heart is analogous to the castle at Montelberry, and yours to the castle at La Rochelle."

Taking God at his word. A pious Irish peasant was for a long time troubled with doubts about the salvation of his soul, arising from false views of the efficacy of the atoning death of Christ. A faithful servant of Christ sought to prove to him, that we must believe or trust God on his word, and related the following account: "Emperor Napoleon once reviewed a regiment. While he was giving orders, the bridle of his horse slipped out of his hand, and the horse ran away. A common soldier, an active man, ran from the ranks, caught the horse by the bridle, and returned him to the emperor, who said to him, "Thank you, captain." "In which regiment, sir?" "In my guards," replied the emperor and galloped away. The soldier had the *word* of the emperor, and depended upon it. He came in his fusiliers uniform to the general of the staff. "This man a captain of the guard!" said one of the generals. "Yes, for *he* has said it," replied the soldier, pointing to the emperor. "O sir, I beg your pardon," said the general. The soldier had not yet taken upon himself the position of a captain, his epaulettes or sword. The word of the sovereign was worth more to him than a uniform He believed." The peasant now comprehended from this narrative, what it is to believe, or take God at his word, and since then he has lived in a new atmosphere.

THE TEMPTATION TO UNBELIEF THROUGH THE DEVIL, THE WORLD, AND THE FLESH.

Scriptural Examples. Adam and Eve, Gen. iii. 1-5; Christ, Matt. iv. 3; Job i. 8-12; ii. 3-6; Judas, Luke xxii. 3; John xiii. 2; Peter, Luke xxii. 31; Adam by Eve, Gen. iii. 6; Joseph by Potiphar's wife, Gen. xxxix. 7-12; Israel by Moab, Num. xxv. 1-3; Job by his wife, Job ii. 9; Christ by the Pharisees, Matt. xxii. 15; The Corinthians by unbelievers, 1 Cor. xv. 33.

The emperor promised to the duke, Philipp, of Hessen, the dukedom of Katzen-Ellenbogen, and the elector, George, of Meiszen, promised him the inheritance of all his goods and lands, if he would forsake the Evangelical faith. But he joyfully declined the offers, and thought of the following verse in a certain hymn:

>All the riches of the earth,
>Silver, gold, or money's worth,
>Have here but a short duration,
>And cannot help in our salvation.

The duke of Venier had engraven on his coat of arms, a tree laden with many fruits and a few broken branches, with the following superscription: *Copia me perdit;* that is, "The abundance is my ruin." This was to signify, that by his possessions, worry and labors he consumed and ruined himself, or that on account of his talents and advantages, he was envied and hated by others.

A misanthropic man in East India violently contradicted and opposed a Christian missionary. The missionary let him scold for a while, and then said quite calmly, "I will tell you a story An ox was grazing quietly in the meadow, when a dog came, barked at him, and drove him away. But the ox said to him, Why do you envy me this good grass, which you can not eat?" The people understood the meaning of this parable and applauded, but the reviler departed with shame.

Johaun Gerhard, one of the most distinguished theologians of the 17th century, rescued the city of Jena, when it was about to experience the calamities of the 30 years' war by the hostile popish troops. He did this at the risk of his own life. The Austrian army was marching towards Jena, with the object of plundering and destroying the city. The courageous and worthy man went out to meet them, and on the bridge, prostrated himself before the general and pleaded for protection. But the general remained unmoved and would not listen to his petition. Gerhard arose, stepped up to him, and called with courage and determination, "If you will not hear me, then God, our heavenly Father, will hear me!" This exclamation reached the heart of the general, and he treated the city and university of Jena with mildness.

A sheriff who was about to levy on the household goods of a poor man, found him and his family engaged in singing the hymn, "Out of the depths we call to thee," etc. By this scene and especially by the hymn, the sheriff was so deeply affected, that he gave his coat to the poor man, that he should sell it and pay his debt.

God tempts no one to sin The temptation here meant is that which proceeds out of an evil cause, and is intended to accomplish a bad end; namely, that we should fall into sin. God tempts no one to do evil.

God, indeed, sends his son into the desert, but it is the devil that tempts him.

"The devil takes no vacation," says the proverb. That is, he does not cease to promote intrigues, by which he can rob believers of their faith and peace. He knows whom he shall incite to fleshly lusts, whom to gormandizing and drunkenness, whom to quarrels and murder, and whom to jealousy and envy. He knows whom he shall depress into discouragements and fear, or to fill with pride by flattery. He takes notice of the habits of all men, he weighs their cares, searches after their minds and inclinations, and studies constantly how he can injure human beings.

Where a church is built for God, the devil seeks to build a chapel beside it.—*Proverb.*

May not deceive us. When the devil would deceive the people, he is beautiful as an angel of light.

The devil goes to work very cunningly. He began by asking Christ to create bread for himself, and ended by asking Christ to worship him.

The ancients related the following legend to illustrate the devil's cunning: The devil once came in the disguise of a pedler with the object of selling *pride* to the people, and called out, "Who wants to buy pride, let him come to me, I will sell it cheap." But the people said, "God forbid, for pride is a mortal sin." Then a wicked woman came and said to the devil, "You fool! Do you think the people will buy pride, when you call it by the right name; you must say, that you have fashion, or gentility for sale, and I'll bet, you will have customers enough." The devil followed her advice and immediately sold all his wares.

The devil takes away from man the sense of shame and fear, that he may commit sin; after he has committed sin, he gives both (shame and fear) back to him again, that he may commit new sins, in order to cover up those which he has committed, without seeking forgiveness of God through Christ. At first he presents sin to him as a trifle, or a grain of sand, but after their commission, as a mountain, which must crush his heart.

The song which the devil sings to men, has three verses;
1. Commit sin;
2. Continue to sin; you have a long time to repent and be converted;
3. Dispair, you have now waited too long; there is now no hope for you; your soul is lost. This is the end of the song.

The World. The world is a crowd of such people, as receive all kinds of good things from God, and repay him with ingratitude and blasphemy.—*Luther.*

The world is the bride of the devil.—*Ger. Proverb.*

Pious people are the step-children of the world, she is not kind to them; she persecutes and oppresses them wherever she can, she takes advantage of them and tries to cheat them out of their inheritance.

As soon as we enter on the way to heaven, a beautiful woman meets us; namely, the *Sweet World*, and lures us by the beautiful apple. To our left appears a hateful woman; namely, the *Bitter World*, who frightens us with the dreadful cross. Now, if the Sweet World can cause us to laugh and the Bitter World can cause us to weep, then the inheritance will soon be spent.

"**Deceive us.**" When the world fondles any one, she is trying to fasten the rope around his neck.—*Ger. Proverb.*

The world gives bad wages.—*Ger. Proverb.*

He who serves the world most faithfully, receives the poorest reward.—*Ger. Proverb.*

The world asks, Is it pleasant? Is it useful? Is it feasible? Is it honorable? But the Christian asks, Is it also Christian?

As soon as man enters into the world an enticing *Jael* goes before him; behind him follows a defrauding *Laban*; to his right walks a smiling *Joab*, with a sword under his mantel; and on the left a false *Judas* offers a kiss. Therefore it is important to keep our eyes open and be on our guard, or else none will escape.

That our flesh may not deceive us. Do not trust him who is nearest to you, who lives in the same house with you, who eats out of the same spoon with you, and sleeps in the same bed with you; namely, *yourself!*

In an old book we find a moth painted to represent how a man may be driven by his own lust to do that which will bring him harm, pain and death. The moth is represented as flying around the flame of a candle, with the subscription, *Ut Patiari Patiar;* that is, "If I catch it, I will suffer for it."

The heart is the fountain of evil. In olden times there lived a man who was very irritable. He became angry at the least provocation, and afterwards was sorry on account of it. Then he thought, "This comes from the bad people, among whom I live; if these did not provoke me, I would be more mild. I will go away and live as a hermit in the wild forest, where I will never see or hear any one, and then I will not become angry any more." Then he went away into the forest and found a place, where a spring of fresh water ran down from the rock; there he built a hut for himself. While he was working at his hut he felt thirsty, went to the spring and set his pitcher down to catch the water. But the pitcher did not stand firm, and fell down. The second time he set it up and it fell down again, when he set it up once more. After a while the pitcher fell down the third time, and instead of setting it up again, he became so enraged, that he struck it against the rock, and broke it into a thousand pieces. But as he stood there, holding the handle of the broken pitcher in his hand, and saw the pieces scattered about on the ground, he came to himself and in alarm said, "O what a fool I have been! I thought the wrath came *into me from without*, now I see that it *comes out of me!* Therefore I will no longer remain a hermit, but I will return to my brethren, that they may give me good advice and help me to pray, that my own heart may be made better."

Once a knight became weary of the world and entered a monastery, where he was received as a lay-brother. Then, when the Abbot told him to clean the stable, or sweep the kitchen, or do any work of that kind, he said, "My dear Abbot, you must remember that I am a nobleman, and stand in high repute before the world; therefore, please do not ask me to do such menial work; it is disgraceful to me." But when the Abbot said, "Get thee ready, Brother Kunrad, to go out riding to-morrow," then he said, "Yes, my dear sir! for this reason I have had my head shaved, in token of my submissive obedience to your orders." This is the answer of the Old Adam: That which is unpleasant to him, he will not do; thinks too much is asked of him; others should do that, although God has commanded him to do it. But when he is told to do something pleasant, he is ready and willing at once, boasts of his obedience, and wishes to receive special praise and honor for doing his duty.

Temptation to false doctrine—and crime. Franciscus Spiera, for worldly gain had permitted himself to deny the faith. When he came to die, his friends tried to comfort him by the mercy of God and the blood of Christ. But he replied, "It is impossible that God should pluck me out of hell."

In the year 1082 a very learned man, in Paris, lay very sick. He had no regard for God's word and a future judgment. While in bed, the 13th chapter of the book of Job was read to him, and when the reader came to the words, (verses 21, 22) "Withdraw thine hand far from me, and let not thy dread make me afraid. Then call thou and I will answer," he sat up in bed and cried out, *Justo Dei Judicio accusatus sum.* That is, "By God's just judgment I am now accused." All present were terrified, and the reading was discontinued. On the next day he exclaimed in connection with the same words, "*Justo Dei Judicatus sum*" That is, "By God's righteous judgment I am sentenced." And on the third day, when he was dying, he cried with a loud voice, that all could hear, "*Justo Dei Judicio damnatus sum.*" That is, "By God's righteous judgment I am damned." So terrible was this cry, that all fled out of the house. With these words he died.

Luther says, We must all feel temptations, although not of the same kind, or of the same degree; some more, some less. Youth has especially temptations of the *flesh*; afterwards those who have grown up or become old, temptations from the *world*; but others, who are engaged in spiritual things have temptations from the *devil*.

. The thief loves to steal especially gold and silver vessels.—*Prov.*

Just as a pirate pursues in preference the richly laden ships, so the hellish pirate, the devil, pursues those most violently, who possess the precious treasures of faith ; namely, the truly regenerated Christians.

We might just as well pray, "Lead us not into any kind of temptation," as a soldier should beg his general not to lead him into *battle*, or the sailor say to his captain, Lead us not out into the open sea.

A Christian's school of suffering contains four classes :
1. In the first class he learns, "*I must suffer ;*"
2. In the second class he learns, "*I will suffer ;*"
3. In the third class he learns, "*I can suffer ;*"
4. In the fourth class he learns, "*I may suffer.*"

He who comes from Gethsemane has overcome death.—*Prov.*

The anvil is not afraid of the hammer.—*Prov.*

He who has not tasted the bitter, does not know what sweet is.—*Prov.*

An aged father said to a sick youth, "My dear son, do not distress yourself on account of your bodily infirmity, for a devout Christian should thank God, even for his afflictions. If you are *iron*, then the fire will take your rust away ; but if you are gold, then the fire will purify you for greater glory. Therefore when God thus visits you, you should not impatiently resist his will, but be resigned, and pray that God shall do with you as seems best to him.

Wenceslaus, king of Bohemia, was taken prisoner by his enemies in battle and treated very harshly. His enemies asked him, "Do you now see the difference between being a king and a prisoner." He replied, "I see the difference very well. While I was a king, I thought only of *worldly* things; now I think of *God* and *heavenly* things. While I was a king, I lived for *myself;* but since I bear these chains, *I live for my God.*"

THE SEVENTH PETITION.

275. *What is the Seventh Petition?*

" But deliver us from evil."

276. *What is meant by this petition?*

We pray in this petition, as in a summary, that our heavenly Father would deliver us from all manner of evil, whether it affect the body or the soul, property or character, and at last, when the hour of death shall have come, grant us a happy end, and graciously take us from this world of sorrow to himself in heaven.

THE MEANING OF THE WORDS.

277. What is the " evil" spoken of in this petition?

By the "evil" from which we pray in this petition to be delivered, is everything that is injurious to us in body, soul, property or character, for time and eternity.

278. By what is evil produced in this world?

Evil is produced

1. By Satan;

Ephesians vi. 12. For we wrestle not against flesh and blood, but against principalities, against powers, against the rulers of the darkness of this world, against spiritual wickedness in high *places*.

1 Peter v. 8. Be sober, be vigilant; because your adversary the devil, as a roaring lion, walketh about, seeking whom he may devour.

2. By sin.

279. What is meant by " deliver us "?

By the words "deliver us" we pray

1. That God would preserve us from the evil that is present;

2 Timothy iv. 14. Alexander the coppersmith did me much evil: the Lord reward him according to his works.

2. From that which is in the future.

John xvii. 15. I pray not that thou shouldest take them out of the world, but that thou shouldest keep them from the evil.

Jonah iii. 4. And Jonah began to enter into the city a day's journey, and he cried, and said, Yet forty days, and Ninevah shall be overthrown.

THE APPLICATION.

280. How do the evils of this world affect us?

The evils affect

1. Our bodies, as in sickness and death;

2. Our souls, as in unbelief, impatience, hatred, jealousy, etc.

281. What is the last evil from which we pray to be delivered?

The last and greatest evil from which we pray to be delivered is

    1. An unhappy death, and

    2. The consequences of an unholy life and a hopeless death.

1 Corinthians xv. 26. The last enemy that shall be destroyed is death.

282. *Who pray this petition to their own condemnation?*

Those pray this petition to their own condemnation,

    1. Who presumptuously persevere in their sins;

Jeremiah xliv. 16. As for the word that thou hast spoken unto us in the name of the Lord, we will not hearken unto thee.

    2. Who despise the means by which they can be delivered from their sins.

Psalm lviii. 4. Their poison *is* like the poison of a serpent: *they are* like the deaf adder *that* stoppeth her ear.

EXPLANATORY NOTES.

To *deliver* us from evil, means to make us free from evil. Instead of "evil," it would be more correct to say the "Evil One;" that is Satan.

In a "*summary*" means, taken all together.

"All manner of evil," means all kinds of evil.

Luther names four kinds of evils:

1. Bodily evils, (*e. g.*, sickness);
2. Evils of the soul, (*e. g.*, sadness, fear, discouragement);
3. Evils of possessions, (*e. g.*, poverty, loss, etc.);
4. Evils of reputation, (*e. g.*, slander, disgrace, etc.)

Of all these four evils, many examples can easily be cited from the Holy Scriptures.

The Lord Jesus endured *all* these four evils for us. This world is called a "vale of tears," because there is so much trouble in it.

Here we pray God, that he would strengthen and comfort us in all trouble, and finally when the hour of death comes, take us to himself in paradise. That is a happy death, when we can depart with prayer and faith in the merits of our Lord Jesus Christ. *Rev. xiv. 13; Psalm xxxi. 5.*

ANECDOTES AND ILLUSTRATIONS.

THE DELIVERANCE FROM ALL EVILS.

Scriptural Examples. Hezekiah, 2 Chron xxxii. 1-24; Manasseh, 2 Chron. xxxiii. 12, 13; Paul, Acts xiv. 19-21; Christ, Matt. xxvi. 39, 41; Heb v 7, 8; Job i. 21; Paul, 2 Cor. iv. 16-18; Paul, 2 Tim. iv. 17, 18; Paul, Phil. i 20-24; Worldly people, Psalm xvii. 13-15; Psalm xlix. 12, 13.

John Tobias Kiesling, the merchant, while on his way to Austria, found, in a village, a little girl sitting at the door, who appeared to be very sad and kept her eyes constantly cast down to the earth. He said to her, "My dear child, why do you sit here with down-cast eyes?" The little girl looked up to the stranger, and he saw that her eyes were very red and inflamed. She replied, "O I am always sick, sad and miserable, and in addition, I have sore eyes." My dear child," said Kiesling, "I think you look too much on the ground, into the dust of the earth; only learn to lift your eyes more toward *heaven*, for which they were given you, then your heart will become glad and cheerful, and you will become healthy, and your sore eyes will be healed." Then the little girl asked the stranger, how this was to be understood? And he explained his meaning to her, so that her eyes overflowed in tears, which indeed, did not injure them. For, behold, when Kiesling on his return came to the same place again, she could look into his face with cheerfulness and joy, and at her eyes it could be easily seen, that they had learned to look upward toward heaven.

The Pharisee and the Publican In olden times, a hermit died, and praised himself extravagantly for the holy life which he had lived. A robber heard him, and became penitent, ran away, confessed his sins and called upon God for mercy. While running, he fell, and broke his neck. All this was seen by a pious man, who wept at the death of the hermit and laughed when he saw the robber break his neck. When he was rebuked for this conduct, and asked, why he acted thus, he replied, "When the hermit died, the devil took him, on account of his pride and hypocricy, therefore I wept; but when the robber broke his neck, the holy angels carried his soul to heaven, on account of his humility and penitence; on this account I was joyful and laughed."

The German poet, Gellert, placed great importance on a good name, and felt very keenly the slanders that were heaped upon him. Therefore, when once a whole year had passed without any slanders having been written or spoken against him, he expressed in his diary his heart-felt gratitude for this, among other blessings, which he had enjoyed during the year.

A sick Negro begged the missionary to give him a shroud in which his body might be buried after he was dead. But the missionary impressed upon him the necessity of caring much more for the robe of Christ's righteousness, to clothe his immortal soul, when he should stand before God, than a shroud to wrap around his dead body, when it should be laid in the grave. This had a good effect, he prayed constantly for mercy, and the forgiveness of his sins. How many are more concerned about the burial of their bodies, than the salvation of their souls!

The Monk, Bonosus, who suffered from defective eyesight, came, like many others, to the distinguished Abbot, Severinus, to be healed by his prayers. But the Abbot exhorted him to pray to God to enlighten his spiritual eyes. These oft repeated exhortations of the worthy Abbot taught him to seek light through his spiritual, rather than bodily eyes, and to forget his ills in communion with God.

Mrs. Anna Catharine Wieglob, of Halle, prayed earnestly during her last illness, that the Lord might soon release her from her sufferings, and take her to himself in heaven. On the morning of Feb. 12, 1719, she related, that during the night the Lord had said to her, "Now all is over; now I will deliver thee from all evil." But soon the thought troubled her, that possibly she had sinned, in praying so urgently to be released by death. She therefore prayed, that God would forgive her, if she had presumed too much.

A HAPPY DEATH.

Scriptural Examples. Jacob, Gen. xlix. 18; Simeon, Luke ii. 29, 30; Christ, Luke xxiii. 46; Stephen, Acts vii. 55-59.

When Christian III., king of Denmark lay critically ill, at Christmas, in the year 1558, he had a singular dream, in which an angel appeared to him and said, "Christian, if you have yet anything to command that is to be done in thy kingdom after thy death, then attend to it in time, for in eight days God will call thee out of thine earthly kingdom into his heavenly kingdom." When he awoke, the pious king rejoiced over this news. On New Year's day he desired to receive the Lord's Supper, and then took farewell of his household, requesting his pastor and the courtiers to sing spiritual hymns. When they hesitated to do this, the king said, "I will sing and you will join me in singing, then it may be said, The king of Denmark sang his own funeral hymns." Then he began to sing, "With peace and joy I pass away;" "In the midst of life we are in death;" "Now sink the body in the grave." At the conclusion of these hymns, he died joyfully on New Year's day, 1559.

An aged lady in England, who had spent her life in the service of Christ's Kingdom, was lying on her deathbed. The well known Dr. Philipp took farewell of her one evening, as he supposed for the last time in this world. When he came home he found a letter, in which the wonderful conversion of the South Sea Islanders was reported. "O," thought he, "If I only had received this letter a few hours sooner, what a joy it would have afforded that dying saint." The next morning his first walk was to her house with the letter in his pocket. When he entered the chamber, he was told, the patient had been lying for several hours with closed eyes, and was speechless. He stepped up to the bed and observed that she appeared to be already dead, or was about dying. But he sat down by the bed, and began to read the letter. He had scarcely read a few lines, when a change on her face was observed; he read on, and her features showed a smile. He still continued to read, and behold! she opened her eyes, and as he continued to read the account of that miracle of grace – she raised her hands, and praised the Lord for what she had heard—then she expired, and her spirit passed over to continue the praises in heaven, which had just been silenced on earth.

Melanchton was lying critically ill during the Easter festival of the year 1560, the hour of his departure came on Friday, after Easter. Hands and feet began to be cold; his pulse failed and his face became pale; then he prayed in these words, "Lord Jesus, into thy hands I commend my spirit; thou hast redeemed me, O thou faithful God." After repeating these words for the third time, he peacefully fell asleep in death.

When the pious John Arndt lay on his deathbed, March 11, 1621, he woke up after a short sleep and exclaimed, "We beheld his glory, the glory as of the only begotten of the Father, full of grace and truth." John i. 14. His wife asked him, *when* he had seen this glory? He replied, "Now I have seen it, O what a glory that is! No ear hath heard it, and it hath not entered into any human heart! This glory I have seen!" His last words were, "Now I have overcome!"

On one occasion, Dr. Mangold, a Christian physician, was suffering severe pains, and a friend was leaving him to go to church; he said to him, "O my dear friend, pray most earnestly, that the Lord would soon relieve me from all evil." But he immediately recalled what he had asked, and said humbly and resignedly, "No, do not pray for that; I do not wish to die one moment sooner, than it is the will of my Lord and Savior."

The distinguished Heinrich Mueller died in Rostock in peace and joy, on Sept. 11, 1675. Before his departure he sang spiritual songs, prayed most earnestly, exhorted his household to prayer, and comforted them with these words, "It is not I, but it is my misery and pain that will die."

The sufferings of Christopher Von Haugwitz, of Alt Seitenberg, were very severe in his last sickness, and he prayed, "O Lord, how long, how long!" His pastor said to him, "The Lord will come and not tarry. You, as an experienced soldier know very well, what was the rule when you stood on guard; no matter whether it hailed or snowed, the soldier must not leave his post, until he has been relieved by his commander." The sick man was pacified by these words.

A Christian youth was lying on his deathbed, and his mother was watching by his side. At length he said, "Mother, it is getting dark; I can not see you any more." After awhile he said again, "Mother, my feet are getting cold, and I feel a chilliness creeping up towards my heart." After awhile he said again, "Mother, it is getting light again! I see the holy angels, and I hear them sing!" After these words he softly expired, and we have no doubt, the holy angels conveyed him on wings of light and glory home to heaven.

THE CONCLUSION.

283. What is the conclusion of the Lord's Prayer?

For thine is the kingdom, and the power, and the glory, forever and ever. Amen.

THE MEANING OF THE WORDS.

284. What do we pray for when we say "Thine is the kingdom"?

By these words we acknowledge him as

1. Our Lord and King to whom we submit as loyal subjects;
2. Our Father, whom we obey as loving children, and
3. To whom we pray for the prevention of evil and the bestowal of all good.

Isaiah lxiii. 16. Doubtless thou art our father, though Abraham be ignorant of us, and Israel acknowledge us not: thou, O Lord, *art* our father, our redeemer; thy name is from everlasting.

285. What do we mean by the word "power"?

By the word "power," we mean, that God is Almighty and can help us in every time of need.

Psalm lxxxix. 13. Thou hast a mighty arm; strong is thy hand, and high is thy right hand.

286. What is meant by the word "glory"?

By the glory of God we mean that he displays his divine attributes before his intelligent creatures to the honor of his name.

287. What do we understand by the word "forever and ever?"

By this word we mean that God is eternal in his existence and unchangeable in his character.

Psalm cii. 27. But thou *art* the same, and thy years shall have no end.

Psalm cii. 28. The children of thy servants shall continue, and their seed shall be established before thee.

288. What is meant by the word "Amen?"

By this word is meant,

That I should be assured, that such petitions are acceptable to God, our Heavenly Father, and are heard by him;

For he himself has commanded us to pray in this manner and has promised that he will hear us. Amen, Amen; this is, yea, yea, it shall be so.

289. What is the application of the word Amen?

The application of the word Amen is, that we have the confident assurance that he will and can do what he promises, because

1. We belong to his kingdom.

Psalm xcvii. 1. The Lord reigneth; let the earth rejoice; let the multitude of isles be glad *thereof.*

2. He has divine power to do whatever he wills.

Psalm lxxxix. 19. Then thou spakest in vision to thy holy one, and saidst, I have laid help upon *one that is* mighty; I have exalted *one* chosen out of the people.

3. **He has commanded us to pray, and**

Ephesians vi. 18. Praying always with all prayer and supplication in the Spirit, and watching thereunto with all perseverance and supplication for all saints.

4. **He has promised to hear our prayers.**

Matthew vii. 7. Ask, and it shall be given you; seek, and ye shall find; knock, and it shall be opened unto you.

EXPLANATORY NOTES.

THINE IS THE KINGDOM, THE POWER AND THE GLORY.

Scriptural Examples. David, 1 Chron. xxx. 11, 12; Paul, Rom. xvi. 27; 1 Tim. i. 17; The 24 Elders, Rev. iv. 11.

On one occasion, a poor man asked Luther for assistance. He gave him what little money he himself had in the house. His wife did not seen to be entirely pleased with this liberality. But Luther said to her, "Dear Katie, God is rich; he will supply all our needs."

While Hayden's musical composition, "*The Creation*," was performed, he himself was affected to tears. But when, after the performance, everybody rushed to him to congratulate him, he exclaimed, "Not to me! The honor belongs not to me, but all goodness comes from above!"

A Negro slave in Virginia, who was endowed with much sound Christian intelligence, was remarkable for his faith in a future life and devoid of all fear. A white man, also a true Christian, said to him, "Jack, you appear to be always confident and assured in your hope of salvation, what is the cause of this?" Jack replied, "Well, massa, I fall right down on the promises, and then pray right up."

Thine is the kingdom, to which we are called; therefore, *God will help;*

Thine is the power, by which we are upheld; therefore, *God can help;*

Thine is the glory, for which we are created, redeemed and sanctified; therefore, God will surely support and glorify us.

On the little word "*Thine*" is built our confidence, that our prayers will be answered, for every petition is based on this kingdom. The kingdom belongs to God; therefore it must remain, yea, rather *come*, as we pray in each petition, even if wicked men and Satan strive to hinder it. Therefore Luther writes so beautifully, Aug. 5, 1530, to Gregory Brueck, Chancellor of the Elector Johann, of Saxony:

"I have lately seen two wonders: The first one, as I looked out of the window, and saw the stars of heaven, and the whole beautiful arch of the firmament, and yet I could see no pillars, upon which the Master Builder had set the arch; notwithstanding the heavens did not fall, and the arch stands firm. Now there are some who search for the pillars and would grasp them, and feel them. But as they can not do this, they struggle and tremble for fear that the heavens would fall, for no other reason, than that they can not grasp and see the pillars that support the heavens. If they could lay hold of the pillars, then they think the heavens would stand firm.

The second wonder that I saw, was thick clouds, which floated over our heads, so great and heavy, that they could be compared to a vast sea; and yet I saw no foundation on which they could rest, and no reservoir, (Kufe, in which they were contained. Yet they did not fall upon us, but saluted us with a frowning countenance, and fled away. When they were passed away the foundation and the covering, in which they had been embraced, shone forth; namely, the *rainbow*, (Gen. ix. 8-17.) That was, indeed, a weak, thin, and insignificant foundation and covering, which also vanished with the clouds and was more like a phantom, or shadow, than a powerful foundation, so that one might be more in dread of the foundation than of the lowering clouds. Yet it appeared, indeed, that this feeble phantom or shadow bore up and protected the great flood of waters. Yet there are some who look upon, regard and fear the flood of waters, thick clouds and heavy burdens, more than this thin, narrow and light phantom; for they want to feel the power and strength of this phantom, and because they can not do this, they fear the clouds may become an eternal flood, like that in the days of Noah."

AMEN

When "Amen" is said after the creed or any utterance of faith in prose or verse, its meaning must be "so be it," for it is true.

When "Amen" is said after any prayer, or blessing, or spiritual good, it must mean "so be it," for it is my desire.

When "Amen" is said after any prayer involving on our part promises of amendment, and such like. it must mean "so be it," for it is my firm purpose.

When "Amen" is said after praise and adoration, it must mean "so be it," for it is the aspiration of my heart.

Amen is the seal of our loving, heavenly Father.—*Ger. Proverb.*

Amen says to you, Live upon it; pray upon it; suffer upon it, and die upon it!—*Ger. Proverb.*

Luther once wrote to Melanchton, "I pray for you ; I *have* prayed for you, and I *will continue* to pray for you ; and I *doubt not*, my prayer has been answered ; for I feel that Amen in my heart." (He meant the Amen at the end of the Lord's Prayer.) God spoke the Amen into Luther's heart. Luther tells his experience, when he says in the Catechism, "I am sure, I feel the Amen of God in my heart." Such petitions are answered at the Throne of Grace.

Amen is also a name of Christ. Rev. iii 14. These things saith the Amen, the faithful and true witness, the beginning of the creation of God." Jesus is meant in this Scripture passage. As his name is, so is he also, the Amen, the truthful one. So the Lord also calls himself : I am the Way, the *Truth* and the Life.

Amen was used by the Hebrews in covenants or oaths. It was customary in apostolic days to say Amen at the giving of thanks. Tertullian says they said Amen at the eucharist—that is, at the end of the prayer.

"So," says Dean Stanley, "in the early Christian liturgies it was regarded as a marked point in the service ; and with this agrees the great solemnity with which Justin speaks of it, as though it were on a level with the thanksgiving : 'The president having given thanks, the whole people shouted their approbation.' In later times the Amen was only repeated once by the congregation, and always after the great thanksgiving, and with a shout like a peal of thunder."

A Hindu and a New Zealander once met on the deck of a missionary ship. They were both converts from heathenism, but could not speak to each other. They pointed to their Bibles, shook hands, and smiled. At last a happy thought occurred to the Hindu. He exclaimed, "Hallelujah." The New Zealander answered in delight, "Amen." In these two Hebrew words, brought into their respective languages by the Word of God, they were able to express their feelings.

Alexander the Great had a famous but indigent philosopher in his court. This adept in science was once particularly straitened in his circumstances To whom should he apply but to his generous patron, the conqueror of the world? His request was no sooner made than it was granted. Alexander gave him a commission to receive of his treasurer whatever he wanted. He immediately demanded, in his sovereign's name, ten thousand pounds ! The treasurer, surprised at so large a demand, refused to comply ; but he waited upon the king, and represented to him the affair, adding withal how unreasonable he thought the petition, and how exorbitant the sum. Alexander heard him with patience, but as soon as he had ended his remonstrance, replied, "Let the money be instantly paid. I am delighted with the philosopher's way of thinking: he has done me a singular honor; by the largeness of his request, he shows the high idea he has conceived both of my superior wealth and my royal munificence." Thus let us honor what the inspired penman styles the "marvellous loving-kindness of Jehovah." "He that spared not his own Son, but delivered him up for us all, how shall he not with him also freely give us all things?" Rom. viii. 32.

"The Amen thus used," says Dean Stanley, "was borrowed from the worship of the synagogue, and hence probably the article is prefixed as to a well-known form. It was there regarded as the necessary ratification of the prayer of blessing. The rabbins say: 'He who says Amen is greater than he that blesseth.' 'Whosoever says Amen, to him the gates of paradise are open.' An Amen, if not well considered, was called an orphan Amen. 'Whosoever says an orphan Amen, his children shall be orphans; whosoever answers Amen hastily or shortly, his days shall be shortened; whosoever answers Amen distinctly and at length, his days shall be lengthened.' Captain Burton noticed the word as uttered by the vast assembly of the pilgrims at Mecca, to express their assent to the great sermon at Kaaba."

"The certainty, Amen, is derived from the truth and faithfulness of God. Christ introduces his most solemn statements with this word; and with it believers close their prayers, in sign and testimony that all human faithfulness and human certitude spring from the faithfulness of God. This word Amen has its great history in Biblical theology, in the services of the Church, and in the lives of believers "—*Lange*.

A milkdealer in London heard, while he was distributing his cans, a man cursing himself in most horrible language. He stepped up to the man and asked him, "My friend, do you know the meaning of the word *Amen?*" "Of course I do," replied the man, "it means, *so may it be.*" "Now," said the milkdealer, "consider how angry you would be, if some one would say Amen to all your curses, which you have uttered against your poor eyes and feeble limbs! But now, if God should say Amen to them, what would then become of you?" The milkdealer related this conversation to his neighbors, when one of them, a short time after, told him that a man had been received into a neighboring church, who said that a milkdealer had reproved him for his cursing and swearing, which was the means, in the hand of God, to convince him of his sins, and induce him to seek the forgiveness of his sins.

The Catechism begins with articles of faith—what we are to believe concerning God. It then considers what duty God requires of man, treating first of the ten commandments of the law as the general duty of man, and secondly of the particular duties of the sinner under the gospel. The concluding parts treat of the means of grace—the word, sacraments, and prayer. Under the last the Lord's Prayer is made, very appropriately, to end the series of questions and answers.—*Steel.*

The following beautiful paraphrase of the Lord's Prayer has been credited to a Frenchman—M. Pierre Bernard; but in the Life of the Rev. William Marsh, D. D., so long known and so highly esteemed in England, it is stated that during a wakeful night Dr. Marsh composed it, and that it was written down from his dictation the next morning. Comparing the two versions, the one ascribed to M. Bernard is more full; but it may be merely an amplification of that of Dr. Marsh. We give the following compilation from both, as a fitting conclusion to this Exposition of the Lord's Prayer :—

THE LORD'S PRAYER PARAPHRASED.

Our Father—
    By right of creation,
    By bountiful provision,
    By gracious adoption ;
Which art in heaven—
    The throne of thy glory,
    The home of thy children,
    The temple of thy angels ;
Hallowed be thy name—
    By the thoughts of our hearts,
    By the words of our lips,
    By the works of our hands.
Thy kingdom come—
    Of providence to defend us,
    Of grace to refine us,
    Of glory to crown us.
Thy will be done in earth, as it is in heaven—
    Towards us without resistance,
    By us without compulsion,
    Universally without exception,
    Eternally without declension.
Give us this day our daily bread—
    Of necessity for our bodies,
    Of eternal life for our souls.

And forgive us our trespasses—
>   Against the commands of thy law,
>   Against the grace of thy gospel ;

As we forgive those that trespass against us—
>   By defaming our character,
>   By embezzling our property,
>   By abusing our person.

And lead us not into temptation, but deliver us from evil—
>   Of overwhelming afflictions,
>   Of worldly enticements,
>   Of Satan's devices,
>   Of error's seductions,
>   Of sinful affections.

For thine is the kingdom, and the power, and the glory, for ever—
>   Thy kingdom governs all,
>   Thy power subdues all,
>   Thy glory is above all.

Amen—
>   As it is in thy purpose,
>   So it is in thy promises ;
>   So be it in our prayers,
>   So it shall be to thy praise.

By this prayer of our Lord—
>   The Father bless,
>   The Son adore,
>   The Spirit praise,
>   For evermore. Amen and Amen.—*Steel.*

MATTHIAS CLAUDIUS' EXPOSITION OF THE LORD'S PRAYER.

The above named distinguished German Christian author has written a classical exposition of the Lord's Prayer, in a letter to his friend Andres, which we will try to translate, although it will be difficult to render many of his idiomatic German phrases into good English. This exposition contains, like a good prayer—*few* words, but *many* and *deep* meanings :

"The Lord's Prayer is, once for all, the best prayer, for you know who composed it. But no man on God's earth, can so pray it, as he meant it; we mutilate it only from a distance, one of us more miserably than the other. But that will do no harm, dear Andres, if we only mean it right, (*gut meinen,*) the dear God (*Liebe Gott*) must always do the best for us, and he knows how it ought to be. As you have requested it, I will tell you sincerely, how I use the Lord's Prayer. But I think it is only very poorly done, and I would gladly let some one instruct me how to do it better.

See now, when I want to pray, then I think first of my sainted father, who was so good and kind to me, and gave me so willingly what I needed. And then I imagine (*stell mir vor*) that the whole world is my Father's house : and all the people in Europe, Asia, Africa and America, are, in my mind, my brothers and sisters ; and God sits in heaven on a golden throne, and stretches his right hand over the sea, to the end of the world, and his left hand is full of blessing and goodness, and the tops of the mountains round about are crowned with glory—then I begin :

Our Father who art in heaven, hallowed be thy name.

This, already, I do not yet fully understand. It is said that the Jews had some special mysteries about the names of God. I will let this pass (*lasse gut sein,*) and only wish that the idea (*Andenken*) of God, and every trace (*pur*), by which we can know him, may be above all things great and holy to me and all mankind.

Thy kingdom come

At this I think about myself, as things go hither and thither within me ; now this and now that controls, which causes all kinds of heart aches. And then I think, how good it would be for me, if God would make an end of all strife, and he himself would rule within me !

Thy will be done in earth as it is in heaven.

Here I think of heaven, with the holy angels who joyfully do His will ; whom no pain or sorrow afflicts, and who overflow with love and happiness, in which they rejoice, day and night. And then I think, O, if it were also thus on earth !

Give us this day our daily bread.

Every one knows, what "daily bread" means, and that we must eat, as long as we are in the world, and that it also tastes good. Then I think about this. My children also come into my mind : how they enjoy their meals and eagerly reach out for their food. And then I pray, that the dear God (*Liebe Gott*) would give us something to eat.

And forgive us our trespasses as we forgive those who have trespassed against us.

It hurts, when we are injured, and revenge is sweet. Thus it appears also to me, and I feel an inclination in that way. But then the wicked servant (*Schalks knecht*) in the gospel comes up before mine eyes, and my heart sinks, and I resolve to forgive my fellow-servant, and never say a word about those hundred pennies.

And lead us not into temptation.

Here I think of all kinds of instances, where people under such and such circumstances departed from the good, and fell, and that this might also happen to me.

But deliver us from evil.

Here I think of the temptations to which we are exposed, and that we are so easily led astray, and lured from the right way. But at the same time I also think of all the ills of life, of consumption and old age, trouble with children, gangrene, and delirium, and the thousand kinds of misery and heartaches in the world, which torment and distress the poor people, while none can help. And you will find, dear Andres, that if the tears have not come before, they will certainly come now, and we long so heartily to be delivered, and feel so sad and cast down, as if there were no help at all. But then we must take caurage again (*sich Muth machen*), lay our hands upon our mouths, and exclaim triumphantly, *Thine is the kingdom, and the power, and the glory for ever. Amen.*"

PART IV.

THE SACRAMENT OF HOLY BAPTISM.

290. What is a Sacrament?

A Sacrament is a holy ordinance, instituted by Christ, whereby, under visible signs, or elements, in connection with the word of God, divine grace is offered and sealed to believers.

291. From what is the word Sacrament derived?

The word "Sacrament" is derived from the Latin word *Saramentum*, which signifies something sacred or holy, and was applied to the oath by which the Roman soldiers bound themselves to be faithful to their general, and was adopted by the early christians to express their fidelity to Jesus as the Captain of their salvation.

292. What are the typical Sacraments in the Old Testament?

The Sacraments of the Old Testament were Circumcision and the Passover.

Genesis xvii. 1-14. I will make a covenant with thee, (Abram), etc.

Exodus xii. 3-9. Speak ye unto all the congregation of Israel, saying, In the tenth day of this month they shall take to them every man a lamb, according to the house of their fathers, a lamb for an house, etc.

Romans iv. 11. And he received the sign of circumcision, a seal of the righteousness of the faith, which he had, yet being uncircumcised; that he might be the father of all them that believe.

293. What are the Sacraments of the New Testament?

The Sacraments of the New Testament are Baptism and the Lord's Supper.

294. What relation do these two Sacraments bear to each other?

By Baptism we enter into a covenant with the Triune God; by the Lord's Supper, this covenant is renewed, confirmed and sealed.

Jeremiah xxxi. 31. Behold the days come, saith the Lord, that I will make a new covenant with the house of Israel and with the house of Judah.

Ephesians v. 25, 26. Christ also loved the church and gave himself for it; that he might sanctify and cleanse it with the washing of water by the word.

EXPLANATORY NOTES.

Definitions of a Sacrament:

Lutheran: A Sacrament is a holy ordinance, instituted by Christ, whereby, under visible signs, or elements, in connection with the word of God, divine grace is offered and sealed to believers.

Ger. Reformed: A holy ordinance, instituted by Christ, whereby, under visible signs, and seals, divine grace is offered and applied to believers.

Episcopal: An outward and visible sign of an inward and spiritual grace given us; ordained by Christ himself, as a means whereby we receive the same, and a pledge to assure us thereof.

Presbyterian: A Sacrament is a holy ordinance instituted by Christ; wherein by sensible signs, Christ, and the benefits of the new covenant, are represented, sealed and applied to believers

I. *The Author of the Sacraments.* Christ, as the Head of his Church: Eph. i. 22. He appointed the ordinances of the New Testament. His express warrant is required for the observance of Sacraments.

II. *The signs in the Sacraments.* They are sensible; they can be seen, touched, and tasted. They are signs of spiritual matters. These signs are of Christ's appointment. The significant actions in use in the Sacraments are also of his appointment.

III. *The design of the Sacraments.*
1. To represent Christ and the benefits of the new covenant. Christ's person and works are set forth by them in relation to believers.
2. To seal Christ and the benefits of the new covenant to believers. The Sacraments are signs and pledges on his part, by which he engages to fulfil the covenant Those who believe on him receive the sacraments in this sense.

3. To apply Christ and the benefits of the new covenant to believers. The signs are channels of the things signified. Faith by the sign takes hold of the thing signified. As the sign is sensibly applied, so the spiritual blessing is received by faith.

IV. *The proper recipients of the Sacraments.* These are believers only. They have a relation to Christ by faith.

LESSONS.

1. Sacraments cannot save.
2. Every lover of Christ loves what he has appointed.—*Steel.*

The New Testament Sacraments come in place of those under the Old Testament. They refer to the same spiritual truths, but occupy a different position. The one class pointed to the future, the other points to the past. Circumcision referred to the spiritual cleansing, as Baptism does; and the Passover was a feast upon the lamb slain, as the Lord's Supper is a feast upon the bread and wine, emblems of the body and blood of Christ.

I. *Baptism was appointed by Christ himself as an ordinance or Sacrament of his church.* Though John baptized, yet it was not Christian baptism. It was not in the name of the Father, the Son, and the Holy Ghost. Christ expressly appointed the formula of baptism: Matt. xxviii. 19.

II. *The Lord's Supper was instituted by Christ.* This was done on the night on which he was betrayed. The apostle refers to this as his authority for the sacred ordinance: 1 Cor. xi. 23.

III. *These are the only Sacraments of the New Testament appointed by Christ.* They have an outward visible sign, and an inward spiritual grace. No other ordinances in the New Testament have such appointed signs.

LESSONS.

1. The way of salvation is the same under the New as under the Old Testament.
2. The sacraments point to the same essential truths of salvation. —*Steel.*

Old Testament types of the New Testament Sacrament of Baptism: 1. Circumcision; 2. The Flood, (1 Peter iii. 21, etc,); 3. The passage through the Red Sea, (1 Cor. x. 2); 4. The pillar of cloud in the wilderness, (Exodus xiv. 19; 5. Naaman's washing in Jordan, (2 Kings v. 14).

Of the Lord's Supper: 1. The Passover; 2. The manna, (Ex. xvi. 15); 3. The water from the smitten rock, (Ex. xvii. and 1 Cor. x. 1-5).

ANECDOTES AND ILLUSTRATIONS.

In classical usage the word "sacramentum" means in general something sacred. In legal proceedings, the money deposited by contending parties was called "sacramentum," because when forfeited it was applied to sacred purposes. In military usage it expressed the obligation of a soldier to his leader or his country; then the oath by which he was bound; and generally an oath. In ecclesiastical use it was something sacred; then something secret or mysterious; then a sign of a mystery.

"On Sabbath last," said a good man, "we were enabled to keep the New Testament passover. It was a good day, a day of salvation. At the sacred banquet my heart melted, and the tears flowed plentifully from my eyes; but they were tears of joy—my heart was full. On Monday Mr. B—— preached from these words, 'And one shall say, I am the Lord's' Oh, what a sermon to me? My heart made the happy claim and cheerful surrender again and again. My soul said, 'I am the Lord's;' and with my heart I subscribed it, and I hope and believe will never unsay it."

> "Sweet was the hour I freedom felt
> To call my Jesus mine,
> To see his smiling face, and melt
> In pleasures all divine.

"'Truly I am thy servant; I am thy servant, and the son of thine handmaid: thou hast loosed my bonds.' Why me, O Lord, why me? What am I, or what is my father's house, that thou hast brought me hitherto?"

> "Low in adoration bending,
> Now our hearts our God revere;
> Faith her aid to sight is lending,—
> Though unseen, the Lord is near;
> Ancient types and shadows ending,
> Christ our paschal lamb is here."

Circumcision was instituted about nineteen hundred years before the incarnation of Christ, and doubtless looked forward to him who was to come. It was a sign of the covenant which God made, or rather renewed, with Abraham his friend in the hundredth year of his age: Gen. xvii. Circumcision represented our natural pollution and depravity, together with the necessity of regeneration, or of being cut off from the first Adam as a federal head and representative, and of being ingrafted into Christ, the second Adam, and washed in his all-cleansing blood : Rom. ii. 28, 29. It was the initiatory Sacrament under the Old Testament dispensation, as Baptism is under the New. Both substantially represent the same thing—the one the putting off of the sins of the flesh, and the other the washing of them away in the blood of Jesus.

"The Passover was instituted on the occasion of the deliverance of the children of Israel out of the land of Egypt; and it had a most important meaning with respect to Christ, who was to come : Ex. xii. No sooner did the destroying angel observe the blood sprinkled where it ought to be, according to the divine command, than he viewed it as their refuge ; so that this evidenced obedience to the divine command, and faith in the blood of Christ which was to be shed. And without doubt this sprinkling of blood typified that it is only in virtue of the blood or satisfaction of Christ that the danger arising from sin can be averted—namely, the curse of the law and the wrath of God, which shall assuredly overtake all those who are not under the sprinkling of the blood of Jesus : Rom. v. 9."—*Paterson.*

The five additional Sacraments of the Romish church were not appointed as ordinances by Christ.

Confirmation, by the laying on of the bishop's hands, along with the sign of the cross and the anointing with oil, has no scriptural authority.

Penance, or repentance, is a state of mind, and not an outward form. Contrition, auricular confession, satisfaction, and absolution by a priest, are not a divine appointment.

Sacred Orders, or ordination to office in the church, was instituted by Christ, but is no symbol of grace.

Matrimony is no special institution of the Christian church, but is common to all mankind.

Extreme unction, or the anointing of a dying person's eyes, ears, nostrils, mouth, hands, feet, etc., with olive oil by a priest, has no appointment by Christ

They have no claim to be Sacraments in the church, and some of them are connected with fundamental errors condemned by the Scriptures.

BAPTISM.

295. *What is Baptism?*

Baptism is not simply water, but it is the water comprehended in God's command, and connected with God's word.

296. What is that word of God?

It is that which our Lord Jesus Christ spake, as it is recorded in the last chapter of Matthew, verse 19: "Go ye and teach all nations, baptizing them in the name of the Father, and of the Son and of the Holy Ghost."

THE NATURE OF BAPTISM.

297. When and by whom was Christian Baptism instituted?

Christian Baptism was instituted by Christ on the day of his ascension.

Matthew xxviii. 19. Go ye therefore and teach all nations, baptizing them in the name of the Father, and of the Son, and of the Holy Ghost.

298. What is a Covenant?

A covenant is a mutual promise between two or more persons to do something for each other.

299. In what does the Baptismal Covenant consist?

The Baptismal Covenant consists in the promise which the Triune God makes to man, and the promise which man makes to God.

300. What blessings does the Triune God promise to us in Baptism?

1. God the Father promises us the adoption into the family of his children ;

Galatians iii. 26, 27. For ye are all the children of God by faith in Christ Jesus ; for as many of you as have been baptized into Christ, have put on Christ.

2. God the Son promises us salvation through the merits of his atonement ;

Romans vi. 3, 4. Know ye not that as many of us as were baptized into Jesus Christ were baptized into his death? Therefore, we are buried with him by baptism into death ; that like as Christ was raised up from the dead by the glory of the Father, even so we also should walk in newness of life.

Mark xvi. 16. He that believeth and is baptized shall be saved.

3. And the Holy Ghost promises his gifts.

Titus iii. 5-9. Not by works of righteousness which we have done, but according to his mercy he saved us by the washing of regeneration and renewing of the Holy Ghost, etc.

301. What does man promise to God in his Baptismal Covenant?

Man promises in his Baptismal Covenant to renounce the devil, that is, his services; and his works, that is sin; and all his ways, that is everything in which he might become like Satan; and he promises to serve the Triune God faithfully until death.

302. Who are proper subjects for Baptism?

All who have truly repented of their sins, and believe on the Lord Jesus Christ, are proper subjects for Christian Baptism.

Matthew xxviii, 19. Go ye therefore and teach all nations, baptizing them in the name of the Father, and of the Son, and of the Holy Ghost.

303. Should children also be baptized?

Children of believing parents should be baptized, because,

1. They are held in high esteem in the eyes of God, and Christ, who has redeemed them also by his blood.

Jonah iv. 11. Should not I spare Ninevah, that great city, wherein are more than six score thousand persons, that cannot discern between their right hand and their left?

Matthew xviii. 10. Take heed that ye dispise not one of these little ones; for I say unto you, that in heaven their angels do always behold the face of my Father which is in heaven.

2. They belong to the nations whom Christ has commanded to be taught and baptized.

Acts ii. 39. For the promise is unto you and your children, and to all that are afar off, even as many as the Lord, our God shall call.

Matthew xxviii. 19. Go ye therefore and teach all nations, baptizing them in the name of the Father, and of the Son, and of the Holy Ghost.

3. They belong to the kingdom of Christ, and are therefore, entitled to all the means of grace in that kingdom.

Matthew xix. 14-15. But Jesus said, Suffer little children, and forbid them not to come unto me, for of such is the kingdom of heaven. And he laid his hands on them.

4. In the Old Testament the children were received into the covenant of God by circumcision, which is the type of the Sacrament of Baptism.

Genesis xvii. 13. He that is born in thy house, and he that is bought with thy money, must needs be circumcised; and my covenant shall be in your flesh for an everlasting covenant.

5. In the New Testament, when the heads of families believed and were baptized, their whole households, consisting partly of children, were also baptized. Instances are, The households of Cornelius, Lydia, the Phillipian Jailer and the household of Stephanus.

6. Origen, who was born only eighty-five years after St. John died, and other christian fathers, assert that *infant baptism was handed down to their age from the days of the apostles?*

7. At the council of Carthage, in the year 253, the question was proposed, "Should children be baptized on the second, third or eighth day after their birth, in like manner as the children of the Israelites were circumcised on the eighth day?" There was, therefore, no doubt among these early Christians in regard to the Baptism of infants.

304. What are the benefits of Baptism?

It causes* the forgiveness of sin, delivers from death and the devil, and gives everlasting salvation *to those that believe*, as the word and promise of God declare.

Mark i. 4. John did baptize in the wilderness, and preach the baptism of repentance for the remission of sins.

Titus iii. 5. Not by works of righteousness which we have done, but according to his mercy he saved us, by the washing of regeneration, and renewing of the Holy Ghost.

Colossians ii. 12. Buried with him in baptism, wherein also ye are risen with him through the faith of the operation of God, who hath raised him from the dead.

305. Which are these words and promises of God?

Those, in which our Lord declares, Mark xvi. 16: "He that believeth and is baptized, shall be saved; but he that believeth not, shall be damned."

---

* That is, it is one of the appointments for obtaining those blessings.

1 Peter iii. 21. The like figure whereunto even baptism doth also now save us (not the putting away of the filth of the flesh, but the answer of a good conscience toward God,) by the resurrection of Jesus Christ.

Hebrews xi. 6. But without faith it is impossible to please *him*; for he that cometh to God must believe that he is, and that he is a rewarder of them that diligently seek him.

306. How may the benefits of Baptism be designated?

The benefits of Baptism may be designated as two-fold; namely, external or visible, and internal, spiritual or invisible.

307. What are the external or visible benefits of Baptism?

By Baptism we are admitted into the visible church of Christ, entitled to all the privileges of church membership and the enjoyment of the means of grace, in like manner as the naturalization of a foreigner entitles him to all the privileges of citizenship, in the country to which he has sworn allegiance.

308. What are the spiritual or invisible benefits of Baptism?

The spiritual benefits of Baptism may be stated negatively and positively:

1. *Negatively:* Baptism is of no spiritual benefit to an unbeliever, or to a person who has no knowledge of the word of God, and has had no instruction in the doctrines of the Christian religion.

2. *Positively:* As in our Baptismal covenant we renounce the devil, the world, and the flesh, and profess our faith in the Triune God, Father, Son, and Holy Ghost, whom we profess to love with all our heart, mind, soul and spirit, and to serve with all the faculties of our minds and the energies of our bodies, so God, on his part, grants us faith, the forgiveness of our sins and imputes to us the righteousness of Christ, spiritual life and salvation, and the inheritance of the kingdom of heaven.

Note 1. In the case of adults, *repentance* and *faith* is required before Baptism; for, without faith, such, indeed, receive Baptism, but deprive themselves of its benefits by neglecting, or violating the terms of the Baptismal covenant.

<small>Acts viii. 37. And Philip said, "If thou believest with all thine heart, thou mayest (be baptized). And he answered and said, I believe that Jesus Christ is the Son of God.
Acts ii. 38. Then Peter said unto them, Repent, and be baptized.
Acts ii. 41. Then they that gladly received his word were baptized.</small>

See also the accounts of the Baptism of Cornelius, Acts v. 29-42; Lydia, Acts xvi. 15, and the Philippian jailer, Acts xvi. 33, all of which indicate faith before Baptism.

Examples of such as were not benefitted by Baptism for want of true faith: Ananias and Saphira, Acts v. 1-11; Simon Magus, Acts viii. 9-24.

Note 2. In the case of infants, *faith,* or at least, membership in the Christian church, is required of the parents or sponsors who present the child for Baptism.

309. How can water produce such great effects?

1. It is not the water that produces them, but the Word of God, which is connected with the water;

2. For without the Word of God, the water is mere water, and no Baptism.

3. But with the Word of God it is a Baptism; that is, a merciful water of life, and a laver of regeneration in the Holy Ghost, as St. Paul says to Titus:

<small>Titus iii. 5. Not by works of righteousness which we have done, but according to his mercy he saved us, by the washing of regeneration, and renewing of the Holy Ghost;
Titus iii. 6. Which he shed on us abundantly through Jesus Christ our Savior.</small>

4. "According to his mercy hath he saved us by the washing of regeneration and the renewing of the Holy Ghost; which he hath shed on us abundantly through Jesus Christ our Savior," that thereby we might be made

righteous, and be heirs according to the hope of everlasting life.

Galatians iii. 26. For ye are all the children of God by faith in Christ Jesus.

Galatians iii. 27. For as many of you as have been baptized into Christ have put on Christ.

310. What are the means by which these benefits of Baptism are conferred and received?

The means of imparting and of receiving the benefits of Baptism are the following:

I. On the part of the administrator,
  1. By the use of the words of the institution.
  2. By the questions asked of the person to be baptized, (or in the case of infants, of the parents or sponsors,) whether he will faithfully enter into, accept and carry out the conditions of the Baptismal covenant.
  3. The act of baptizing by pouring or sprinkling water upon the person to be baptized.

Ephesians v. 26. That he might sanctify and cleanse it with the washing of water by the word.

1 Peter iii. 21. The like figure (Noah saved from the flood) whereunto *even* baptism doth also now save us (not the putting away of the filth of the flesh, but the answer of a good conscience toward God,) by the resurrection of Jesus Christ.

II. On the part of the person to be baptized,
  1. That he confidently believe and trust the Word connected with the water;
  2. That he heartily and with a good conscience enter into and accept the Baptismal covenant.

311. What does such baptizing with water signify?

1. It signifies that the Old Adam in us is to be drowned and destroyed by daily sorrow and repentance, together with all sins and evil lusts;

2. And that again the New Man should daily come forth and rise, that shall live in the presence of God in righteousness and purity forever.

THE MEANING, DUTIES AND EFFECTS OF BAPTISM.

312. What is meant by the words, " The Old Adam?"

The words, "Old Adam," signify original sin, or depravity, which is a natural disposition to do evil, and is so called, because we have inherited it from our first parents.

313. In what does original sin consist?

Original sin consists in a destitution of every thing that is good in man, and an inclination to every thing that is evil, which leads to the commission of actual sin, and extends over the whole man; namely, his understanding, will, walk and conversation.

Romans iii. 23. For all have sinned and come short of the glory of God.
Romans iii. 11. There is none that understandeth, there is none that seeketh after God.
Romans iii. 12. They are all gone out of the way, they are together become unprofitable; there is none that doeth good, no, not one.

314. Why is natural depravity called " The Old Adam?"

Natural depravity is called The Old Adam, because it began with Adam, the first man, and cleaves to us through life, and we grow old with it.

315. What is meant by the words, " The new man?"

By the words "new man" is meant the divine image and likeness in which man was created.

316. Why is he called " The new man?"

He is called "The new man," because the new or regenerated nature extends over the whole man, as to his body and soul, his will, his memory, etc., which becomes manifest by his walk and conversation; and he becomes a new man through faith.

Romans vi. 13. Neither yield ye your members *as* instruments of unrighteousness unto sin: but yield yourselves unto God, as those that are alive from the dead, and your members *as* instruments of righteousness unto God.

317. What is meant by the words, " The new man shall come forth and rise?"

The words, "The new man shall come forth and rise," mean, that this renewal shall be wrought in us and continue more and more.

<small>Romans vi. 3. Know ye not, that so many of us as were baptized into Jesus Christ were baptized into his death?
Romans vi. 4 Therefore we are buried with him by baptism into death: that like as Christ was raised up from the dead by the glory of the Father, even so we also should walk in newness of life.</small>

318. Where is this recorded?

St. Paul, in the Epistle to the Romans, chapter vi., verse 4, says: "We are buried with Christ by Baptism into death; that like as he was raised up from the dead by the glory of the Father, even so we also should walk in newness of life."

319. What is meant by being "buried with Christ in Baptism?"

Being buried with Christ means,

1. That we appropriate the merits of Christ's death to ourselves.

2. That we derive from his death life and resurrection, and

3. That we frequently renew our Baptismal covenant, and continue to live in covenant with God,

4. For by being unfaithful to our covenant, we become covenant breakers.

320. What is meant by "Shall be drowned and destroyed?"

The meaning of these words is that the natural depravity in us shall be suppressed and overcome, although it may be difficult and painful.

321. By what means shall this natural depravity be suppressed and overcome.

Our natural depravity is to be suppressed by daily sorrow and repentance, which is produced by contemplation of the violated covenant and its sad results.

EXPLANATORY NOTES.

Definitions of Baptism:

Lutheran: Baptism is not simply water, but it is the water comprehended in God's command and connected with God's word.

Ger. Reformed: Baptism is a covenant of grace of the Triune God with man, whereby God promises forgiveness and salvation, and man vows obedience and devotion to him.

Episcopal: Baptism is an outward and visible sign of an inward and spiritual grace given unto us, ordained by Christ himself, as a means whereby we recieve the same, and a pledge to assure us thereof.

Presbyterian: Baptism is a sacrament wherein the washing with water in the name of the Father, and of the Son, and of the Holy Ghost, doth signify and seal our ingrafting into Christ, and partaking of the benefits of the covenant of grace, and our engagement to be the Lord's.

Scriptural Examples. John's Baptism of repentance, Luke iii. 3, Matt. xxi. 25; The disciples of Jesus, John iv. 1, 2, 3; iii. 25, 26; Christ's Baptism, Matt. iii. 13-15; The divine institution of Baptism, Matt. xxviii. 19; The Baptism of the first believers, Acts ii. 41; of the Eunuch, Acts viii. 35; of the disciples at Ephesus, Acts xix. 1-8.

BAPTISM OF CHILDREN INDICATED.

Mark x. 13-16; Children Baptized in Christian families, Acts ii. 39; 1 Cor. vii. 14; Lydia and her house, Acts xvi. 14, 15; The jailer at Philippi, Acts xvi. 33.

I. *The sign used in Baptism.* Water.
  1. Because of its cleansing properties.
  2. Because it is thus made to represent the blood and Spirit of Christ, which cleanse the soul.

  The mode of Baptism is by pouring, sprinkling, or dipping.

II. *The formula of Baptism.* The words to be used were prescribed by Christ himself, and to be in the name of the Father, of the Son, and of the Holy Ghost. The three persons in the Godhead are equally engaged in salvation.

III. *The design of Baptism.* It teaches great truths connected with salvation.
  1. It signifies and seals our ingrafting into Christ. The soul must be as closely united to Christ as the branch is to the tree. This is pledged by Christ to all his believing people.
  2. It signifies and seals our partaking of the benefits of the covenant of grace. These are, pardon of sin, Acts. ii. 38; regeneration, Titus iii. 5; and the resurrection to life everlasting, Rom. vi. 4.

3. It signifies and seals our engagement to be the Lord's.
  (1.) It is a profession of faith in him as our Savior.
  (2.) It is a public form of joining the communion of the visible church.
  (3.) It binds us, therefore, to be the Lord's.

LESSONS.

1. The Baptism of the Spirit is essential : John iii. 5.

2. All who are Baptized into Christ should put on Christ : Gal. iii. 27.—*Steel.*

"It is admitted—1. That Baptism is a sign, and that the blessing which it signifies is purification from sin. 2. That the theocratical purifications, having the same general import, were effected by immersion, affusion, and sprinkling. 3. That the soul is cleansed from the guilt of sin by the blood of Christ. 4. That under the Old Testament the application of the blood of the sacrifices for sin was expressed by the act of sprinkling. It was sprinkled on the people (Ex. xxiv. 8) for whose benefit the sacrifices were offered; it was sprinkled upon the altar; and, by the high priest, upon the mercy-seat. In the New Testament the application of the blood of Christ is expressed by the same word: 1 Peter i. 2; Heb. xii. 24. 5. It is admitted, further, that the purification of the soul from the moral pollution of sin is effected by the renewing of the Holy Ghost. 6. It is admitted that the communication of the sanctifying influences of the Spirit is expressed in the use of two familiar figures, that of anointing with oil, and that of the pouring of water. Kings, priests, and prophets were anointed. The people of God are called his 'anointed': 1 John ii. 20, 27. The other figure is no less familiar: Isa. xxxii. 15; Joel ii. 28. The Spirit's influences are compared to rain which waters the earth, and to the dew which falls on the mown grass. From all this it appears that the truth symbolized in Baptism may be signified by immersion, affusion, or sprinkling; but that the ordinance is most significant and most conformed to Scripture when administered by affusion or sprinkling."—*Hodge.*

ANECDOTES AND ILLUSTRATIONS.

The Rev. Titus Coan, D. D., missionary at the Sandwich Islands, in the course of forty years baptized 13,000 persons. Of these, 5,000 were baptized in one year, and 1,700 in one day, at a great period of awakening in 1838. Of the last number he says that more water flowed from their eyes than he sprinkled on their faces.

"If the church is one under both dispensations, if infants were members of the church under the theocracy, then they are members of the church now, unless the contrary can be proved."—*Dr. Hodge.*

"A credible profession of Christianity is all that the church may require in order to communion. She may be deceived; her utmost caution may be, and often has been, ineffectual to keep bad men from the sanctuary; and this, too, without her fault, as she is not omniscient. But she has no right to suspect sincerity, to refuse privileges, or inflict censure, where she can put her finger upon nothing repugnant to the love or the laws of God."—*Dr. Mason.*

"It is plain that, according to the standards of the Reformed Church, it is the children of the members of the visible church who are to be baptized. Agreeably to scriptural usage, such members are called '*fœderati*,' saints, believers, faithful, holy brethren, partakers of the heavenly calling. The apostles, in addressing professing Christians, in the use of such terms did not express any judgment of their state in the sight of God. They designated them according to their profession.

"1. The visible church has always consisted of those who professed the true religion, together with their children.

"2. The terms of church membership under both dispensations have been the same—namely, profession of faith, and promise of obedience.

"3. The requirements for participation in the sacraments have been the same. That is, any one entitled to the rite of circumcision was entitled to partake of the passover; those under the Christian dispensation entitled to baptism are entitled to the Lord's Supper. Those who, unbaptized, would be entitled to baptism for themselves, are entitled, and they only, to present their children for baptism.

"Those, therefore, who have been themselves baptized and still profess their faith in the true religion, who have competent knowledge and are free from scandal, should not only be permitted but urged and enjoined to present their children for baptism, that they may belong to the church, and be brought up under its watch and care."—*Abridged from Dr. Hodge.*

"I spent some time," says Mr. J. Baily, of New England, "in offering up myself and my child to the Lord, and in taking hold of the covenant for myself and him. It is actually to be done to-morrow in baptism. I prayed hard to-day that I might receive help from the Lord. It is not easy, though common, to offer a child to God in baptism. Oh, that is a sweet word, 'I will be a God unto thee, and to thy seed after thee.' No wonder Abraham fell on his face at the hearing of it."

Mr. Philip Henry drew up the following short form of the baptismal covenant, for the use of his children.

"I take God, the Father, to be my chiefest good and highest end.
I take God, the Son, to be my Prince and Savior.
I take God, the Holy Ghost, to be my sanctifier, teacher, guide and comforter.
I take the word of God to be my rule in all my actions.
And the people of God to be my people in all conditions.
I do likewise devote and dedicate unto the Lord, my whole self, all I am, all I have, and all I can do.
And this I do deliberately, sincerely, freely, and for ever."

This he taught his children, and they each of them solemnly repeated it every Lord's day in the evening, after they were catechised, he putting his *Amen* to it, and sometimes adding, "So say, and so do, and you are made for ever."

A Greenlander, who for many years had communication with the Moravian missionaries, but could never resolve to forsake his land, where he was held in great respect, being at the Capelin fishery, got a sight of his daughter, who had removed from him, and was baptized, and showed his resentment at it. But she modestly told him the reasons that induced her to it; set forth the happiness of believers, concluding with these words: "So happy may *you* also be; but if you will not, I cannot stay and perish with you. This softened his heart, and he began to weep, went with her to the missionary, and declared, his intention now was, not to take away his daughter from the baptized, but rather go with her. He expressed his resolution to remain with the missionaries, and his wish that the rest of his children might be baptized. "As to myself," said he, "I dare not think of baptism, as I am very bad, and old too, and incapable of learning much more; but yet I will live and die with you, for it is very reviving to me, to hear of our Savior."

As an instance of the misapplication and abuse of the sacred ordinance of baptism, the author of the *Protestant*, publishes in that excellent work, a description sent him by a correspondent, of the ceremony of the baptism of a *bell*, which took place at Naples. A noble lord was godfather to the bell, and a lady of quality was godmother. Most of the prayers said on the occasion, ended with the following words: "That thou wouldst be pleased to rinse, purify, sanctify, and consecrate these bells with thy heavenly benediction." The following were the words of consecration: "Let the sign be consecrated and sanctified in the name of the Father, and of the Son, and of the Holy

Ghost." The bishop then turning to the people, said, "The bell's name is Mary." He had previously demanded of the godfather and godmother, what name they would have put upon the bell, and the lady gave it this name.

A gentleman in Vermont, who had lived to middle age without religion and without family prayers, was thus accosted by his little son, not quite seven years old : " Papa, you have taught me to pray morning and evening, and now I want *to know if you ever pray?*" The father, conscious of his failure in this duty, and astonished at this unexpected question, was at a loss for a reply. At length recollecting that he had sometimes attempted to pray in secred, replied, "I hope I have sometimes endeavored to pray that you might be a good boy, and that I might also be enabled to do my duty." The child replied, "Well, papa, Mr. and Mrs.—— pray in their families, and sometimes, when they have been here, you have asked them to pray. Is it wicked Pa?" "O no, my child, all good people pray, and it is right they should." "Well, papa, if it is right *they* should, is it not right that *you* should?" "I suppose it would be, my son, if my heart was right." "Well, papa, were my sister and I ever baptized?" "No," says the father, sighing with a heavy heart; "No, you are neither of you baptized." "Why not papa? I have seen several little children baptized, when I have been at meeting. Is it wicked, papa, to baptize children?" "O no, my son, I do not conceive it to be wicked, but I cannot get you baptized." "Why not, papa?" "Because I do not belong to the church." "Why do you not belong to the church, papa? is it wicked!" "O no, my son; nothing, I suppose, debars me, but my own wicked heart." "Well, pa, if it is right you should, why will you not belong to the church, and so get sister and me baptized?"

These solemn inquiries were directed by the Holy Spirit to the conversion of the father, who soon commenced family prayer, and is now a distinguished member of the church.

He who is born but once must die twice; but he who has been twice born will die only once.—*Ger. Proverb.*

Our forefathers used to kiss their little children after they were baptized, saying, "My darling, before you were my child, now you are God's child."

When saint Remigius, of Rhiems, baptized king Chlodwig, he consecrated him with these words : " Burn what thou hast heretofore worshiped, and worship what thou didst formerly burn."

After Adalgisus, king of Friesland, had been baptized, Ebrain, duke of Frankonia, wrote him a letter, in which he promised him a rich reward, if he would apostatize from the Christian religion. But Adalgisus threw the letter into the fire in the presence of his courtiers, and said, "Just as this paper is burned, so may he burn who breaks the covenant which he has made with a friend."

The Old Adam shall not only die, but shall also be buried, and it is the new man that buries him.—*Ger. Proverb.*

An aged heathen woman in the Bethany mission station in South Africa, remarked that "she also desired to be received by baptism into the covenant with God. But she felt her unworthiness; she appeared to herself like a little child." To this the missionary replied, that this was exactly the state of heart which the Lord required, for he had said, Except ye be converted and become as little children, ye shall not enter into the kingdom of heaven. Matt. xviii. 3.

A poor, miserable woman, who had been a servant in Luther's house at Wittenberg, had sold herself, soul, body and to the devil. When she had fallen into great distress on this account, Luther visited her and asked, why she was so distressed, "O dear sir," said she, "why should I not be distressed? I have turned away from God, and given myself over to the devil." "Be comforted," said Luther, "This is comparatively a trifling sin. Have you not committed a greater sin?" She replied, "O dear Doctor, what greater sin could I have committed?" "That would be the greatest sin," replied Luther, "if you would continue in this folly, and yield yourself to despair. Listen to this, dear Elsa, Can you give away Mr. Froeshlins money, or book, or his coat?" "No," said she, "they are not mine." "Well, then," replied Luther, "you can not give yourself away, for you are not your own. You have not redeemed yourself; the Lord Jesus has redeemed you. You are *bap!ized in his name.* You belong to him. You have no authority over yourself. Break off your contract with the devil, and say to him, Hence thou lying spirit, go to my Lord Christ. If you want anything, ask him for it; he will pour the fire of hell upon your head!"

Lewis IX., king of France, was baptized in the village of Poisy, and crowned at St. Dennis. He usually signed himself Lewis of Poisy. For, said he, at St. Dennis I received an earthly crown, but at Poisy I received a heavenly crown. In reference to his baptism he used to say, "Three handfulls of water are worth more to me than a royal crown!"

The sainted jailer, Erdle, of Nurnberg, often accompanied his godfather, in his childhood, to church. At his entrance into the church, the pious man usually prayed somewhat audibly for his little Godchild by name, which had a very wholesome, spiritual effect upon him.

A baptized Christian child is like the child of a king, when in its cradle; it is the heir of a crown, although not conscious thereof.

Here are a few words from the writings of Dr. Luther:

1. What is the Old Adam? It is that nature with which we were born. The Old Adam is angry, hateful, envious, unchaste, stingy, lazy, proud, unfaithful, beset with all kinds of vice, and has by nature nothing good about him. Now when we come into the kingdom of Christ, all these things shall daily decrease, we shall in the course of our lives, become more mild and patient and meek, and break off more and more from our unbelief, stinginess, hatred and envy. This is the proper use of Baptism among Christians, and which is signified by water Baptism. Where this is not the case, but the reins are left to the Old Adam, that he may grow still stronger, this is not making a proper use of, but is in opposition to Baptism.

2. Unfortunately many conduct themselves, as if they might always continue in their old ways (*alten Haut*), live according to their lusts, and thus disgrace their holy Baptism; as though they had been called into the kingdom of grace, that they might have the liberty to do what they pleased, trusting, that God would be gracious to them, and thus comfort themselves, "I am an imperfect man; God will graciously excuse and forgive me." No, not in this way, dear brother. I have not taught you that Baptism shall give you freedom to sin; but the contrary. Your sins are remitted and you have received the grace of God, because you now lead a different life, and have forsaken your sins. It is not consistent to be baptized and live in sin.

DR. SCHMUCKER'S HINTS ON CATECHISATION.

The following extract from Dr. Schmucker's Catechism may be helpful to the pastors in the instruction of their classes:

In a course of instruction for *confirmation*, an excellent method is the following:

1. The pastor may divide the entire series of questions into as many parts as he expects to hold meetings, and assign one portion for each meeting. The pupils should not attempt to memorize the answers verbatim, but should attentively read and prayerfully reflect on them, and when questioned, answer in their own words, as in Bible lessons.

2. The pastor should make the same portion of the catechism the subject of premeditation for the day. He should first address one question by name to each of those pupils whom he deems best qualified to answer, in order to encourage the others, and on subsequent days, pass questions regularly along to the pupils, as they may be seated. He may explain the subject of each question after the answer is recited, or may reserve his explanations until all the questions have been answered by the pupils; and then give them in the form of a paraphrase of the whole lesson, or in a separate lecture.

3. In either case, he should himself repeat aloud the answer to each question as he comments on it, in doing which he will find additional materials for remark by casting his eyes on the connected Scripture proofs.

4. The *Introduction* might be taken up last, if sufficient time remains, after the great subjects of doctrine, experience, and duty have been fully discussed, and the pupil led to the Savior.

5. After the pupil has repeated an answer, especially when timidly done and in a low voice, or not correctly, the minister also should repeat it aloud, so that all can hear; for in order that all may be benefited, all must hear. And even when he reserves his principal remarks to the close of the entire exercise, he ought, as he repeats each answer, to add a few words of confirmation or explanation.

6. The utmost simplicity of matter and manner should be aimed at, that the timid may not be embarrassed, and that all may feel at ease. Ministers should also seek to gain the affection and confidence of their children; should notice them when they meet them elsewhere; cultivate a personal acquaintance with them in the week, and take delight in teaching them

7. In the elucidation of the answers, the minister should study variety; and for this purpose cast his eye on the proof-texts before him, which were selected with the utmost care, and will furnish new and abundant materials for his remarks. By this course the congregation will become well *indoctrinated*, be proof against the extravagances and errors of the age, and be an active, devoted Church of Christ. Such an early religious training will, moreover, by the divine blessing, save the rising generation from the corruptions of the world, make them affectionate, obedient, and faithful children, and prepare them for being zealous and active disciples of the Lord.

S. S. SCHMUCKER.

GETTYSBURG, *October* 31, 1871.

CONFIRMATION.

322. What is Confirmation?

Negatively: Confirmation is not a sacrament, divinely instituted;

Positively: 1. It is a solemn and impressive ceremony established by the church, in which those who profess Christ are publicly received into the visible church of Christ.

2. It is the ceremony by which persons, who were baptized in their infancy and have been instructed in the doctrines of our holy religion, publicly renew and confirm their Baptismal Covenant.

323. Of how many parts does Confirmation consist?

Confirmation consists of three parts:

1. Public confession of the Christian faith;
2. A solemn vow to lead a Christian life; and
3. The consecration by prayer and the laying on of hands by the minister.

324. What qualifications should be required of those who wish to be confirmed?

Those who wish to be confirmed should,

1. Possess a correct knowledge of the fundamental doctrines and the duties of the Christian religion;
2. They should exhibit credible evidence that they have been taught by the Holy Spirit to see, deplore and renounce their sins, and
3. Exercise a living faith in Jesus Christ, and consecrate themselves unconditionally and forever to the service and glory of God.

325. What are some of the particular duties of those who are confirmed?

It should be the special effort of those who are confirmed,

1. To be faithful to the covenant engagements into which they have entered with God and his people;

2. To adorn their Christian profession by a well ordered walk and conversation;

3. With this view they should be particularly attentive, to the public ordinances of God's house, such as public worship, social prayermeetings, Sunday-schools, contributions to missionary purposes, as well as the support of the gospel at home; private and family worship, and take an active part in the benevolent efforts and all other duties of the church.

EXPLANATORY NOTES.

Scriptural Examples. Analogies of confirmation, Jesus and the twelve, John vi. 66-71; Those who were baptized at Samaria, Acts viii. 14-17; Those who were baptized at Ephesus, Acts xix. 6; The Collossians, Col. iii. 1-19; The Hebrews, Heb. v. 12-14.

Confirmation is a rite, whereby a person, arrived at the age of discretion, undertakes the performance of every part of the baptismal covenant made for him by his sponsors.

In the ancient church it was done immediately after baptism, if the bishop happened to be present at the solemnity. Throughout the East it still accompanies baptism, but the Romanists make it a distinct, independent sacrament. Seven years is the stated time for confirmation; however, they are sometimes confirmed after that age. In the church of England the age of the persons to be confirmed is not fixed.—*Howe's Episcopacy.*

Public confirmation was introduced in the Lutheran church in the year 1737.

As the rite of confirmation was not divinely instituted, but is only a ceremony of the church, it is not essential to salvation. Yet it is a sacred, important and impressive transaction, and may be the means of great blessing to the participants.

Confirmation may be embraced in two principal things:
I. Profession of religion on the part of the persons confirmed;
II. The consecration on the part of the minister.
I. *The Profession.* Children become members of the Christian chruch by baptism. Confirmation is not, therefore, the entrance into the Christian church, as some suppose.

The sponsors have promised to see that the child shall be trained up in the Christian religion, and be taught to believe in the Triune God, and lead a holy life.

But the Christian congregation now also wishes to hear from the mouth of the child itself, its confession of faith, after it has been taught in all things which Christ commanded. The catechumen confirms, ratifies everything that has been done in his name in holy baptism.

The vow of the catechumen to live and die in faith and holiness is very solemn. It is expressed

1. With the mouth. To the question of the minister, the divinely appointed servant of the church, he answers, Yes;
2. With the hand. The minister then says, Give me thy right hand, in token, that thou wilt faithfully keep thy vow. The giving of the right hand is a token of faithfulness and truth in fulfilling a promise or a vow.
3. In the presence of the all-seeing God. He hears your vow.
4. In the presence of the congregation. The congregation accepts your profession and vow, and regards you now as a communicant member.

II. *The Consecration* consists of the laying of the hands of the minister on the head of the catechumen, and his prayer. The imposition of hands is a symbol of the communication of spiritual gifts.

The preparation for confirmation is a sacred and solemn time. It should be devoted to prayer, that the Holy Ghost might open the heart, to the love and service of Christ; for grace and strength to keep the vow made on the day of confirmation; there should be much self-examination and reflection on the instructions that have been received; there should be diligent study of the holy Scriptures, and avoidance of all distracting company and worldly amusements.

ANECDOTES AND ILLUSTRATIONS.

On one occasion, when the sainted pastor Gonthier, had assembled his catechumens in the church on the occasion of their first communion, he saw in the midst of them an old soldier, who took a deep interest in the whole proceeding. Gonthier preached a sermon on the words, "For what knowest thou, O wife, whether thou shalt save thy husband, or how knowest thou, O man, whether thou shalt save thy wife?" 1 Cor. vii. 16. The text and the sermon made such a deep impression on the heart of the soldier's wife, that she continued from time to time to urge her husband to make a visit to the minister. He consented to do so, and came to the pastor, but could give him no reason for his visit, but the desire of his wife, whom he sincerely loved. She spoke every day, especially since that sermon, about things to him, of which he had never heard in his life and in which he took no interest, and she thought if he would only come once to the minister, he would take an interest in these things. Gonthier received him very kindly, and secured his confidence in his first conversation with him, to get him to promise to come again. In the second conversation the man had progressed so far as to ask for instruction in religion, and in the third conversation he declared that in future he would not enter secretly, as he had done, by the back door into the parsonage. At last he requested, as he did not now wish needlessly to interfere with the pastor's time, that he might take part with the catechumens in the religious instruction, and finally was admitted with them to the communion table.

Dr. A. F. Bushing, school-director in Berlin, was, after proper instruction by a worthy minister, confirmed in the spring of the year 1741, and died in the year 1793. He wrote on the occasion of his confirmation, for himself and his friend Dilthey, a covenant with God. Both friends, although far separated from each other, renewed this covenant every year on the anniversary of their confirmation, for the strengthening of their faith and love.

Beautiful is the way in which Tobias Kiesling, of Nürnberg, prepared his son, the younger Tobias, for his first communion. A few days before the confirmation he went with him to the minister and formally confided him to the spiritual supervision as his pastor. On the day, when the preparatory services were held, he took his son into his closet and with tears and prayer commended him to the grace and mercy of Christ.

The departure of one of the children from the homestead, was always a very affecting time in the family of the sainted pastor Rauschenbusch, of Elberfeld. To the affectionate admonition, addressed to the departing son or daughter, during the last meal, was added a fervent prayer. The departing one could not help but feel, that the father had not yet given up his guiding influence, but now pled for him by his intercessory prayer, at the throne of grace.

PART V.

THE SACRAMENT OF THE ALTAR OR THE LORD'S SUPPER.

326. What is the Sacrament of the Altar?

It is the true body and blood of our Lord Jesus Christ, under the bread and wine, given to us Christians to eat and drink, as it was instituted by Christ himself.

327. For what purpose was the Sacrament of the Lord's Supper instituted?

The Lord's Supper was instituted,

1. For the commemoration of the death of Christ;
2. For the renewal of our Baptismal Covenant, and
3. For the union of believers with Christ and among themselves.

1 Corinthians xi. 23, 24. The Lord Jesus, the *same* night in which he was betrayed took bread: And when he had given thanks, he brake *it*, and said, Take, eat: this is my body, which is broken for you:

1 Corinthians xi. 24. This do in remembrance of me.

1 Corinthians xi. 26. For as often as ye eat this bread, and drink this cup, ye do shew the Lord's death till he come.

Matthew xxvi. 27. And he took the cup, and gave thanks, and gave *it* to them, saying, Drink ye all of it;

Matthew xxvi. 28. For this is my blood of the new testament, which is shed for many for the remission of sins.

1 Corinthians x. 16. The cup of blessing which we bless, is it not the communion of the blood of Christ? The bread which we break, is it not the communion of the body of Christ?

1 Corinthians x. 17. For we *being* many are one bread, *and* one body: for we are all partakers of that one bread.

328. By what names is the Sacrament of the Lord's Supper called?

It is called by the following names:

1. The Lord's Supper, (1 Cor. x. 21) because it was instituted by Christ at night;

2. The Lord's Table, (1 Cor. xi. 20) because it was first partaken of by the disciples, while reclining around a table, and this custom was doubtless followed by the early Christians;

3. The Communion, (1 Cor. x. 16, 17) because it is a celebration of the union of believers with Christ and among themselves;

4. The Eucharist, or giving of thanks, (Matt. xxvi. 30) because it is customary to sing hymns of thanksgiving during the celebration of the Lord's Supper, which is a "commemoration of all the blessings of God, that culminate in redemption by the blood of Christ;"

5. It is also called the Sacrament of the *Altar*, (Heb. xiii. 10) "as a celebration of the atoning sacrifice of Christ."

329. Which are the words of the institution of the Lord's Supper?

The holy Evangelists, Matthew, Mark and Luke, together with St. Paul, write thus:

"Our Lord Jesus Christ, the same night in which he was betrayed, took bread; and when he had given thanks, he brake it, and gave it to the disciples, and said, Take, eat; this is my body which is given for you: this do in remembrance of me."

"After the same manner also he took the cup, when he had supped, gave thanks, and gave it to them, saying, Drink ye all of it: this cup is the new testament in my blood, which is shed for you, for the remission of sins: this do ye, as oft as ye drink it, in remembrance of me."

330. What is meant by the consecration of the elements?

By the consecration of the elements is meant the setting apart, or devoting a sufficient quantity of bread and wine for use in the Holy Sacrament by prayer and the repetition of the words of the institution.

331. Who should consecrate and administer the elements in the Holy Communion?

Only properly appointed ministers of the Gospel should consecrate and administer the elements in the Holy Communion.

1 Corinthians ix. 13 They which minister about holy things.
1 Corinthians xiv. 40. Let all things be done decently and in order.

332. Which are the external elements used in the Lord's Supper?

The external elements are bread and wine. The bread may be either leavened or unleavened, and the wine should be the uncorrupted, unadulterated "fruit of the vine."

Matthew xxvi. 29. But I say unto you, I will not drink henceforth of this fruit of the vine, until that day when I drink it new with you in my Father's kingdom.

333. Who should be admitted to the Lord's Supper?

All Christians who have been baptized and have united with the church by a profession of faith, and whose life corresponds with their profession.

334. What should communicants do before partaking of the Lord's Supper?

Before partaking of the Lord's Supper communicants should examine themselves, confess their sins, pray for forgiveness, and resolve by the help of God to live a holier life.

1 Corinthians xi. 28. But let a man examine himself, and so let him eat of *that* bread, and drink of *that* cup.

335. Who commune worthily?

Those commune worthily, who have repented of their sins, humbly trust in Christ, and truly believe these words, "Given and shed for the remission of sins."

336. Which is the chief thing in the Lord's Supper?

Besides the bodily eating and drinking the chief thing in the Sacrament is faith in these words, "Given and shed for you for the remission of sins." For where there is remission of sin, there is also life and salvation.

337. Who is unprepared and unworthy to come to the Lord's Supper?

He who lives in known and voluntary sin, and has no true faith, or doubts in his mind the truth of Christ's words; for the words, " Given and shed for you," require truly believing hearts.

Romans xiv. 23. And he that doubteth is damned if he eat, because *he eateth* not of faith : for whatsoever *is* not of faith is sin.

338. What threatning is pronounced against those who commune unworthily?

Those who live in known and voluntary sin, and do not recognize the body and blood of Christ in the Sacrament, but partake of it as if it were an ordinary meal, eat and drink condemnation to themselves.

1 Corinthians xi. 27. Wherefore whosoever shall eat this bread, and drink *this* cup of the Lord, unworthily, shall be guilty of the body and blood of the Lord.

1 Corinthians xi. 29. For he that eateth and drinketh unworthily, eateth and drinketh damnation to himself.

339. In what does our true preparation to receive the Lord's Supper consist?

We become worthy participants of the Lord's Supper,

I. Not by bodily discipline, or external preparation, such as fasting, bodily purifications, etc.

Isaiah lviii. 5. Is it such a fast that I have chosen? a day for a man to afflict his soul? is it to bow down his head as a bulrush, and to spread sackcloth and ashes under him? wilt thou call this a fast, and an acceptable day to the Lord?

Isaiah lviii. 6. Is not this the fast that I have chosen? to loose the bands of wickedness, to undo the heavy burdens, and to let the oppressed go free, and that ye break every yoke?

Isaiah lviii. 7. Is it not to deal thy bread to the hungry, and that thou bring the poor that are cast out to thy house? when thou seest the naked, that thou cover him ; and that thou hide not thyself from thine own flesh?

1. Which are, indeed, good and commendable, when they are done in order to clear the mind and make it capable of appreciating the importance of our communion.

1 Corinthians xi. 28. But let a man examine himself, and so let him eat of that bread, and drink of that cup.

2. But which are not of themselves sufficient, because God requires the whole heart and its worthy preparation by purification from sin.

Matthew vi. 24. No man can serve two masters: for either he will hate the one, and love the other; or else he will hold to the one, and dispise the other. Ye cannot serve God and mammon.

Isaiah i. 16. Wash you, make you clean; put away the evil of your doings from before mine eyes; cease to do evil.

II. But it consists in awakening and promoting a living faith, which is done, when we examine ourselves by asking, How do I stand with God? In his grace and service? or in his displeasure?

340. By what standard should we examine ourselves?

We should examine ourselves

1. By the law which requires perfect obedience, and threatens inevitable punishment on its transgressors;

Galatians iii. 10. For as many as are of the works of the law are under the curse: for it is written, Cursed *is* every one that continueth not in all things which are written in the book of the law to do them.

2. By the gospel which invites to the exercise of faith, and offers and grants grace.

Romans iii. 24. Being justified freely by his grace through the redemption that is in Christ Jesus:

Romans iii. 25. Whom God hath set forth *to be* a propitiation through faith in his blood, to declare his righteousness for the remission of sins that are past, through the forbearance of God.

Romans i. 16. For I am not ashamed of the gospel of Christ: for it is the power of God unto salvation to every one that believeth: to the Jew first, and also to the Greek.

EXPLANATORY NOTES.

Definitions of the Lord's Supper:

Lutheran: It is the true body and blood of our Lord Jesus Christ, under the bread and wine, given unto us Christians to eat and drink, as it was instituted by Christ himself.

Ger. Reformed: A communion of the body and blood of Christ, whereby the souls of believers are nourished, unto everlasting life.

Presbyterian or Calvinistic: The Lord's Supper is a sacrament, wherein, by giving and receiving bread and wine, according to Christ's appointment, his death is shown forth ; and the worthy receivers are, not after a corporal or carnal manner, but by faith, made partakers of his body and blood, with all his merits, to their spiritual benefit and growth in grace.

Moravian: 1. It is a memorial of the sacrifice of Christ, whereby we commemorate his sufferings and death on our behalf;

2. It is a communion of the body and blood of Christ, whereby we are assured of the forgiveness of sins, and are nourished unto eternal life ;

3. It is a communion of believers with each other, as members of the church, which is the body of Christ.

Protestant Episcopal: 1. The outward part or sign of the Lord's Supper are bread and wine, which the Lord hath commanded to be received ;

2 The inward part, or thing signified : The body and blood of Christ, which are spiritually taken and received by the faithful in the Lord's Supper.

Romish : By the consecration of the bread and wine, a conversion is made of the whole substance of the bread into the substance of the body of Christ our Lord, and of the whole substance of the wine into the substance of his blood ; which conversion is, by the Holy Catholic Church, suitably and properly called Transubstantiation.

—*Council of Trent.*

The Lutheran church maintains that the Savior fulfills his promise and is actually present, especially present, at the holy supper, in a manner incomprehensible to us, and not defined in Scripture. And why should it be thought a thing impossible, that he, who fills immensity with his presence, should be there where his disciples meet to celebrate his dying love?—*Dr. S. S Schmucker.*

The passage, John vi. 63, furnishes the key to the interpretation of the preceding section, verses 51-58, and the words of Christ generally, which are spirit and life, and should be understood accordingly. It excludes all those theories on the Lord's Supper which either carnalize or materialize it, or which resolve it into a mere symbol or figure, and empty it of its profound and spiritual mystery.—*Schaff.*

The account of the institution of the Lord's Supper occurs four times in the New Testament, which we here give in parallel columns:

Matt. xxvi. 26-28.	Mark xiv. 22-24.	Luke xxii. 19, 20.	1 Cor. xi. 23-29.
And as they were eating, JESUS took bread, and blessed it, and brake it, and gave it to the disciples, and said, Take, eat; this is My Body.	And as they did eat, JESUS took bread, and blessed, and brake it, and gave to them, and said, Take, eat: this is My Body.	And He took bread, and gave thanks, and brake it, and gave unto them, saying, This is My Body, which is given for you: this do in remembrance of Me.	The LORD JESUS the same night in which He was betrayed took bread: And when He had given thanks, He brake it, and said, Take, eat: this is My Body, which is broken for you: this do in remembrance of Me.
And He took the cup, and gave thanks, and gave it to them, saying, Drink ye all of it; For this is My blood of the New Testament, which is shed for many for the remission of sins.	And He took the cup, and when He had given thanks, He gave it to them: and they all drank of it. And He said unto them, This is My blood of the New Testament, which is shed for many.	Also the cup after supper saying, This cup is the New Testament in My blood, which is shed for you.	After the same manner also He took the cup, when He had supped, saying, This cup is the New Testament in My blood: this do ye, as oft as ye drink it, in remembrance of Me For as oft as ye eat this bread, and drink this cup, ye do shew the LORD'S death till He come. Wherefore whosoever shall eat this bread, and drink this cup unworthily, shall be guilty of the body and blood of the LORD For he that eateth and drinketh unworthily, eateth and drinketh damnation (or rather condemnation) to himself, not discerning the LORD'S body.

Add these following, and we have all the direct references to the Eucharist to be found in the New Testament:

The cup of blessing which we bless, is it not the Communion of the blood of CHRIST? The bread which we break, is it not the Communion of the body of CHRIST? (1 Cor. x. 16.)

CHRIST our Passover is sacrificed for us; therefore let us keep the feast. (1 Cor. v. 7.)

We have an altar, whereof they have no right to eat which serve the tabernacle. (Heb xiii. 10.)

The celebration of the Lord's Supper has been continued in the Christian church from the night of its institution to the present time, and will continue to be celebrated till the end of the world. In the early ages of the church it was celebrated in its beautiful simplicity just as Christ had instituted it. Justin Martyr's account, describing it to the emperor, Antoninus Pius, the earliest we have, shows how it was administered about the year of our Lord, 150. He says, "On the day called Sunday they meet together, and instruction in Scripture is given and prayer offered Then, when our prayer is ended, bread and wine and water are brought, and the president in like manner offers prayers and thanksgivings, according to his ability, and the people assent, saying, Amen; and there is a distribution to each, and a participation of that, over which thanks have been given, and to those who are absent a portion is sent by the deacons. This food is called among us Eucharistia." (Apol. Book I, lxvii.)

There has been much controversy in the Christian church in regard to the nature of Christ's presence in the Lord's Supper. There are three principal views taught by the Romanists, Calvinists and Lutherans:

1. The Romish church teaches that the bread and the wine in the Sacrament are instantly changed, when the priest speaks the words of the institution with the sign of the cross, into the literal body and blood of Christ. Consequently there are no more bread and wine present, but only their outward appearance. This is called Transubstantiation. The Romish church also teaches that the priest alone shall receive the sacrament in both kinds, bread and wine, but the laity, the people, shall receive only the bread, namely, the unleavened wafer, or *host*. The reason given is, that the blood of the Lord is already in the body or host. In accordance with this the Romanists worship the host, and believe that this is the living body of Christ, and will remain such, even if no one should partake of it, but should remain in the monstrance, that is, the casket or box in which it is locked up. They therefore regard the sacrament of the Lord's Supper as an unbloody repetition of the sacrificial death of Christ, in direct contradiction to the Scriptures, Heb. vii. 27; x. 10. All these false doctrines are concentrated in the Romish *mass*. The priest consecrates the bread and changes it into the flesh of Christ. By this means he professes to offer in an unbloody manner again and again, a sacrifice to God, (Sacrifice of the mass) The wafer (host) kept in the pix (box) is carried about in the streets with great solemnity and is worshipped. All true Protestants from the reformers down to the present time reject and abhor these Romish doctrines of the Lord's Supper.

2. The Reformed churches teach that the bread and wine in the Lord's Supper are only signs and emblems of the body and blood of Christ, which are not present with the bread and wine, but are in heaven. Only believers are fed with the heavenly gifts of grace; the others receive only earthly bread and common wine.

3. The Lutheran church teaches, that *in, with,* or *under* the bread and wine, Christ imparts to us his body and blood, and that unbelievers, as well as believers receive the sacrament; the former to their condemnation, the latter to their edification. Bread and wine are not changed, but are only the bearers or conveyers of the body and blood. The bread and wine left over after the communion are no longer bearers or conveyers of the body and blood, but remain simply bread and wine; for to the full reality of the sacrament belongs also the reception thereof.

The Lutheran doctrine of the Lord's Supper is very frequently misunderstood or misrepresented. Many are mislead by the little words, *in, Con and sub,* (in, with, or under), and think it means that the body and blood of Christ are so combined with the bread and wine, as to become one substance with them. This is called Consubstantiation. But this is not taught, as the following note from Dr. Mosheim, the Lutheran historian, shows:

"What the nature of this presence is, we know not. The thing itself we know; but the mode of its truth is a mystery which we cannot comprehend. We deny that Christ is present and received in a physical or material manner. But should any one ask, How is he present? our answer is, We know not. We commonly call his presence in this holy ordinance, a 'sacramental presence.' This might seem to be an attempt to define the mode of his presence; but by this word we mean nothing more than that we are ignorant of the mode.—They therefore err who say that we believe in *impanation,* or that Christ is *in* the bread and wine. Nor are those correct who charge us with believing in *subpanation,* that is, that Christ is *under* the form of bread and wine. And equally groundless is the charge of *consubstantiation,* or the belief that the body and blood of Christ are changed into one substance with the bread and wine."

THE NATURE AND DESIGN OF THE LORD'S SUPPER.

I. Its author is Christ, whom we regard
  1. As an Almighty Savior, who can and will perform what he has promised. Matt. xxviii. 18; 1 Peter iii. 22.
  2. As a dying Savior, wherefore his words are to be regarded as a testament, which dare not to be changed, nor interpreted differently from what they were spoken by him. Heb. ix. 16, 17; Gal. iii. 15; Rev. xxii. 18, 19.

II. The Lord's Supper was instituted in the night in which he was betrayed and given over to his sufferings and death, whereby the following things are to be noted :
  1. Some things were done, which were not commanded to be continued ; namely, Christ ate the Passover in the same night as he sat or reclined at the table with his disciples, previous to the Lord's Supper ; brake the unleavened bread, etc. Exodus xii. 18, 19, 34.
  2. Some things were positively commanded ; for the command is, "Take, eat," etc. "This do in remembrance of me," where we note that,
     a. The bread is to be eaten, and not to be locked up in a box, to be worshiped and carried about the streets ; he does not say, this is no longer bread, or is changed into my literal flesh and blood, (Transubstantiation), but it is still called bread, "As oft as ye eat of this bread."
     b. With the cup he commands positively, that *all* should drink of it ; therefore it was not intended for the priests alone, but also for the laymen, none of whom should be excluded from it.
     c. That we should receive it with the confident belief and assurance, that Christ's body was broken and his blood was shed for us ; that is, he died in our stead, for our reconciliation with God, and our salvation. Heb. ix. 12. Christ calls the cup "The New Testament," (Luke xxii. 20); his "blood of the New Testament," (Matt. xxvi. 28,) and by this puts it in the place of the wine, that was drank at the passover ; also in place of the blood of the Passover lamb, that was sprinkled on the door posts of their dwellings in Egypt, and on the altar in the temple at Jerusalem. Exodus xii. 7 ; 2 Chron. xxx. 16.
III. The design of the Lord's Supper :
  1. We partake of the Lord's Supper in remembrance of our Savior. 1 Cor. xi. 24.
  2. To show the Lord's death till he come again. 1 Cor. xi. 26.
  3. To appropriate by faith the benefits of his death for the forgiveness of our sins. Matt. xxvi. 28.

Note : Christ ordained bread and wine to be used in the Lord's Supper, not only because they are the most natural strengthening means, (Psalm civ. 15), and can be everywhere obtained ; but also represent the intimate union with Christ and believers among themselves ; namely, the bread is composed of many grains, and the wine is composed of many grapes, which are brought together and united into one bread and one wine; also, nothing becomes so intimately united with us as our food and drink.

THE PREPARATION FOR THE WORTHY RECEPTION OF THE LORD'S SUPPER CONSISTS

I. Not in external or bodily discipline, such as fastings, purifications, etc, Isaiah lviii. 5-7.
   1. Which are, indeed, good and commendable, when done in order that the mind may be clear and capable of appreciating the importance of this ordinance. 1 Cor. xi. 28;
   2. But are not sufficient, because God requires the whole heart and its proper preparation by purification from sin. Matt. vi. 24; Isaiah i. 16; Joshua vii. 13.

II. But it consists in awakening and promoting a living faith, which is done, when one examines himself; that is, inquires and asks, How do I stand with God? in his grace and service? or in his displeasure? etc. This examination should be according to the law, as well as according to the gospel.
   1. According to the law, which requires perfect obedience, and threatens inevitable punishment on its transgressors. Gal. iii. 10.
      a. We should realize the number and enormity of our sins (Psalm xxxviii. 5-9) with godly sorrow (2 Cor. vii. 10), in which we must especially feel, that we have offended such a gracious God, who has done us so much good, and that we justly deserve the punishment for our sins. Psalm l. 21. Worldly sorrow is not sufficient; yea, injurious, because it concerns itself only with worldly loss, or the disgrace, which is a natural consequence of sin. Prov. v. 22; Prov. xxii. 8; Jeremiah xxxi. 19.
      b. We must realize our inability to help ourselves, (Rom. vii. 1-24,) and permit ourselves to be driven to Christ. Gal. iii. 24
   2. According to the gospel, which invites to the exercise of faith, and offers and grants grace; (Rom. iii. 24, 25; Rom. i. 16.)
      a. Namely, The gospel awakens an inward desire in us to accept by faith the merits of Christ. Isaiah xlv. 22-24; Isaiah liii. 4, 5; Rom. viii. 38, 39.
      b. The gospel encourages us, with childlike confidence to seek our refuge in Christ. Heb. iv. 16.

    c. In faith on Christ, confidently to expect the grace of God. 2 Timothy i. 12.

    d. To continue constantly therein to the end. Matt. xxiv. 13. Thus shall we be worthy communicants.

AND THUS WE ATTAIN THE GRACE OF GOD AND SALVATION,

Through God as the author and originator of our salvation;
Through Christ as our divine Teacher and Guide;
Through the gospel as our assurance, (Rom. i. 16);
Through the Sacraments, as the seals of our redemption;
Through faith as the hand by which we take hold of the offered grace in Christ.

THE BENEFITS OF THE LORD'S SUPPER

are the same as those which have been received in Baptism; only those benefits are renewed, confirmed and sealed; that is, a visible pledge is given; namely,

    1. *The forgiveness of sin,* because Christ has shed his blood; (that is, given his life) for us, and thus redeemed us from the guilt and punishment of our sins; (Matt. xviii. 27; Eph. i. 7) and we become partakers by faith of the salvation wrought for us by Christ's sufferings and death.

    2. The spiritual life, by the awakening of a pious disposition, the desire and power to do that which is good is imparted, maintained and increased in us. This is also called "The life of my Spirit," (Isaiah xxxviii. 16, 17) on account of its similarity with the bodily life; (because the soul governs the body), and manifests itself, when we permit ourselves to be governed by the Spirit of God. Gal. v. 17; Rom. viii. 14.

    3. Eternal salvation (Psalm xxxii. 1, 2); namely, when believers remain intimately united with Christ. Rom. viii. 1; 1 Tim. i. 19.

THE MEANS BY WHICH WE OBTAIN THESE BENEFITS.

    1. Not by the mere outward reception with the mouth, because it is not designed to appease bodily hunger, but it is designed for the strengthening of the soul in spiritual things; also they receive the sacrament unworthily, who make no proper distinction between the sacrament and an ordinary meal. 1 Cor. xi. 26, 29

    2. But by the necessary appropriation of the atoning death of Christ. This is done when we confidently, without doubting, apply to ourselves the words *for you,* and say in faith: Given and shed for *me.* 2 Cor. v. 14, 19.

ANECDOTES AND ILLUSTRATIONS.

Scriptural Examples. Types of the Lord's Supper in the Old Testament, The Passover Lamb, Exodus xii. 3-13; I Cor. v. 7; The manna, Exodus xvi. 15; I Cor. x. 3; The water from the smitten rock, Exodus xvii. 3-6; I Cor. x. 4; The institution of the Lord's Supper, as recorded in the gospels and first Epistle to the Corinthians; The first believers, Acts ii. 42, 46.

George Buchholtzer received the Lord's Supper, shortly before his death, and expressed himself as follows: "Why should I be afraid of death; Do I not have him in my heart who has conquered death? Lord Jesus, I am weary of this life, certain to die, and desirous of eternal life. Receive my spirit."

When Luther heard that the king of Denmark had ordered a fast of three days for all the people in his kingdom, he said, "It is right—I wish this custom were again introduced. It is the external humiliation, and it is well when the internal humiliation accompanies it."

Valerius Herberger relates the following words of a pious woman on her deathbed: My Lord Jesus shed drops of blood in the garden of Gethsemane; from these flowers have sprung up, which are called, Forgiveness of sins, The grace of God, Heaven and eternal life. I thank and praise God, that these flowers are also blooming in my heart.

In the Eastern church the communicant exclaims when he receives the Lord's Supper, "My Savior, I will not kiss thee like Judas did, but I will call upon thee like the thief on the cross, Lord, remember me!"

Many excuse themselves from coming to the Lord's Supper on account of their unworthiness. They do not consider, that the greater the sickness, the more need of a physician. Christ came not to call the righteous, but sinners to repentance.

The Rev. John Brown of Haddington said: "I reflect on it as a great mercy that I was born in a family which took care of my Christian instruction, and in which I had the privilege of God's worship morning and evening. About the eighth year of my age, I happened in a crowd to push into the church at Abernethy on a communion Sabbath. Before I was excluded I heard a minister speak much in commendation of Christ; this in a sweet and delightful manner captivated my young affections, and has since made me think that children should never be kept out of church on such accasions."

Take care that it may not go with you as it did with that young man, who, while he was receiving instruction as a Catechumen, was a pious youth. But after his confirmation and first communion he loved the world, forgot his baptismal covenant and confirmation vow, and at last died miserably in a distant hospital. There he exclaimed, "Alas, it has gone with me as it did with Noah's raven. When it found the carcass it did not return to the ark. So I also satisfied myself with the stinking vices of the world, and forgot the church of Christ, in which I was born, baptized and confirmed. When all the other faithful ones shall stand upon the mount of God, from whom our help comes, then I shall stand without as one who has forsaken his inheritance, and shall be reserved unto the judgment of the great day in the bonds of eternal darkness."

On account of an uproar in an ancient Christian church in Thessalonica, the emperor Theodocius had, in his anger, caused many innocent persons to be slain with the guilty ones. Ambrosius refused on this account to permit him to come into the church and receive the sacrament, unless he would confess his sin, and repent. Theodocius replied, "See here, has no one else made mistakes before? Did not king David also do wrong? But Ambrosius answered, How canst thou excuse thyself with the example of David and other people's sins? David not only committed grievous sins, but he also publicly repented of his crimes, which will be spoken of to the end of the world. If you have sinned with David, then repent also with David! Then Theodocious began to weep publicly in the congregation. This affected the congregation deeply, insomuch that they all shed tears with him. The emperor then confessed with penitent sorrow, that in his passion he had done that which was not right before God, asked forgiveness, and was again admitted to the sacrament.

Bread is most necessary for preserving the natural life. It is prepared by bruising, etc., for use. It is pleasant and profitable to the body. The wine is also pressed out of the grape before it is used.

"Supposing," said Archbishop Tillotson, "the doctrine of transubstantiation had been delivered in Scripture in the very words in which it was decreed in the Council of Trent, by what clearer evidence could any man prove to me that such words were in the Bible than I can prove to him that bread and wine after consecration are bread and wine still? He could but appeal to my eyes to prove such words to be in the Bible; and with the same reason and justice might I appeal to several of his senses to prove to him that the bread and wine after consecration are bread and wine still."

The doctrine of transubstantiation— that the elements of bread and wine are changed into the body and blood of Christ— is the very heart and marrow of the Romish system. It is repugnant to the senses, to reason, and to Scripture. Yet it is taught by the church of Rome, and made the basis of many deadly errors and corrupt practices. It is pretended that it is a sacrifice for the sins of the living and the dead; and that Christ is corporeally received by the living. It leads to the adoration of the elements. It dishonors the perfect work of Christ, and leads people to build their hopes upon a false foundation. It is made an article of merchandise, by which so many masses or celebrations of the sacrament are made for the dead.- *Steel*.

"Here, O my Lord, I see thee face to face;
Here would I touch and handle things unseen;
Here grasp with firmer hand the eternal grace,
And all my weariness upon thee lean.

"Here would I feed upon the bread of God;
Here drink with thee the royal wine of heaven;
Here would I lay aside each earthly load;
Here taste afresh the calm of sin forgiven.

"This is the hour of banquet and of song;
This is the heavenly table spread for me;
Here let me feast, and, feasting, still prolong
The brief, bright hour of fellowship with thee."
—*H. Bonar*.

Philip Henry was accustomed to advise people to put to themselves, in self-examination, these three questions—What am I? What have I done? What do I want?

When William IV. was Duke of Clarence, he was on one occasion on the bench at the examination of men for military service. Having put the questions, he signed the papers. A surgeon who was present remarked how well His Royal Highness wrote. The Duke said, "The fact is, when I served as midshipman—and you must know I served my regular time—I was obliged to keep a log-book; and my captain had a particular aversion to bad writing. I then acquired a habit which has been of the greatest consequence to me through life; that is, of recording the occurrences of the day, and by so doing submitting my actions to the scrutiny of self-examination. This habit is a good one; I have tried and proved it."

"Know thyself," was the great counsel of a heathen sage.

"To-morrow," said Dr. James Hamilton in his youth, "the sacrament of the Lord's Supper is to be dispensed here. Oh, for the wedding garment! . . Lord, grant that in encompassing thy table my faith may be strong, my love to thee ardent, my sorrow and humiliation for sin greater than they have ever been heretofore. Open the windows of heaven and pour out a blessing, till there be not room enough to receive. I have renewed my covenant with thee. Enable me to remember and keep it. May it be an everlasting covenant, ordered in all things and sure, and never to be forgotten."

While the American army, under the command of Washington, lay encamped in the environs of Morristown, New Jersey, the service of the communion was to be administered in the Presbyterian church of that village. In the previous week the general visited the house of the Rev. Dr. Jones, then pastor of that church, and thus accosted him: "Doctor, I understand that the Lord's Supper is to be celebrated with you next Sunday. I would learn if it accords with the canons of your church to admit communicants of another denomination?" The doctor replied, "Most certainly. Ours is not the Presbyterian table, General, but the Lord's table; and we hence give the Lord's invitation to all his followers, of whatever name." The general replied, "I am glad of it; that is as it ought to be. But as I was not quite sure of the fact, I thought I would ascertain it from yourself, as I propose to join with you on that occasion. Though a member of the church of England, I have no exclusive partialities." The general was found seated with the communicants next Sabbath.

"I have observed that children when they first put on new shoes are very careful to keep them clean. Scarce will they set their feet upon the ground, for fear to spoil the souls of their shoes. Yea, rather, they will wipe the leather clean with their coats; and yet, perchance, the next day they will trample with the same shoes in the mire up to the ankles. Alas! children's play is our earnest. On that day whereon we receive the sacrament we are often over-precise, but are not so careful the next, and too often (what shall I say?) go on in sin up to the ankles; yea, our sins go over our heads."—*T. Fuller.*

A notorious drunkard and swearer once coming to partake of the Lord's Supper from the hands of Mr. Higginson, the good man warned him to withdraw. On which the wretch went away, venting his resentment, but filled with horrors of conscience; under which continuing a few days, he at length cried out, "He was damned, he was a dog, and was going to the dogs forever." And in this miserable condition he died.

"There are many false pretenders to religion," says Boston, "from off whose faces Christ will draw the mask." See Matt. vii. 22, 23; Luke xiii. 25-27.

> " O feed me daily on the living bread,
>   Refresh me hourly with the living wine ;
>   O satisfy my famished soul with food,
>   And quench my thirst with fruit of the eternal vine.
>
> " Thy flesh is meat indeed, my God and Lord ;
>   Thy blood is drink indeed for evermore ;
>   On thee alone I feed, of thee I drink,
>   That into this sick soul the heavenly health may pour."
>
> —*H. Bonar.*

"Do you believe in transubstantiation?" said a protestant to a papist. "Yes, I do," was the reply. "Why," said the other, "the thing is impossible." "And I," said the papist, "believe it *because* it is impossible!"

In a speech in the house of Lords, in 1719, Lord Lansdowne said, "The receiving of the Lord's Supper was never intended to be as a qualification for an office ; but as an open declaration of one's being and remaining a sincere member of the church of Christ. Whoever presumes to receive it with any other view, profanes it, and may be said to seek his promotion in this world, by eating and drinking his own damnation in the next."

During the ministry of Mr. Andrew Gray at Glasgow, Mr. William Guthrie of Fenwick, on one occasion, assisted him in the dispensation of the Lord's Supper. Some of Cromwell's officers, then in Glasgow, acting on the principle of promiscuous admission to the Lord's table, were coming irregularly, without having acquainted the minister, or giving evidence that they were prepared for the observance of that holy ordinance. Mr. Guthrie addressed them, when leaving their pews to come to the table, with such gravity, resolution, and zeal, that they were quite confounded, and sat down again, without giving any further disturbance.

What did Christ do with the bread and wine, after he had given thanks? He gave it to the disciples. He did not keep it with himself. Thus he showed, that this, his sacrament was to be distributed to the people, and that it should not be partaken of by any one man, while the others looked on, as is done in the popish mass.

What is the Lord's Supper?

1. *It is a feast of love.* "With desire have I desired to eat this passover with you, before I suffer."
2. *A feast of grace.* "Given for you; shed for you, for the remission of sin."
3. *A memorial feast.* "Do this in remembrance of me."

How shall it be celebrated?

We are commanded by Christ to eat the bread and drink the wine. Without the eating and the drinking it is no sacrament; and it is of no benefit, when, as in the Romish church, it is locked up and carried about in the church or on the street.

Why does the Savior say expressly, Drink ye ALL of it? No doubt he foresaw that in the future times the cup would be withheld by the Romanists; therefore he emphasized the little word *all*, which includes the laity as well as the ministry.

John Locke, so much distinguished for his learning (died 1704), had not for a long time been able to attend public worship, on account of his bodily infirmities. A few months before his death, he desired to receive the Lord's Supper in his own house. He partook of it in communion with two of his intimate friends. After the reception he assured the minister, that he felt a true love for all men, and a sincere union with all true Christians of whatever name or denomination.

Dr. Jerome Weller, of Freiburg, was severely afflicted in his old age, and he strengthened himself very much by the reception of the Holy Communion. As often as he received it, he noted it down, and added, Thanks and praise to God; to-day I have again partaken of the Lord's Supper by which I am strengthened against evil.

Lucia Ursula Stern, wife of the Courtpreacher Stern, desired before the close of her life (May 19, 1709,) once more to receive the Holy Communion. She received it with such an impression of God's holiness, that she exclaimed, "Never in my life have I had such an impression of the infinite mercy of God. I am astonished at the great love which the Lord manifests to such a poor worm of the dust."

A pastor in Wurttemberg called on a tailor, who was a member of his congregation, and asked him why he did not come to the communion of the Lord's Supper. The man replied, I would have no objection to go to the Lord's Supper, but previously in the confession to say, "I, poor sinner." No, dear pastor,—that appears too mean for me! The pastor replied, You need not say that, you can say, "I the proud self-righteous tailor."

When Francis Von Sickingen lay upon his deathbed, he was asked by his chaplain, whether he wished to confess to him? Sickingen replied, "I have in my heart confessed to God."

Frederick II., king of Prusia, had a very high regard for General Von Ziethen, who had led his army during the seven years war. He frequently invited him to dine at the royal table, and when no persons of nobility were present, always ordered him to sit by his side. On one occasion the king had invited him to dine with him on Good Friday. But Ziethen excused himself, because on this solemn festival he always received the Lord's Supper, and desired to maintain a devotional frame of mind. When Ziethen appeared the next time at the royal table, and the conversation had assumed a rather hilarious character, the king asked him in a jocular and scoffing manner, "Well, Ziethen, how did you enjoy the Lord's Supper. Did you properly digest the body and blood of Christ?" A loud laughter from all the guests sounded through the hall on hearing this profane question. The old general arose, and after bowing to the king, he addressed him in a firm voice as follows: "Your majesty knows, that in war I fear no danger and that wherever it was necessary, I risked my life for you and the fatherland. This disposition I still retain, and if it were needed and your majesty commanded, I would lay my gray head obediently at your feet. But there is ONE above us, who is greater than your majesty and I, greater than all men. That is the Savior and Redeemer of the world, who died for you, and has redeemed us all with his precious blood. This Holy One I will not permit to be touched or reviled, for on him is built my faith, my consolation and my hope in life and death In the power of this faith your noble army bravely fought and conquered. Let not your majesty undermine this faith; for then you will undermine the safety of the state." The king was visibly affected by these words of his brave general. He arose and extended to the noble Christian general his right hand, laid his left hand on his shoulder and said, Happy Ziethen! I wish I could have your faith? I have all respect for your faith; hold fast to it; this shall never occur again! A deep and solemn silence prevailed; no one had the courage to utter a word. The king dismissed the guests, gave his hand to Ziethen, and said, Come with me into my cabinet

The Sacrament in both kinds: During the time of the Reformation, Luther's doctrines penetrated to other countries, where the popish church would not tolerate evangelical doctrines and usages. The cup was withheld from the laity, who consequently received only half of the sacrament. A Christian in Bohemia, whose mind had become enlightened on this suject, wrote to Dr. Luther for advice, and received the following letter in reply :

' "To my good friend, the honorable and wise Martin Laninger, in Gastein, Peace in Christ.

My dear brother, against the impossible there is no help. As you are aware, that it is right to receive the sacrament entire, and not half, it is better for you to abstain from it altogether, and content yourself in the mean time with the faith and the desire for the entire sacrament, by which means you receive it spiritually. But if you by all means desire to receive the sacrament bodily and entire and your government will not permit it, then you must leave that country and seek elsewhere. Christ says, "If they persecute you in one city, flee ye to another." Beside these I can give you no other advice. Herewith I commend you to the grace of God."

Wittenberg, Tuesday, after St. Bartholomews, 1533.

DR. MARTIN LUTHER.

"In all the world there is nothing more holy than the word of God; for the sacrament itself is made and blessed and hallowed through God's word, and thereby all of us are spiritually born again and consecrated to be Christians." . . . "Where God's word is not preached, it were better that there were not singing, or reading, or assembly. The greatest and the principal part of the worship of God is the preaching and teaching of his word."—*Luther*.

Shining more and more In the Christian life Baptism is the morning star; Confirmation is the dawn of day, and the Holy Communion is the rising sun. As the sun shines brightest at noonday, so the love of God shines brightest and most glorious in this wonderful ordinance. Here the loving heart of God opens wide, as an expanding rose in all its loveliness and beauty. "God so loved the world, that he gave his only begotten Son, that whosoever believeth on him, should not perish, but have everlasting life."

The blood is the life. Jesus says, Drink ye all of this; this cup is the New Testament in my blood, which was shed for you and for many, for the remission of sins. "The blood is the life," for when the blood is shed, the life is gone. The meaning therefore is, I give my life for the remission of your sins. I die that you may live. By faith in Jesus Christ we appropriate his meritorious sufferings and death. By his death we obtain forgiveness of sins, eternal life and salvation. The words "Given and shed for you for the remission of sins," are the chief thing in the Sacrament, for, as Luther says, "Where there is forgiveness of sins, there is life and salvation."

The food of the soul. As our natural bodies are nourished and sustained by food and drink, so the Lord, in addition to his inspired word, has appointed a spiritual food and drink, in the Lord's Supper, that those who are weak in faith, sorrowful in spirit, sick in soul, may obtain spiritual nourishment, strength and consolation.

This is my body; this is my blood In the night in which he was betrayed, Christ ate for the last time the Passover of the Old Testament with his disciples During its celebration it was customary to ask this question: What is the meaning of this ordinance? And the answer was given: This is the body of the lamb that was slain, when our fathers came out of Egypt; and this cup is the blood of the lamb, which was sprinkled on the door-posts, and saved our fathers, when the angel of death passed over the land

Now Christ institutes the Lord's Supper in place of the Passover, to become the Sacrament of the New Testament, and to the question, What is this? he says, This is (not the body of the lamb that was slain in Egypt, but it is) my body, it is the body of the Lamb of God, that was slain for the redemption of the world; and this cup, of which you drink, is (not the blood of the lamb which was sprinkled on the door-posts of the Israelites, to save them from temporal death, but it is) my blood of the New Testament, the blood of the Lamb of God, which is shed on Calvary to save you from eternal death.

How unspeakably more precious and glorious is the Sacrament of the New Testament, than that of the Old Testament!

Thanks be to God that we live in the New Testament dispensation, and partake in this holy Sacrament, not of the body and blood of the lamb that was slain in Egypt for the redemption of the Israelites, but of the Lamb of God that was slain on Calvary, for the sin of the world!

A positive command. When you surround this communion table you are obeying a positive command of the Savior, which is just as binding on every Christian as any other command in the Bible. The Lord says, "Do this in remembrance of me." "Drink ye all of this cup, which is the New Testament in my blood." No obedient subject of Divine Grace can wilfully refuse to obey this solemn injunction of our Savior, without forfeiting the favor of God and a saving interest in the atonement, which is symbolized in the Lord's Supper. May you therefore continue to obey this solemn command of Christ, as well as all other commands, which are enjoined upon us in the word of God. And finally the Lord will say to you, "Well done, thou faithful servant, enter thou into the joy of thy Lord," and you will enter into the great marriage supper of the Lamb, where we shall see Jesus face to face and be like unto him.

The living bread, which came down out of heaven. Jesus said, "I am the living bread, which came down out of heaven. If any man eat of this bread he shall live forever. I say unto you, except ye eat the flesh of the Son of man, and drink his blood, ye have not life in yourselves." The Jews understood these words literally, and exclaimed, "How can this man give us his flesh to eat? This is a hard saying; who can hear it?" And when Jesus in the words of the institution says, "Take, eat; this is my body. Drink ye all of it; for this is my blood of the New Testament." The Roman Catholics take the words literally, and teach that the bread is no longer bread, and the wine is no longer wine, but are changed by the priestly consecration into the literal living flesh and blood of Jesus Christ, which we eat and drink in the Lord's Supper.

But Jesus explains his own words when he says, "It is the spirit that quickeneth; the flesh profiteth nothing; the words that I have spoken unto you are spirit and are life."

Drink ye all of this Why did the Lord put the word *all* into the Sacrament? No doubt he foresaw the perversion of the Holy Communion by the Papists, who withhold the cup from the laity, and administer to them only the bread, against his express command in the words of the institution. We Protestants therefore emphasize the word *all*. The cup of blessing which we bless was not designed for priests only, but for *all* Christians without distinction. Ministers and laymen, male and female, we *all* have an equal interest in Christ's salvation, and have an equal right to the *whole* sacrament in both of its elements. Therefore the Savior says, "Drink ye *all* of this cup." His blood was shed for us *all*.

The three forms of the word God's Spirit operates in our minds and hearts through the truths of his Holy Word. There are three forms in which the Word is addressed to us: In the Bible we have God's inspired and written Word; in the preaching of the Gospel we have the spoken Word; and in the Sacraments we have the visible Word.

The written word we receive by the sight of our eyes, the spoken word is communicated to us by the hearing of our ears, and the visible word is administered to us through our sight, touch and taste. In the sacraments the spoken and the visible word are combined, in order to constitute a sacrament. Water alone, without the word, is no baptism, and bread and wine alone, without the word, is not the Lord's Supper. But with the words of the institution, as given and commanded by Christ, they constitute a blessed and holy sacrament, to the joy and comfort of every true believer in the Lord Jesus Christ.

Show forth the Lord's death till he come "As oft as ye eat of this bread and drink of this cup ye do show forth the Lord's death till he come."

There are two momentous facts referred to in these words of St. Paul. One is the most important event that has happened since the foundation of the world, and which occurred nearly two thousand years ago; namely, the death of Jesus Christ by crucifixion on Mount Calvary. That event is symbolized in this sacrament by the emblems of his broken body and his shed blood.

The other event referred to is the second coming of Jesus Christ on the day of judgment. He himself declares that he will come in the glory of his Father, accompanied by the holy angels, with the voice of God and the trumpet of the archangel; and the dead shall rise, and stand before him in judgment. "Great day, for which all other days were made, for which earth rose from chaos, man from earth, and an eternity, the date of God, descended on poor, earth-created man."

What the Lord gives us In the Holy Communion the Lord gives us not silver and gold, not earthly crowns and sceptres, nor anything which the world holds in high esteem, but he gives himself to us, with all his worthiness; with his whole heaven; with his full salvation. There is an intimate communion between Christ and the believer; here my soul is united with his soul; my body with his body; my blood with his blood; my heart with his heart; my weakness, my poverty, mine infirmities are absorbed in his divinity, glory and holiness. Christ is mine and I am his. Hallelujah! Praise, honor and glory be to God, who hath loved us and the Lamb that hath redeemed us with his blood.

Shed for the remission of sins. Jesus says, "This is my blood of the New Testament, which is shed for many for the remission of sins."

Our sins are remitted, that is forgiven, not because we come to the Lord's Supper, nor because of anything we have done, or can do; but our sins are forgiven, because Christ's blood was shed and he died to make an atonement for our sins

Luther says, "The words given and shed for you," are the chief thing in the sacrament. Whoever doubts these words is unfit, for the words, "for you," require truly believing hearts. We might, therefore, come to the Lord's Supper every day of our lives, and if we did not believe, or trust in Christ's blood shed for our sins, it would do us no good.

I trust our sins were forgiven us when we were regenerated, converted and sanctified, and he still daily forgives our sins, when we repent and trust on Christ for pardon.

Do this in remembrance of me. In that solemn night, when Jesus was betrayed, when he knew that he must be separated from his loving disciples and suffer that awful death on the cross, he instituted this holy sacrament, saying, "Do this in remembrance of me." Jesus speaks these loving words also to us now! If he did not care for us, and did not love us, it would make no difference to him whether we remembered him or not.

When we separate from a dear friend, we usually say, now, brother, or sister, don't forget me, remember me, remember me in your prayers If we did not love our friends, we would not make such a request. So the loving heart of Jesus goes out to us in this holy communion. It is the strongest proof of his love to us, when he says, "Do this in remembrance of me." May our hearts also flow out in love to Jesus, who first loved us, even unto death, and gave himself for us.

Our faith strengthened. The worthy reception of the Lord's Supper strengthens our faith. The Christian's living, saving faith is a sure confidence that Christ's precious blood was shed for his redemption. Jesus says, "This is my body, given into death for you, This is my blood shed for the remission of your sins." Whereby our Christian graces, such as faith, hope and love are strengthened. O Lord Jesus, we believe, help thou our unbelief. Strengthen our faith and hope, that we may exclaim with the Patriarch, "I know that my Redeemer liveth, and I shall see him with mine own eyes."

The New Testament in my b'ood. When a man expects to die soon he usually makes his last Will and Testament, in which he bequeaths his earthly goods to his family or friends, or to some benevolent institution. So our Lord Jesus Christ, in that solemn night before his death, gave the cup to his disciples, saying, "Drink ye all of it; for this is my blood of the New Testament, which is shed for many for the remission of sins." This is therefore Christ's last Will and Testament, or Covenant, written and sealed with his own blood. In this Testament we, who have put on Christ, become his heirs. And what does he bequeath to us in this Testament? He bestows upon us unspeakably great and precious things Forgiveness of our sins, Justification before God, Redemption from eternal Death and Hell, and Life eternal. We are received as the Children of God, become Heirs of the kingdom of heaven, joint heirs with Jesus Christ, the Son of God, to a crown of glory which fadeth not away, but is eternal in the heavens. Rejoice, therefore, and be exceeding glad, for ye are the children and the heirs of the King Eternal.

The New Testament. Jesus calls this holy ordinance "The New Testament in his blood." The Old Testament consisted in the blood of the Passover Lamb, that was slain for the redemption of the children of Israel from Egyptian bondage. The New Testament consists in the blood of the Lamb of God, that was slain for the redemption of the world from the bondage of sin and Satan.

The Last Will and Testament. The last will and testament of a dying friend has always been regarded as a very solemn and sacred document. While the testator lives he may, if he choose, change, or amend, or even annul his testament. But after the death of the testator, and after his will has been signed, witnessed, sealed and probated, it is regarded in law as a criminal offence for any one to altar or efface any part of that will and thus defeat the intention of the testator. This was done to this holy sacrament when by the doctrine of Transubstantiation the bread and the wine were made objects of idolatrous adoration, as is done in the popish mass; and also when the cup was withholden from the laity, who thus receive only half of the sacrament.

Christ's last Will and Testament was made for us. We are therein constituted his heirs. Let us therefore hold fast with jealous care both to the letter and the spirit of our Lord's last Will and Testament.

The Lord's Supper on the Lord's Day. There are two ordinances of the New Testament which have been observed for nearly two thousand years. One is the Lord's Supper, and the other is the Lord's Day. And these two correspond with two ordinances in the Old Testament. One of these is the Passover and the other is the Sabbath The Passover commemorated the deliverance of the Israelites from the bondage of Pharaoh by the blood of the paschal lamb sprinkled on their doorposts. The Lord's Supper commemorates the death of Jesus Christ, the Lamb of God, whose blood was shed on Calvary for the sin of the world and to deliver us from the bondage of Satan. The Old Testament Sabbath was observed in commemoration of a finished creation on the seventh day of the week; the Lord's Day is observed in commemoration of a finished redemption through the resurrection of Christ on the first day of the week.

The sheltering blood. That was a dark night for Egypt, when the destroying angel passed over that land. It was a sad, sad night in every home, where was not found the sheltering blood of the paschal lamb upon the door-posts of the dwelling.

The Judgment day is coming. The Archangel's trump proclaims his advent. My brethren, will he find our hearts sprinkled with the blood of the Lamb of God?

The Names of Our Holy Ordinance. There are a number of terms by which this holy ordinance is named.

It is called the Lord's Supper, because Christ instituted it in the night in which he was betrayed.

It is called the Breaking of Bread, because Christ blessed and brake the bread, when he instituted the Lord's Supper.

It is called the Eucharist, because during the administration we sing hymns of praise and thanksgiving, as the Lord and his disciples also did after the institution.

It is called the Lord's Table, because the emblems of Christ's broken body and shed blood are exhibited on a table.

It is called the Sacrament, because we here renew our Baptismal Covenant and vow again our eternal faithfulness to Christ, the great Captain of our salvation.

It is calllled the Communion. Communion means coming together. Christ meets with us at his table, and his gracious presence cheers our hearts. It is also a communion among Christians. We surround one common table; there is no difference made, as is often done in the world, between rich and poor, high and low, learned and unlearned; we all partake of the same bread and drink of the same cup. If the emperor of Germany, or the queen of England should commune with us, they would get nothing more, and nothing less than the least of us. We are all brethren and sisters in Christ. The Lord God is our Father in heaven, Jesus Christ is our Savior, and the Holy Ghost is our sanctifier. I love this name, *Communion*, and as we have such a sweet communion here, I hope we may all have part in the blessed and glorious communion at the marriage feast of the Lamb in heaven.

My body broken—my blood shed. Jesus took the bread and brake it in the sight of his disciples, and said, "Take, eat, this is my body, broken for *you*." In this action and these words he portrayed to them, how on the morrow, his body should be broken, tortured, lascerated by the crued Roman scourge, wounded by the thorny crown pressed upon his sacred head, and his hands and feet pierced by the rugged iron nails. Thus his body was broken for *us;* that is, to atone for *our sins*

The wine in the cup, of which he gave them to drink, was an emblem of that precious blood of Christ, which flowed from his thorn-crown wounded head, and pierced hands and feet. "It is my blood of the New Testament," said Jesus, "which was shed for *yon* and for *many*, for the remission of sin" "He was wounded for our transgressions, he was bruised for our iniquities; the chastisement of our peace was upon him, and with his stripes we are healed."

Show forth the Lord's Death. The Apostle Paul says, "As often as ye eat this bread and drink of this cup, ye do show forth the Lord's death till he come." 1 Cor. xi 26.

The Lord's Supper was therefore not instituted to commemorate the birth of Christ, nor to extol his miracles, nor to set forth any special work that he did, or doctrine that he taught—these are all important and demand our attention at the proper time - but it was instituted for the express purpose of setting forth his sufferings and death on the cross as an expiation for our sins. And what could be better adapted for this purpose? Here we have before us the emblems of his broken body and his shed blood, and our minds are directed to his sufferings and death. We behold him in his agony and bloody sweat in the garden of Gethsemane; we see him at the mockery of his trial, buffeted and spit upon; we follow him to Pilate's judgment hall, where he was rejected, scourged and crowned with thorns; we accompany him on his way to Calvary, bearing his cross. There we hear the strokes of the hammer, as the iron nails are driven through his hands and feet; we hear him praying for his murderers, opening the gates of Paradise to a penitent and believing sinner, providing a home for his aged and grief-stricken mother. We see the supernatural darkness, we feel the earth quake beneath our feet, hear the rocks rending and observe the graves opening and the dead come forth, while we mark the awfully mysterious cry, "My God, my God, why hast thou forsaken me," until at last our bleeding, suffering, dying Savior can exclaim, "It is finished," resign his spirit into the hands of his Father, bow his head and expire.

And we remember, all this was done and suffered on account of our sins. It was our sins that caused him the agony in the garden, the mockery, scourging and thorny crown. It was our sins that laid the cross upon his shoulder and drove the nails through his hands and feet, and it was our sins that caused him that awful feeling of being forsaken of his God. The Holy Communion should therefore cause us to hate sin, as the most abominable thing on earth, which made it necessary in God's sight for his beloved Son to endure such suffering and such a death in order to make it possible for us to be saved.

CHRONOLOGY OF THE REFORMATION IN GERMANY.

Luther, born at Eisleben, November 10,	1483
Luther attends the school at Mansfeld until	1496
Luther is sent to Magdeburg	1497
Luther comes to Eisenach	1498
Luther goes to the university at Erfurt	1501
Luther becomes a baccalaureate	1503
Luther enters the monastery in the night of 17 July,	1505
Luther is ordained a priest	1507
Luther is called as a professor to the newly established university of Wittenberg	1508
Luther becomes preacher in Wittenberg	1509
Luther is sent on business of his order to Rome	1510
Luther becomes Doctor of Divinity	1512
John Tetzel sells indulgences	1516
Luther nails his 91 theses to the door of the castle church, October 31,	1517
Luther is cited to Rome, but befends himself before Cardinal Cajetan at Augsburg, in October,	1518
Philipp Melanchton, born at Bretten, February 16,	1497
Philipp Melanchton becomes professor in Wittenberg	1518
Luther has a discussion with the Pope's Legate, Carl Von Miltitz, at Altenburg, January,	1519
Luther disputes with Dr. Eck at Leipsic, where he attacks the Hierarchy,	1519
Luther burns the papal bull, December 10,	1520
Luther defends himself at the Diet of Worms, on the 17th and 18th of April	1521
Luther is carried to Wartburg to shield him from the ban, May 4th,	1821
Luther there begins to translate the Bible into the German language	1521-34
Luther returns to Wittenberg on account of Karlstad and the Zwichan prophets, March 7,	1522
Thomas Muenzer and the war of the peasants	1524-25
Luther marries Catharine Von Bora, June 13th,	1525

The first Diet of Speier, August,	1526
Luther, Bugenhagen, and Jonas visit the churches of Saxony	1527-29
Luther writes his Larger and Smaller Catechisms	1529
The second Diet of Speier, the friends of the Reformation protest	1529
The Diet of Augsburg, the Augsburg Confession is read and handed to the emperor, Charles V., June 25,	1530
The Apology appears, 22 September,	1530
The Schmalkald League	1531
Death of Zwingle	1531
The peace at Nurnberg, 23 July,	1532
The Schmalkald Articles appear, 15 February,	1537
The Roman Catholic League	1538
The order of the Jesuits organized by Loyola, about	1540
The Council of Trent	1545-63
Luther died at Eisleben, 18 February,	1546
The Schmalkald war	1546-47
John Frederick of Saxony and Philipp of Hessen taken prisoners	1547
The Interim	1548
Moriz of Saxony conquers the treaty of Passau	1552
The Peace of Augsburg	1555
The Formula of Concord	1577
Melanchton dies, 19 April,	1560
The Union League (Evangelical), the Catholic Liga	1608-9
The 30 year's war begins in Bohemia and ends there	1618-48
Frederick, king of Bohemia conquered at White Mount	1620
Christian IV, king of Denmark defeated at Lutter	1626-27
The peace of Lubeck	1629
The Restitution Edict	1629
Gustavus Adolphus, king of Sweden, landed in Germany, 24th of June	1630
Magdeburg falls into the hands of Tilly, 10th May,	1631
The battle of Lutzen and death of Gustavus Adolphus, 6th Nov.	1632
The peace of Westphalia, which secures equal rights to the Protestants and Catholics	1648

CONTENTS.

Preface,	iii
Introduction,	v

PART I.
THE TEN COMMANDMENTS.

Introduction to the Commandments,	9
The First Commandment,	10
Anecdotes and Illustrations,	12
The Second Commandment,	18
Anecdotes and Illustrations,	21
The Third Commandment,	26
Anecdotes and Illustrations,	30
The Fourth Commandment,	37
Anecdotes and Illustrations,	40
The Fifth Commandment,	49
Anecdotes and Illustrations,	53
The Sixth Commandment,	58
Anecdotes and Illustrations,	62
The Seventh Commandment,	66
Anecdotes and Illustrations,	71
The Eighth Commandment,	77
Anecdotes and Illustrations,	80
The Ninth and Tenth Commandments,	85
Anecdotes and Illustrations,	93

PART II.
THE CREED.

The First Article,	101
Explanatory Notes,	104
Anecdotes and Illustrations,	107
The Second Article,	114
Explanatory Notes,	120
Anecdotes and Illustrations,	124
The Third Article,	131
Explanatory Notes,	137
Anecdotes and Illustrations,	141

CONTENTS.

Sanctification,	143
A Holy Christian Church,	147
The Forgiveness of sin,	150
The Resurrection of the Body,	151

PART III.
THE LORD'S PRAYER. 155

Prayer in General,	157
Explanatory Notes,	157
Anecdotes and Illustrations,	158
The Lord's Prayer in Particular,	164
Explanatory Notes,	164
Anecdotes on the Lord's Prayer in General,	165
Introduction to the Lord's Prayer,	166
Explanatory Notes,	167
Anecdotes and Illustrations,	168
The First Petition,	171
Explanatory Notes,	172
Anecdotes and Illustrations,	173
The Second Petition,	177
Explanatory Notes,	179
Anecdotes and Illustrations,	180
The Third Petition,	187
Explanatory Notes,	190
Anecdotes and Illustrations,	191
The Fourth Petition,	197
Explanatory Notes,	200
Anecdotes and Illustrations,	202
The Fifth Petition,	211
Explanatory Notes,	214
Anecdotes and Illustrations,	216
The Sixth Petition,	223
Explanatory Notes,	226
Anecdotes and Illustrations,	227
The Seventh Petition,	236
Explanatory Notes,	238
Anecdotes and Illustrations,	239
The Conclusion of the Lord's Prayer,	242
Explanatory Notes,	244
Meaning of the word Amen,	245
Anecdotes and Illustrations,	246
The Lord's Prayer Paraphrased,	248
Matthias Claudius' Exposition of the Lord's Prayer,	249

CONTENTS.

PART IV.

THE SACRAMENT OF HOLY BAPTISM. 252

Explanatory Notes on the Sacraments, ... 253
Anecdotes and Illustrations, ... 255
Baptism, ... 256
    Explanatory Notes, ... 265
    Anecdotes and Illustrations, ... 266
Confirmation, ... 273
    Explanatory Notes, ... 274
    Anecdotes and Illustrations, ... 275

PART V.

THE SACRAMENT OF THE LORD'S SUPPER. 277

Explanatory Notes, ... 281
Definitions of the Lord's Supper, ... 281, 282
The words of the institution of the Lord's Supper in parallel columns, ... 283
Explanatory Notes on the Lord's Supper, ... 184
The Nature and Design of the Lord's Supper, ... 285
The preparation for the worthy reception of the Lord's Supper, . 287
The benefits of the Lord's Supper, ... 288
Anecdotes and Illustrations, ... 289
Chronology of the Reformation in Germany, ... 304

www.ingramcontent.com/pod-product-compliance
Lightning Source LLC
Chambersburg PA
CBHW031902220426
43663CB00006B/730